Stealing from the Rich

The Story of the Swindle of the Century

David McClintick

Quill • New York • 1983

For Judy

Library of Congress Cataloging in Publication Data

McClintick, David, 1940-
Stealing from the rich.

Reprint. Originally published: New York: M. Evans,
1977.
Includes bibliographical references and index.
1. Securities fraud—United States—Case studies.
2. Home-Stake Production Company. 3. Petroleum
industry and trade—United States.   I. Title.
HV6698.Z9H655   1983   364.1'63'0973   82-21495
ISBN 0-688-01967-6 (pbk.)

Printed in the United States of America

First Quill Edition

1 2 3 4 5 6 7 8 9 10

BOOK DESIGN BY AL CETTA

Contents

Acknowledgments

I am very grateful to a newspaper, and to a number of people for their help and support during the often difficult process of producing this book. The newspaper, *The Wall Street Journal*, is one of the relatively few publications in the world that encourages and enables its writers and editors to practice journalism as a profession rather than as an assembly-line craft. I began investigating the Home-Stake affair for the *Journal* on March 1, 1974; stayed with the story full-time for more than a year; and continued to devote substantial time to it until mid-1976. That work for the paper became the core of this book. Although the *Journal* bears no responsibility for the opinions and conclusions of *Stealing from the Rich* (the book goes far beyond the *Journal* articles and required substantial additional research), the paper's strong commitment to thorough reporting as the story unfolded was an essential foundation of the larger undertaking.

Many thanks to Stewart Pinkerton, the *Journal's* New York bureau manager; Mary Bralove, the assistant bureau manager; Donald Moffitt, columnist and member of the page-one editing staff; banking editor Charles Stabler; page-one editor Glynn Mapes, and assistant page-one editor Mack Solomon; as well as to managing editor Fred Taylor.

I am also indebted to the late John Barnett, who until his death in August 1975, was page-one editor of the *Journal* and supervised the editing of the paper's first Home-Stake stories.

Particular thanks to Nancy Uberman, the senior editor of M. Evans and Company; to Sterling Lord; and to Robert Sack.

I owe considerable gratitude to James Landis, Senior Vice President and Editorial Director of William Morrow & Company, and Publisher of Quill; and to my representatives, Kathy Robbins and Richard Covey.

In addition, I deeply appreciate the generous and crucial help of several people who figure directly in the Home-Stake case but for various valid reasons cannot be identified here.

Most of all, I want to thank my wife, Judy, whose love and encouragement have been a source of great sustenance.

Dry sherry in hand, Reg Dawson eased through the cocktail crowd into the lavishly furnished living room.

Dawson, a rather provincial New Yorker, knew little of life-styles in the Southwest. But he was somewhat surprised to find that the decor of this sprawling ranch house in Tulsa, Oklahoma, was dominated by European furnishings: French chairs and tables, a tufted velvet sofa, an antique Louis XVI marble fireplace, crystal chandeliers, and a number of English and Italian pieces, all set in a color scheme of pink, blue, and purple.

A bit garish but obviously very expensive, Dawson decided.

He also sensed an impermanence about the place. It didn't look lived in; everything seemed to be in perfect condition, as if the house had been totally remodeled just for this dinner party and might be stripped bare the next day. Dawson[1] guessed that such an appearance wasn't unusual in an oil town like Tulsa, where, it is said, people make money quickly and lose it just as quickly.

Actually, Dawson had come to Tulsa hoping to learn something about oil. It was Monday evening, May 24, 1971, and he had spent the day acquainting himself first-hand with an oil company called Home-Stake Production in which he had invested $160,000 over the past nineteen months. From the opulent setting of the dinner party, it seemed that one might be better off as an officer of Home-Stake than as an investor in the company.

---

[1] Reg Dawson is the only pseudonym used in this book.

The party, hosted by Harry Fitzgerald, executive vice-president of Home-Stake, was the fifth such affair given by the company's executives in as many days for about 150 investors, stockbrokers, and financial analysts, mainly from New York and Los Angeles. They had come to Tulsa at Home-Stake's urging for the company's annual shareholders' meeting. In years past, these meetings had been brief and perfunctory, attended by few out-of-towners. But 1971 was different. Without saying so explicitly, Home-Stake was trying to save its reputation.

Three months earlier the U.S. Securities and Exchange Commission had accused Home-Stake of selling $23 million worth of interests in a Venezuelan oil-drilling venture the previous year under false pretenses. Claiming that Home-Stake had substantially inflated the amount of oil it could prove it had in Venezuela, the SEC had forced Home-Stake to scale down its estimates and offer a full refund to any of the 890 people who had invested in 1970 and who had found the reduced income projections unattractive.

Reg Dawson had put $20,000 into the Venezuelan venture. The rest of his $160,000 was invested in Home-Stake properties in central California, where the company had been drilling for oil since 1965. The SEC hadn't investigated the California properties, but there were vague rumors that Home-Stake might have misrepresented them, too. More than two thousand investors had poured $68 million into the California drilling from 1965 through 1969. Home-Stake hadn't said profits would be quick, but payments to investors were even slower than expected. Some people doubted that the company had spent all the money drilling for oil as promised.

Harry Fitzgerald's party buzzed with talk of the California and Venezuelan drilling and whether to take the refund from the Venezuelan venture or leave the $23 million with Home-Stake.

The company had told all its investors that they could expect profits of three to four times their investment, aside from tax savings. The tax breaks, of course, were as important to most investors as oil profits. Like many similar companies, Home-Stake was sold as a tax shelter. The favored status of oil made drilling investments tax deductible. But if the company didn't drill as much as it said, or inflated the amount of oil it could produce, it not only couldn't make the projected profits, but might even jeopardize the tax deductions, whose viability depended on commitment of the investors' money to the tax-sheltered activity for which it was intended.

Reg Dawson, and many other visitors to Tulsa, had asked Home-Stake officers some pointed questions, but no one seemed to have been able to substantiate the negative reports. Home-Stake executives pooh-poohed the SEC's doubts about the Venezuelan drilling. Skeptics were shown two engineering surveys in which Home-Stake's original estimates appeared reasonable. The executives did acknowledge there were some knotty technical problems in California but claimed that the company was making excellent progress toward solving them.

Dawson liked the Home-Stake people he had met that day. They seemed honest, competent, and conscientious. Harry Fitzgerald was especially popular among Home-Stake investors. A charming, informal man of sixty, Fitzgerald looked a bit like Henry Fonda and spoke a little like Peter Lisagor, the Washington journalist who appeared on so many television news-interview programs.

Dawson was even more impressed with Conrad Greer, the earnest, articulate young engineer who managed the California drilling. Greer had explained how the drilling was hampered by difficulty separating a fine-grained sand from the oil before it was extracted from the ground. He described a special filter and pump he had designed to do the job.

But everyone knew that the most important man at Home-Stake wasn't Harry Fitzgerald or Conrad Greer. It was Robert Simons Trippet, the company's fifty-two-year-old founder and president.

Trippet wasn't like a lot of southwestern oil promoters who had gone to Manhattan and Beverly Hills selling tax-sheltered drilling investments. He didn't wear a ten-gallon hat and cowboy boots, or a leisure suit, suede shoes, and tinted glasses. And he didn't fly around the country in a Lear jet.

To all appearances, Bob Trippet was the quintessential conservative businessman of means. Five feet nine, bespectacled, and slightly plump, he usually dressed in a dark pin-striped suit, white shirt, and quiet tie. He stood erect, and his stride, demeanor, and resonant voice revealed a large measure of self-confidence, even a little arrogance. But he wasn't overbearing. He was gregarious without being loud, smooth without being slick.

Above all, he was smart. Anyone who had ever spoken with Bob Trippet for any length of time came away knowing he was exceptionally intelligent. (Trippet never let anyone forget that he was a lawyer, not just an oil man.)

His poise never failed him. He was as comfortable chatting with top executives of the General Electric Company in their plush Manhattan offices as he was playing bridge with friends in Tulsa.

It was well known that more than three dozen high-ranking General Electric officers, including board chairman Fred J. Borch, had invested in Home-Stake's drilling programs. So had top people at the First National City Bank of New York, the Western Union Corporation, the United States Trust Company of New York, the Procter & Gamble Company, and some of Wall Street's most prestigious law firms.

Then there were the show-business people. Jack Benny, Liza Minnelli, Andy Williams, Walter Matthau, and many others had entrusted hundreds of thousands of dollars to Home-Stake. Of course, Trippet hadn't sold investments to them directly. He had wooed their financial advisers—astute, highly paid lawyers and certified public accountants whose main function was to protect their clients from thieves and the Internal Revenue Service.

In short, Robert Trippet enjoyed the confidence of some of the most sophisticated financial minds in America. It seemed obvious to Reg Dawson that these people wouldn't have chosen Home-Stake if they hadn't first analyzed all the available oil investments and oil men and concluded that Home-Stake and Trippet were the best.

The Securities and Exchange Commission's accusations, therefore, had to be seen in perspective. The SEC was forever complaining about something. Oil-drilling companies always inflate their claimed oil reserves, at least a little. It was accepted practice to portray drilling prospects as favorably as possible. In-

vestors knew it and the drilling companies knew they knew it.
The trick was to find the company that inflated the least and
could produce the most.

Even though Home-Stake had to lower its production estimates for Venezuela to satisfy the SEC, Bob Trippet had ridi-
culed the agency's petroleum engineers who had challenged
Home-Stake's figures. "Such men are poor-as-church-mice punks
making about $18,000 a year and lucky to be doing that because
they can't make anyone's team," Trippet said. He had always
had great contempt for government bureaucrats.

The Home-Stake shareholders meeting that Monday morning
had been held in the Crystal Ballroom, on the sixteenth floor of
the Mayo Hotel, Tulsa's largest and most elegant old downtown
hotel. The large, white-walled room, with its four crystal chandeliers and rich burgundy carpets and draperies, offered a
panoramic view of Tulsa, the rolling green prairie and wood-
lands around it, and the Texaco and Sunoco-DX oil refineries
beyond the bend in the sluggish Arkansas River on the west edge
of the city. Bob Trippet had run the meeting with flair, introduc-
ing most of the out-of-towners by name and home city without
a pause, or notes to guide him.

After the formal meeting had adjourned, Reg Dawson had
spent about ten minutes alone with Trippet. He had told Trippet
that he sympathized with Home-Stake's problems in California
but wanted to stress that $160,000 was, for him, a major outlay;
he was counting on receiving a substantial return.

Trippet had listened attentively. He had assured Dawson
that there was every reason to have confidence in the drilling
programs. But if Reg felt he had overextended himself, Home-
Stake might be able to repurchase 20 or 25 percent of his investment, in addition to the refund to which he was entitled under
the SEC lawsuit. Dawson had demurred; surely Trippet
wouldn't make such an offer if the investment were in danger.

Harry Fitzgerald's party lasted past midnight. The guests dined
by the light of Tahitian torches on an immense, luxuriantly
landscaped patio at the rear of the house. At the center of the
patio was an elaborate swimming pool designed to resemble a

natural pond. The pool was edged with flower beds and large stones and rocks, and partially encircled a spacious gazebo, which was linked to the opposite sides of the pool by two footbridges.

The highlight of the evening was the appearance of an Indian, in full native garb, from a local tribe, the Sauk and Fox. In addition to honorary membership in the tribe, all the guests received beaded headbands and certificates bearing an Indian-sounding variation of their own names. The visitors loved it. Home-Stake paid the tribe five dollars per guest.

Reg Dawson left the party at half-past twelve and flew back to New York the next morning.

He and most of the other investors in the Venezuelan drilling venture—those who hadn't gone to Tulsa as well as those who had —decided not to withdraw their money. Only $5 million in refunds were asked, leaving Home-Stake with more than $18 million.

It was well into 1972 before Dawson and others began to suspect that they might have made a mistake. Many investors didn't fully realize that they had been swindled until 1973 or later.

It was small comfort to learn, too, that they weren't the first people to misjudge Bob Trippet.

Robert Simons Trippet was born on June 16, 1918, in Enid, a town of fifteen thousand situated on the central Oklahoma plains. His father, a Texan named Hosea Wesley Trippet, had settled in Enid in 1914 at the age of twenty-two when he married Mary Simons, the daughter of a prominent Enid lawyer. Mary's father, P. C. Simons, had been attorney general of Oklahoma from 1904 to 1906 before it became a state.

Bob Trippet was an only child, growing up in a home that, economically at least, was secure and stable. His father, whom friends called Trip, was a bank officer in Enid until 1922, when he took a job as a state banking regulator in Bartlesville, Oklahoma, best known as headquarters of the Phillips Petroleum Company. In 1933 he was named president of the Home Savings & Loan Association in Bartlesville and quickly became one of the town's most prominent citizens. Bright, assertive, and glib, he served terms as president of the Bartlesville Chamber of Commerce, the Rotary Club, and the local baseball club.

Trip Trippet liked the obligatory socializing that accompanied his position in the community. He enjoyed the dinners and receptions at the Hillcrest Country Club. Even more, he liked the constant round of bridge and poker parties. But his social life caused a degree of quiet tension at home. Mary Trippet, an intelligent and exceptionally independent woman, was not the gregarious joiner that a bank executive's wife was expected to be; she endured the essential social functions but avoided others whenever possible. The country club ladies found her somewhat disconcertingly exotic. She wore heavier makeup, dressed less conventionally, and drove her car more aggressively than they did. The pleasure she derived from their company was negligible.

Mary Trippet's world was music—a world populated by her piano, her piano students (she played well and taught privately), her Victrola, her radio and her monthly copy of the *Étude* music magazine.

Although her son had a good voice, he sang only enough to indulge his mother, not enough to please her. Aside from music, however, Bob Trippet achieved, rather nonchalantly, most of the goals that his parents set for him: superior grades in school, social polish and acceptance, and an active extracurricular regimen. He was an Eagle Scout as a young teenager, but in high school he settled into a routine of somewhat more leisurely activities, mostly centered at the Hillcrest Country Club. He and eleven other sons of the local gentry, all members of the Bartlesville High School class of 1935, formed the Club of 35, whose main purpose was to lend gentility and exclusivity to weekly country club poker games.

Bob also played golf; weak eyes kept him out of other sports. And he was something of a prankster. He and a few friends, for example, once figured out a way to activate the slot machines at Hillcrest with bogus coins. The club discovered the scheme. Trip and Mary, angry and disappointed, hoped that their son's flirtation with fraud was an isolated episode.

Although the slot machine caper caused a stir, it was sensational only by Bartlesville standards. Fifty miles south in Tulsa, the nearest sizeable city, some wealthy youngsters were participating in a subterranean sex-and-drug scene featuring a murder and at least three suicides. Such radical conduct shocked the Bartlesville boys of the Club of 35.

Like many similarly talented and privileged young people in the small midwestern towns of the 1920s and 1930s, Bob Trippet had the intelligence and polish to have gone to an Ivy League college. But in the midst of the Depression, such thoughts occurred to few families, even those who could afford an expensive education. Success for most bright young men meant going to a state school and then launching a career in business.

Bob Trippet enrolled at the University of Oklahoma in Norman in September 1935, and pledged the Phi Gamma Delta fraternity. The Phi Gams sought out smooth young men who showed potential as successful campus politicians. Trippet wasn't a disappointment. He became president of several campus organizations, including the fraternity itself. His grades were high enough to get him into Phi Beta Kappa in his junior year.

Despite his political success, or perhaps because of it, Trippet had few close friends at the university and was considered somewhat two-faced by many who knew him. "He was pleasant, considerate, and helpful to others, but still was rather impersonal and didn't form close alliances," a former fellow student says. "He would try to give the impression he was happy-go-lucky and would go out drinking with the boys, but he really didn't drink much, and usually would slip away early and either hit the books or attend to his political duties."

In his junior year the Who's Who section of the university yearbook carried a photograph of Bob—dark-haired, rather handsome, and dressed in a dark double-breasted pin-striped suit. He is seated alone at a small table and has just dealt a row of cards, as if starting a game of solitaire. The picture is captioned: "Smooth is the word."

By his senior year Trippet's campus popularity had ebbed. The yearbook referred to Phi Gamma Delta as the "Robert Trippet Enterprises Association." The book said that the fraternity's "committee for enhancing of efficiency in cribbing devised a new system which won for them the inter-fraternity council's brand new scholarship cup." (Neither Trippet nor anyone else was accused personally of cheating.)

The razz section of the yearbook had this to say about Trippet:

> Just call me "Boss," Trippet clucks to his adoring flock (at
> 25¢ an adore, which makes the flock cost him $1.00). In all
> seriousness, though, Bob really is a big man on campus . . .
> as is obvious by his overbearing attitude. "The Boss" drowns

his sorrows in activities and can be seen continuously flitting from one organization to another. He's past president of everything that he isn't present president of. In fact, he's past; period.

Trippet's senior year doubled as his first year at the university law school, where he continued his superior academic performance. His high grades were a surprise to some first-year law students who had transferred to the university from other schools and hadn't known Trippet as an undergraduate. He sometimes fell asleep in class. The first time the new students noticed this, on a morning in the early fall of 1938, one turned to another and said, "What a loser. He'll never get anywhere." But when the semester ended, and again when the class completed law school in 1941, Trippet ranked at or near the top.

While in law school he married Helen Grey Simpson, daughter of a wealthy Tulsa oil man. They had met while both were undergraduates. The wedding was lavish and gay. At the reception Helen Grey slid down the stair banister of her parents' home balanced on a mink coat.

Over the years a story spread that Trippet got one of the highest scores on the Oklahoma bar examination ever recorded. But the state bar association says that it is impossible for anyone to know that information, since scores at the time were recorded only as pass or fail.

In any case, Trippet did well enough to be admitted in 1941 for a year of graduate work at Columbia University law school, in New York City. (Because of his poor eyesight, he didn't serve in World War II.) He worked for a year at the War Department in Washington before returning to Oklahoma. By the late 1940s, after a stint in the legal department of the Cities Service Oil Company, Trippet had gained a reputation as one of the most skilled writers of oil contracts in Tulsa. The booming oil town possibly deserved the title some no doubt still claim for it: Oil Capital of the World.

On May 1, 1948, Trippet began private law practice as the junior partner in a firm of four lawyers. His three partners —Russell F. Hunt, Morris L. Bradford, and Charles March— were, and still are, men of good reputation. Russell Hunt went into banking and eventually became vice-chairman of the First National Bank & Trust Company of Tulsa, one of the largest banks in Oklahoma. After years of law practice, Morris Bradford was named a U.S. magistrate for the Northern Judicial District of Oklahoma. Charles March still successfully practices law in Tulsa.

During Bob Trippet's early professional years, the personal traits observed by his university classmates continued to be evident. He displayed a quick, incisive mind, and was affable but aloof from his colleagues. While they played golf, went fishing, or sat around drinking at the Tulsa Club (a plush private downtown gathering spot frequented by local lawyers and businessmen), Trippet stayed home with Helen Grey and his three daughters; he spent a lot of time reading on legal and financial subjects.

Other personal characteristics that hadn't been so noticeable before also emerged during these years. Trippet wasn't as nonchalant as he had been when he was a youth. He was extremely ambitious and seemed impatient to inject himself into situations where he could make a lot of money. "More than anything else, he wanted the goddamned almighty dollar," says one former associate. Since he had access to family wealth, Trippet's yearning for money surprised many people. Apart from his wife's wealth, both his father and maternal grandfather were well off, and he must have known or at least suspected that he would inherit hundreds of thousands of dollars from them. But Trippet was too bright, energetic and ambitious to be content to rely on family assets. He was eager to prove to Helen Grey and the Simpson clan that he could make money on his own. Moreover, people who knew him noticed that he seemed to get a great deal of emotional as well as intellectual pleasure from exercising his superior intelligence and knowledge of the law. He knew he was smarter than most of his peers, and seemed to revel in trying to manipulate business situations to his advantage.

He also occasionally displayed an attitude of feisty defiance toward certain laws and government authorities. Acquaintances have cited a relatively trivial example of this attitude from the early 1950s, but in retrospect they say that it foreshadowed more important manifestations of the same trait in later years. Before 1949, to save money, people nationwide bought cigarettes by mail from states with lower tax rates than where they lived. Then a federal law was enacted requiring dealers to report mail-order purchasers to their home states so that the government could collect taxes from them at the local rates. While most Oklahomans stopped their usual practice of ordering cigarettes from Missouri, Bob Trippet made it known that he felt the new law was unconstitutional and that he intended to ignore it. Years later, after the state threatened to have the Tulsa County sheriff seize property from him, Trippet finally paid $55.64 in cigarette taxes, penalties and interest dating back to 1950.

As he was establishing himself as a lawyer in Tulsa during the early 1950s, Trippet was in a position to observe the activities of a number of small oil promoters who have inhabited the fringes of Tulsa's oil fraternity for years. Many of the promoters were honest, but some were not and cheated investors with abandon.

One of the most notorious promoters was Russell ("Rusty") Cobb, Jr., the son of a former Tulsa police and fire commissioner. The senior Russell Cobb committed suicide with a .38 caliber revolver in a bathtub at the Hotel Tulsa one night in 1961.

In the 1950s and 1960s, Rusty Cobb, Jr., chartered planes and flew groups of prospective oil investors to Las Vegas for weekends of gambling and revelry. Legend has it that he once arrived by helicopter at the first tee for a golf match with clients. A heavy, flamboyant drinker, he frequently started the day with a double Black Russian, which a waiter brought from the Tulsa Club bar, across the street from his office.

Cobb's clients might have tolerated, even enjoyed, his showiness if he had made money for them. Instead he occasionally cheated them. Typically, he would collect, say, $20,000 from a group of New York bankers or Hollywood actors (he listed Adlai E. Stevenson as a reference); spend $1,000 drilling a hole in the ground; pocket the rest of the money; and tell the investors it was a dry hole but' that the drilling had consumed their entire $20,000.

Rusty Cobb's luck finally ran out in 1965. He declared himself bankrupt, listing assets of $73,508 and liabilities of $1,088,836. His debts included $11,972 owed to novelist Irwin Shaw, who had obtained a court judgment against Cobb in an oil deal. Other debts were $4,552 to the Beverly Hills Hotel and $4,528 to a men's apparel shop in the hotel; $3,654 to the Deauville Hotel in Miami Beach; $4,977 to American Airlines; $652 to Abercrombie & Fitch in New York; $1,000 to the Tropicana Hotel in Las Vegas; and $7,867 to Neiman-Marcus in Dallas.

Cobb died broke in 1968 at a Veterans Hospital in Muskogee, Oklahoma. But an optimist to the last, he had made reservations in Acapulco for himself and a girl friend only days before his death.

Among the Tulsa oil promoters of Cobb's generation, only one, a man named Paul C. Edwards, is known to have been prosecuted. Although he promised investors that they would receive ten times their original outlay in profits, he in fact cheated them the same way that Cobb did. He even convinced a Roman Catholic priest to invest the funds of a church school in his oil projects. Edwards was convicted of fraud and sentenced to four years in prison.

Although promoters such as Cobb and Edwards were ostracized by the Tulsa oil establishment, few respectable Tulsans felt obliged to warn investors about them. "There are people in this part of the country who wouldn't think of cheating anyone themselves, but who get a certain devilish thrill out of seeing someone else rip off a bunch of effete eastern snobs or kinky Hollywood types," says a man who is intimately acquainted with the Tulsa oil community. "That sort of thing is fodder for a lot of knee-slapping stories in the locker room of the Tulsa Club."

One of Tulsa's honest oil men in the 1950s was Trippet's law partner, Charles March. In 1953 March began managing oil investments for some wealthy friends who lived in Wisconsin and Massachusetts. Initial drilling ventures were successful.

Trippet learned a lot from March and from another Tulsa friend who developed oil properties for the Bronfman family of New York and their Seagram liquor empire. By late 1954 and early 1955, Trippet was telling friends that he planned to start his own drilling company. "If March can do it, I can do it better," he said.

"I know you're a smart oil lawyer, Bob, but what do you really know about finding oil—drilling for it and getting it out of the ground?" a friend asked at lunch one day.

"Not much," Trippet replied. But that didn't deter him. Other promoters had demonstrated that one needn't know a great deal about drilling to sell investments in it. Furthermore, Trippet was smarter, subtler, more sophisticated and more ambitious than the Rusty Cobbs of the world.

Trippet also had good connections. He started the Home-Stake Production Company in April 1955, with the help of his wife's brother, O. Strother Simpson, who operated two other Tulsa petroleum companies—the Home-Stake Oil & Gas Company and the Home-Stake Royalty Corporation. Simpson's companies always have been respected both in and out of Tulsa, and Simpson is reputed to be scrupulously honest.

Simpson's family were among the pioneers of the Oklahoma oil business; his grandfather founded Home-Stake Oil & Gas in 1917, and his father started Home-Stake Royalty in 1929. After graduating from Harvard law school in 1936, Strother Simpson practiced law in Houston for seventeen years before returning to Tulsa in 1953 to take over his family's businesses.

Simpson agreed to serve as president of the Home-Stake Production Company, and a friend, Ben Gutman of Saint Louis, became board chairman. Both positions were titular; the real boss of the company was Bob Trippet, whose title was executive vice-president. Trippet used the Simpson name and reputation to good advantage. He raised his initial capital by selling Home-Stake Production common stock to many of the same people who owned stock in the other Home-Stake companies. Then he began seeking places to drill for oil and soliciting buyers for Home-Stake Production's principal product—oil tax-shelter investments.[1]

[1] Home-Stake Production sold tax-shelter investments in specific annual drilling ventures, often called programs. Beginning in 1964 Home-Stake

The way that tax shelters work and the concepts on which they are based always have been something of a mystery to most people. Tax shelters have been the private preserve of the rich. Other people's understanding usually doesn't penetrate beyond a vague perception of the *impact* of shelters—a substantial easing of the tax burden on the wealthy—and a feeling that this is inherently unfair.

It's no secret why tax shelters are confusing. The laws governing them are very complex, and people who use shelters like to keep the laws that way. Complexity itself inhibits understanding by the uninitiated. Users are reticent, moreover, to talk about their tax shelters, except with each other. They fear that broad public debate about shelters might lead to curbs on their use.[2]

Complex as the laws are, the basic idea of a tax shelter is simple. In essence, a shelter is nothing more than a very large tax deduction. Anyone who itemizes deductions knows that a person in the 30-percent tax bracket who contributes $1,000 to charity, pays $1,000 in interest on a bank loan, or incurs $1,000 in business expenses can deduct that $1,000 from his taxable income, thus saving $300 in federal income tax. What isn't so well known is that these common deductions aren't the only ones allowed by the Internal Revenue Code. The law provides that investments in certain types of businesses also are deductible. Theoretically, these tax-favored businesses meet two criteria: There is a strong national interest in the development of the business; and the business is unusually risky, requiring more than a normal incentive to attract investment to it. By no means all shelters meet both criteria; some exist for far less public-spirited reasons, for example, skillful exploitation by lawyers of quirks in the tax law or unusual court interpretations of the law.

---

would form a new subsidiary corporation each year to offer a drilling program. Investments in these programs were known as units, interests, participations, or shares. The buyers were referred to as participants or simply as investors. The drilling investments were distinct from Home-Stake's common stock, which was sold on a much more limited scale.

[2] Wide dissemination of the exact numbers of wealthy people who pay minimal federal income taxes has been crucial in building support for certain restrictions on tax shelters that have been enacted in recent years.

One of the most favored businesses historically has been oil. The current public interest rationale, of course, is that the United States has a vital stake in reducing dependence on foreign petroleum by developing sufficient quantities domestically. But the economic risk to the driller-investor is great; many wells produce no oil or far less than expected. So to induce investment Congress has awarded tax incentives not only to people and companies actually deriving their livelihoods from oil drilling but also to outsiders willing to invest. The power and self-interest of oil state representatives, such as senators Russell Long of Louisiana and the late Robert Kerr of Oklahoma, also helped spur enactment and preservation of these incentives.

Under the law, much of the drilling expense is totally deductible for income-tax purposes in the year the expense is incurred. The typical oil-investment program is structured so that the investor's funds are used for these drilling expenses, and most if not all of the investment is deductible. For example, if a $200,000-a-year executive does nothing to shelter his income from taxation, he might have to pay more than $100,000 in taxes. But if he invests, say, $100,000 in oil drilling, he can deduct that $100,000 from his taxable income, reducing it to $100,000.

Thus it has cost the executive $100,000 to cut his tax bill by probably $50,000 to $70,000.[3] The $100,000 investment becomes an asset on his personal balance sheet, but its true worth remains to be determined. He hopes, of course, that his shelter will generate income in future years. Such income is taxable, but tax rates on oil income are lower than on other income. Ideally the investor will have found another shelter by then to protect the income produced by the first investment. Even if he sells his first investment before the oil program is fully developed, the proceeds from the sale historically have been taxed at capital gains rates, which are lower than ordinary income-tax rates. Furthermore, by the time he begins receiving income, the investor may be in a lower tax bracket because of retirement or other reasons, thus reducing the tax on the income from his shelter investment even further. The true purpose of tax-

---

[3] These figures are used merely to illustrate the shelter principle. Tax rates change over the years, and always vary according to the nature of one's income.

shelter investment, therefore, isn't to avoid taxes altogether; it is to *defer* tax until a future time when one's rate is lower.

There are several reasons why tax shelters are sold mainly to the wealthy. Because of their higher tax brackets, both their need for shelter and their ability to absorb losses are greater than the comparable need and ability of people in lower brackets. If a man whose oil outlay would have been taxable at 70-percent receives no return from his investment, he has the consolation of knowing that 70 percent of the money would have gone to the government in taxes anyway. An individual in the 30-percent bracket, on the other hand, must consider the possibility that if he hadn't made a tax-shelter investment that went sour, only 30 percent of the money would have gone to the government, and he would have had 70 percent to spend on something else.

Another reason why shelters are sold primarily to the rich is that most businesses offering tax-shelter investments require substantial amounts of money; it costs upwards of $100,000 to drill a typical oil well. Naturally, it is easier and more efficient to sell a few large investments to a limited number of people who need them badly than to sell many small investments to a lot of people whose need is much less.

It is possible to mount solid arguments both for and against tax shelters. One's stance would depend largely on how one perceives the equity of the U.S. tax system as a whole, and a discussion of that topic is beyond the scope of this book. The crucial point here is that, even if one considers the basic concept of the tax shelter to be equitable, it must be acknowledged that equity depends on the investors' money being spent in good faith on the tax-favored business activity for which it was intended. It is squarely up to the Internal Revenue Service to ensure that the money is so spent; if it isn't, the IRS is required to bar the tax deduction.

In 1955 it remained to be seen how much of the investors' money Bob Trippet actually would spend on oil drilling. But Home-Stake's pitch was plausible and appealing. Trippet, in fact, was one of the first men in America fully to discern the appeal of oil-tax shelters to wealthy people, and to devise a workable plan for marketing them on a large scale. Trippet understood three crucial things about wealthy people, and about the Internal Revenue Code and the federal government's enforcement of it.

First, the higher the tax rate, the more most people, including the rich, resent taxes. In the 1950s, tax rates were as high as 90 percent, and some wealthy people invested indiscriminately to avoid turning over most of their income to the government. This attitude didn't change much when the maximum rate was lowered to around 70 percent in the 1960s and 1970s.

Second, the wealthy don't necessarily handle their money any more wisely or carefully than other people do nor are they necessarily any smarter or less susceptible to fraud. On the contrary, some are more careless with their funds because they have more and can afford losses. And some compound their vulnerability by entrusting the management of their money to incompetent or unscrupulous people.

Third, although the IRS claims to audit a larger percentage of rich people's tax returns than of people in lower brackets, audits of the wealthy sometimes are perfunctory and don't penetrate complex tax-shelter transactions deeply enough to test their legality. Thus the taxpayer and the tax-shelter promoter stand a good chance of having questionable aspects of an investment go undetected. (This was particularly prevalent in the 1950s, and despite some improvements, has remained a serious problem in the 1970s.)

Partly by using Strother Simpson's contacts, Home-Stake Production immediately started attracting out-of-state people seeking tax-sheltered drilling investments.[4] But it wasn't long before Trippet's running of the company began to disturb some of his associates. They were bothered, for example, by one of the men Trippet hired—Charlie Plummer.

In 1955 Charles Ellis Plummer was forty years old, three years older than Trippet. A gregarious, aggressive, and bright

[4] Most oil tax-shelter companies in Oklahoma and nearby states have tended to sell investments mainly to people in other parts of the nation. The heaviest concentrations of wealth—and thus most potential buyers—are on the East or West Coast or in the upper Midwest. If a company is fraudulent or its executives have questionable reputations, there is less chance of exposure if its investors live out-of-state than if they reside in the company's home city.

man, Plummer had been a controversial figure in Oklahoma since 1950, when he managed the winning gubernatorial campaign of Johnston Murray, the state's governor from 1951 until 1955.

Shortly after Johnston Murray took office, it was alleged by State Representative Robert Cunningham on the floor of the Oklahoma legislature that Charlie Plummer had collected campaign contributions by threatening potential contributors with loss of state contracts if they didn't make donations, that he had not accounted for all the campaign money collected, and that he was conspiring with underworld figures to take over illegal liquor and gambling traffic in Oklahoma. Plummer, he said, was a close friend of people associated with Kansas City and Dallas mobsters.

Claiming that the allegations were lies, Plummer asked the county attorney in Oklahoma City to bring criminal libel charges against Cunningham, and threatened to file a civil libel suit himself. But the county attorney said that there wasn't sufficient evidence to sustain a criminal case, and Plummer ultimately decided against a suit because Cunningham, he claimed, didn't have enough money to make it worthwhile.

The allegations against Plummer never were thoroughly investigated, and he wasn't formally charged or prosecuted. But his reputation in Oklahoma, justly or unjustly, remained stained.

Trippet and Plummer became good friends in Tulsa in the early 1950s. Plummer used to hang around Trippet's law office, and when Trippet decided to start Home-Stake, Plummer was one of the first people he asked to join the company. Plummer's checkered reputation didn't concern Trippet. Few people, if any, outside Oklahoma knew about it, and Trippet didn't plan to sell oil investments in Oklahoma. What attracted Trippet was Plummer's intelligence and his skill as a salesman and public relations man.

Plummer received a law degree from the University of Georgia in 1940. He served as a U.S. Navy intelligence officer in World War II and saw action in Iwo Jima and Okinawa. The war left him with a mental disorder, however, that made him vulnerable to occasional deep depressions for the rest of his life.

In 1946 Plummer went to work for Bill Doenges, a Ford dealer in Bartlesville, Oklahoma, Trippet's hometown. Doenges owned several Ford agencies in the area and put Plummer in charge of one in Baxter Springs, Kansas. Plummer quickly succeeded as a Ford salesman. In 1949 Doenges moved him to Tulsa, making him vice-president of sales for the entire Doenges chain. When Doenges decided to put his substantial financial resources behind Johnston Murray's 1950 candidacy for governor, Charlie Plummer was an obvious choice to run the campaign. Doenges and Plummer had a falling-out a few years later, but fortunately for Plummer, he had become friendly with Bob Trippet by then and became Trippet's second-in-command at Home-Stake.

Strother Simpson didn't like Plummer personally and didn't like having a man of his reputation as a Home-Stake officer. But even though Simpson was president, he considered Home-Stake Production his brother-in-law's company and hesitated to interfere in Trippet's choice of subordinates. There were other disturbing aspects of Trippet's management, however, that Simpson found more difficult to overlook.

At nine o'clock Monday morning, February 25, 1957, the certified public accountants who had been auditing Home-Stake's books held a secret meeting with a few Home-Stake directors in Simpson's office. The accountants reported that Trippet had removed company funds and placed them in five separate bank accounts that weren't shown in Home-Stake's records. The auditors said Trippet had withdrawn money from the accounts purportedly to pay various company expenses, but that "billings used to withdraw these funds were unsupported in fact and billings on drilling costs had been altered." In essence, the auditors charged, Trippet had collected more money from investors to pay certain costs than was needed and had removed the difference from the company.

Trippet angrily rebutted the accusations. He said he had always considered the funds in question—roughly $30,000—to be Home-Stake's rather than his own. But he added that he believed Home-Stake's contract with investors entitled the company to keep what they paid in, whether or not Home-Stake

spent all the money. Although Trippet insisted that the sums
in the five bank accounts were within the amount the company
was entitled to keep, the directors disagreed. They adopted a
motion that the difference between the amounts collected from
investors and the amounts actually spent should be returned
to the investors. For bookkeeping purposes the board decided
to consider the money Trippet had taken as a loan that he would
be required to repay. He agreed to give the company a promissory note for $29,275 and to close the five bank accounts. (It
also turned out that Charlie Plummer had taken $1,500, for
which he gave a promissory note.)

The directors passed a resolution that "any future conduct
[such as Trippet's] by any officer or employee . . . will be
severely dealt with by the board." It also was stated explicitly
that Simpson and the company's secretary-treasurer, James G.
Blount, hadn't known of the irregularities until the auditors had
revealed them. Blount, disappointed that the board didn't take
stronger action against Trippet, announced his immediate resignation from Home-Stake Production.

In an effort to soothe Trippet's hurt feelings, the board praised
his management of the company, particularly his sales efforts.
The board said that although it disagreed with Trippet's inter-
pretation of the current contract with investors, a provision
permitting the company to keep all money taken in should be
included in future contracts. (Such a provision eventually
became common in tax-shelter drilling contracts. Under the
standard provision, investors agreed to pay a predetermined
amount. If drilling the wells cost less, the company could keep
the excess. If the drilling cost more, the company itself had
to provide the additional amount; it couldn't dun the investors.
Such contracts assumed, of course, that a company would make
a legitimate effort to estimate drilling costs accurately and to
carry out drilling plans as stated in its sales literature.)

Nothing was said formally to the other directors or to Home-
Stake Production's investors about the disclosures at the February
25 meeting, and someone later removed the minutes of the
meeting from the company's master file.

Three weeks later the company issued its annual report and

financial statement to stockholders on activities in 1956.[5] A sharp-eyed skeptic might have wondered about the $30,775 listed under "non-current assets" and labeled "notes receivable from officers," and about a comment in the auditors' letter: "We have extended our examination through February 28, 1957 . . . to reflect happenings subsequent to 1956, including authorizations and approvals of the board of directors." But the events of February 25 weren't mentioned specifically. Nor was anything officially said about them at the regular directors meeting on March 25. Although the minutes state that the directors "ratified, approved and confirmed" the two promissory notes from Trippet and Plummer, no reason is given for the notes.

James Blount's successor as secretary-treasurer of Home-Stake Production was W. Keith Schuerman, an accountant who had worked previously for one of Trippet's former law partners, Charles March. March advised Schuerman against going to work for Trippet, and Schuerman soon wished he had taken the advice.

In mid-1957 Schuerman complained to Simpson that Trippet was continuing to tap company money and was accepting kickbacks from suppliers. Simpson, who had hoped the February 25 confrontation had taught his brother-in-law a lesson, was deeply concerned. But Trippet denied Schuerman's accusations and Schuerman couldn't prove anything. The auditors also were unable to substantiate the new charges, which left Simpson in the difficult position of believing either his own brother-in-law or the company secretary-treasurer. Lacking tangible evidence, he had little choice but to back Trippet although the incident shook his already ebbing faith in Trippet's operation of Home-Stake Production.

Trippet fired Keith Schuerman. But the accountant addressed his letter of resignation to Strother Simpson instead of to Trippet.

[5] Home-Stake was required to send its annual report only to owners of its common stock, not to investors in its annual drilling ventures. But annual reports were sent to many drilling investors anyway and were

In tendering this resignation, I wish to clearly disassociate myself from any of the irregularities in accounting procedure and unsound business practices which have occurred in the past, both with respect to those which were disclosed in the audit for the year 1956 and to those which I believe to have occurred since Jan. 1, 1957. . . . I desire it to be a matter of record that this resignation is solely the result of my disclosure to you of such practices during the current year which, though not provable in a court of law, nevertheless I believe to be true.

Schuerman sent copies of the letter to each member of the board of directors.

By the beginning of 1958, Simpson had had enough. Torn by his family connection to Trippet on the one hand and his deepening suspicions on the other, he finally decided to sever his ties with Home-Stake Production. He resigned as the company's president in January, and announced his decision to the directors and others who had bought stock in the company upon his recommendation. Many of them promptly sold their stock back to the company.

Simpson didn't explain his resignation publicly, but whatever prestige his presence had lent to Home-Stake Production in Tulsa oil circles began to erode. "Everybody knew there was something strange about that set-up when Strother left," a prominent Tulsa businessman recalled later, citing Simpson's good reputation. Most of Simpson's friends on the Home-Stake Production board of directors also resigned within the next several months. Only Saint Louis-based Ben Gutman stayed on as absentee chairman.

Simpson had achieved his immediate aim: to dissociate himself and most of his friends from a company and a man —Trippet—he didn't trust. But the long-term and ultimately devastating result of his action was to give Trippet total control of the company. Trippet appointed himself president and treasurer and named Charlie Plummer executive vice-president. He hired two other Tulsa cronies, J. D. Metcalfe and

---

available to them upon request. It can be assumed, therefore, that drilling investors had ready access to information in the parent company's annual report.

H. Brooks Gutelius, to serve on the board. Eventually the company moved into a suite of offices in the building where the other Home-Stake companies were quartered, the ornate old twenty-two-story Philtower Building, a downtown Tulsa landmark and a prestigious address.

The 1957 annual shareholders report, published on February 5, 1958, was signed by Trippet. It said everything was going well. Nothing was mentioned about Strother Simpson's departure; in fact, he was still listed as president. The non-current assets section of the balance sheet still listed, without explanation, more than $30,000 as notes receivable from officers.

In 1957 Trippet had had his first opportunity to nurture a skill he would soon master: fielding accusations of wrongdoing with one hand while continuing to sell investments with the other. During the same period that Keith Schuerman and the other accountants were accusing him of irregularities, Trippet and Plummer were selling nearly a million dollars worth of drilling investment to out-of-staters.

Home-Stake sold many of its 1957 investments in Memphis, Saint Louis, and other midwestern and southern cities. In 1958, however, Trippet began a serious effort to tap the lucrative tax-shelter market of New York City. Since much of the nation's wealth was concentrated in New York and California, any tax shelter that was sold successfully in one or both of these states didn't need to attract many clients from other areas.

In the spring of 1958, Trippet established contact with a group of New York investors that included William Rosenblatt, a wealthy businessman; Martin M. Frank, a judge in the appellate division of the New York State Supreme Court; and Albert S. Lyons, M.D., a Park Avenue physician and later secretary of the Medical Society of New York County. William Rosenblatt, then sixty-four years old, had been a successful Wall Street broker and was director of a bank and several large corporations. He had heard about Home-Stake from friends who had invested in 1957. Trippet began sending the Rosenblatt group Home-Stake literature, purporting to show that the company's drilling programs were achieving excellent results. The solicitation set the stage for an investment by the group the following year.

Trippet met two other men in 1958 who were to become extremely important to the future success of Home-Stake. One of them was William Edwards Murray, a socially prominent New York tax lawyer and cousin of a Home-Stake vice-president in Tulsa, Thomas Matson, who introduced Trippet and Murray. A native of South Carolina, Murray graduated from the state law school and received a master's degree in law from Harvard. After a stint as an attorney in the U.S. Treasury Department, he joined the well-known Wall Street law firm of Jackson, Nash, Brophy, Barringer & Brooks. By the late 1950s he had established a reputation as an imaginative tax- and estate-planning specialist. He was an official of the American Bar Association's taxation section, and his expanding clientele included top executives of major corporations.

Trippet and Murray had somewhat similar personalities. Both adroitly mixed southern folksiness with big-city polish and exceptional ability as lawyers. They became friends. Murray helped Trippet refine Home-Stake's drilling offerings so that they would have more appeal to sophisticated investors.

Over the next several years, Murray suggested Home-Stake as a possible tax shelter for a number of his clients and put them in touch with Trippet. Among them were officers of the General Electric Company, the Warner-Lambert Company and other major corporations. They invested in Home-Stake, and their names were used by the company in selling to others. These contacts developed gradually, however. Trippet, already raising nearly $1 million a year, could afford to proceed carefully and deliberately.

Another talented lawyer Trippet met in 1958 was Harry Lewis Fitzgerald. Fitzgerald was a Tulsa native, and he and Trippet became acquainted at a rather unlikely spot for two Tulsans to discuss business—a treatment center for alcoholism near Hartford, Connecticut, where both men were visiting patients. Fitzgerald himself was an alcoholic and an out-patient at the Hartford facility.

The first meeting was just a brief encounter on the hospital grounds. But Fitzgerald and Trippet soon got to know each other better, and it didn't take Trippet long to grasp that despite Fitzgerald's personal problems, he was a very able man.

The two lost touch. Harry Fitzgerald was in and out of other alcoholism facilities in subsequent months. His wife divorced him in Mexico. Trippet heard he had died. But the two men met again by chance on a blustery day in New York City in front of the Winslow Hotel, at Fifty-fifth Street and Madison Avenue. Trippet did a double-take. "I thought you were dead."

"Almost but not quite," Fitzgerald said. He had been released from a treatment facility but still was having difficulty controlling his drinking and was out of work and nearly penniless. He was living on what he could make washing dishes and sweeping out Alcoholics Anonymous meeting halls, where he spent part of each day.

Trippet, in New York completing the sale of $870,000 in Home-Stake interests, was feeling benevolent. He asked Fitzgerald if he would be interested in selling oil-drilling investments. Fitzgerald, who had had considerable oil business experience, said he was interested and would contact Trippet soon. Fitzgerald would always remember that meeting in front of the Winslow as a turning point in his life.

On Thursday, November 20, 1958, an article appeared in the Tulsa newspapers saying that the Home-Stake Production Company was planning to sell 116,667 shares of its common stock to the public. Among those who saw the article was Keith Schuerman, whom Trippet had fired from Home-Stake a year earlier. Schuerman, by then working for another Tulsa oil company, called in his secretary and dictated a letter to the SEC.

It has come to my attention that Home-Stake Production Co. of Tulsa has made application to register 116,667 shares of its common stock to be offered at a public sale at $6 a share.

As the former secretary-treasurer of the company . . . I am aware of certain serious circumstances which might cause you to deny the application to protect the investing public. . . .

the past operations of the company should be thoroughly investigated before you take any action on this application.

Coming three years and seven months after Home-Stake was founded, Schuerman's letter marked the first time the company had been called to the attention of the federal regulatory agency responsible for combatting fraud in the sale of securities. Schuerman received only a perfunctory form-acknowledgment from the commission. In future years he and others learned that it takes much more than a vaguely worded letter from a Tulsa, Oklahoma, accountant to galvanize the SEC, which receives hundreds if not thousands of such letters each year and can give close attention to relatively few. Deployed against the vast amount of fraud practiced in the United States, the agency was hopelessly understaffed in the 1950s, and still is today. Trippet, of course, knew that all along.

In January 1959, Harry Fitzgerald's father, Harry senior, a well-known oil man, died in Tulsa at the age of eighty-four. Harry junior returned for the funeral. While in Tulsa he found it necessary to attend to another matter as well. The senior Fitzgerald's lawyer and his guardian had both accused Harry junior of removing assets, including a block of Texaco stock, from his father's estate before the old man died. The guardian charged that Harry junior owed the estate at least $229,000. The younger Fitzgerald denied the allegations. He said that his father had given him the stock and that he had sold it with his father's permission.

Harry's appointment as executor of his father's estate was opposed by the lawyer on the grounds that state law disqualified anyone possessing qualities of "drunkenness, improvidence, and want of understanding and integrity." The case eventually was dismissed. A judge ruled that Harry had done nothing wrong. Furthermore, he was his father's only heir and probably would have gotten the assets anyway.

Trippet contacted Fitzgerald while he was in Tulsa. Trippet recalled their meeting on the street in New York and asked if Harry still was interested in becoming a Home-Stake salesman. Fitzgerald agreed to start selling for commissions. Trippet was delighted; as Harry's rescuer, he figured he could count on a lot of loyalty. And he had learned enough about Fitzgerald's background to know that Harry had grown accustomed to wealth in past years and would work hard to achieve it again.

Harry Fitzgerald, Jr., grew up in Tulsa but attended Washington and Lee University in Virginia, his father's native state. An excellent athlete, Ftizgerald was offered $10,000 to sign a baseball contract with the Detroit Tigers after his first year of college. His parents forbade it, and Harry was bitterly disappointed. To console him, they sent him to Paris for the summer. One of the first things he did upon arrival was to purchase a copy of James Joyce's *Ulysses*. Fitzgerald's freshman English professor had gotten him interested in Joyce, whose works were then banned in the United States.

"At first I just hunted for the dirty parts," Fitzgerald said later. "But then I developed a curious fascination for his use of words and the various levels on which he could be interpreted." It was the beginning of a serious life-long interest in Joyce. Fitzgerald collected his writings and lectured on the author to various groups in Tulsa.

After a summer of motorcycling around France and England with two friends, Fitzgerald returned to Washington and Lee. He had completed college and one year of law school when baseball again tempted him. This time he signed, and played first base during the summer of 1933 for the Springfield, Illinois, minor-league farm team of the Saint Louis Cardinals. He was told he was a promising player, but his parents convinced him to finish law school.

Fitzgerald worked as a lawyer for a Tulsa oil company through the late 1930s. He also obtained a pilot's license, and in World War II was a navy flight instructor and test pilot.

After the war Fitzgerald married a wealthy Dallas debutante, and for the next few years he played more than he worked. In 1949 he entered law practice with another Tulsa lawyer. But in 1951 Fitzgerald invested in an extremely lucrative oil field near Tulsa, and left law practice to devote part of his time to the oil business, and part to playing and drinking.

Fitzgerald spent most of a year in Las Vegas living with a

friend who owned one of the first big hotel-casinos to be built on the Strip. Harry's drinking worsened. By the late 1950s he knew that he was an alcoholic and required help.

Bob Trippet turned out to be just what Harry Fitzgerald needed.

On February 11, 1959, Trippet published Home-Stake's third annual stockholders report. It said that inflation was sure to drive up petroleum prices but that "our reserves of oil and gas are contained in the ground, which is free storage." Some 153 wells were to be drilled or rehabilitated in Home-Stake's 1959 drilling program, all of them "extremely low risk."

"We have been able to eliminate entirely from this program any wildcats or semi-proven prospects," Trippet assured investors. This statement referred to an unusual approach Trippet had decided to use in Home-Stake's drilling ventures. Rather than drilling exploratory wells, or wildcats, many of which fail, Home-Stake would engage mainly in "secondary recovery" of oil. That is, Home-Stake was to drill on property that had been abandoned by conventional, or primary, drillers but that was known still to contain significant quantities of oil not accessible by conventional means. Home-Stake proposed to use water-flooding, and later steamflooding—both proven techniques—to extract the oil. In simplest terms, water or steam is injected into the ground to force the oil out.

The secondary-recovery approach enabled Trippet to distinguish Home-Stake in sales literature from more conventional tax-shelter drilling programs, many of which drilled only exploratory wells. Trippet not only promised investors tax deductions, he also projected profits, apart from tax breaks, of more than 400 percent of an investor's outlay.

Trippet didn't mention it in his letter to shareholders, but the 1958 annual report also revealed that Strother Simpson and four other directors had left the company, and that the certified public accounting firm that had pointed out the 1957 irregularities, W. O. Ligon & Company, had been replaced by another Tulsa accounting firm, Eberhart and Brown.

In April and May 1959, Trippet stepped up his efforts to sell investments to the New York group—William Rosenblatt and several of his relatives; Judge Martin Frank; and Dr. Albert Lyons. Trippet told Rosenblatt, who handled most of the group's contacts with Home-Stake, that the 1959 program was a "low-risk venture, since there is no doubt about recovering oil from the waterflood projects and thus the only chance involved would be a sharp drop in the price of oil." Trippet said that profits would at least reach and possibly surpass those projected in the company's "profit analysis summary" (three to four dollars for every dollar invested). He added that since it always took two or three years to develop a waterflood project, investors shouldn't expect a lot of money immediately.

Trippet gave Rosenblatt the names of some people he said would vouch for Home-Stake's legitimacy. One was R. Burdell Bixby, chairman of the New York State Thruway Authority and a law partner of Thomas E. Dewey, former governor of New York. Bixby owned a small amount of stock in Home-Stake. Dewey, too, was an investor. Bixby had been introduced to Trippet one evening in the bar of New York's Roosevelt Hotel by Samuel Nakasian, a New York lawyer who had been advising Samuel Bronfman, head of the Seagram Corporation, on oil matters. Trippet, who had met Nakasian before starting Home-Stake, had done some legal work for a Seagram-related oil company in Tulsa.

Bixby told Rosenblatt that Home-Stake seemed okay to him, and in early June the Rosenblatt group invested $52,800 in the 1959 drilling venture—three units at $17,600 each. Trippet, who was even more charming and skillfully ingratiating in letters than he was in person or on the telephone, wrote to Rosenblatt:

By golly, I believe you are the best salesman we have. I certainly appreciate the expression of confidence in us which you have manifested by having us include Judge Frank and your nephew [David Rosenblatt]. You may rest assured that we will never violate your confidence in any way and will always do everything in our power to do the most profitable job possible.

To Judge Frank, Trippet wrote:

I have just received word from Mr. Rosenblatt that you have decided to participate with us in our 1959 oil development program. It is indeed a pleasure to welcome you as a part of our group and is a compliment to us to have a man of your standing doing business with us. We regard the investments of our participants . . . as a trust. We shall always do everything in our power to make you the highest possible return on your investment.

By December, Trippet, Charlie Plummer, and Harry Fitzgerald had sold $2.2 million worth of interests in the 1959 drilling program. How much of the money actually was invested in drilling isn't known. It was later alleged, however, that the same month, Trippet and Plummer began stealing in earnest from Home-Stake and its investors. They created several companies that purportedly were to perform various services for Home-Stake. Trippet ensured that the companies billed Home-Stake for the services and that Home-Stake paid the bills. But for the most part, the companies either existed only on paper or rendered services worth far less than what Home-Stake paid. Trippet and Plummer allegedly pocketed the money.

The companies were called the Waterflood Construction Company, the Oil Engineering Company, Pipeline Systems Inc., and the Producers Servicing Company. Between 1960 and 1962 Home-Stake paid Waterflood Construction (owned by Trippet) $87,533; Oil Engineering (owned by Plummer) $165,320; Pipeline Systems (owned by Plummer) $101,257; and Producers Servicing (owned by Trippet) $276,574. Between 1960 and 1965 another Plummer-owned company, the Secondary Recovery Servicing Company, received $139,644. From 1960 to 1966 a company with a similar name, the Secondary Recovery Operating Corporation, which Trippet owned, received $1,119,287. During that period, it repaid Home-Stake $783,384, leaving Trippet with $335,903.

In Home-Stake's annual report for 1959, issued February 10, 1960, Trippet told shareholders that he had "every reason to believe 1960 will be another good year." It was disclosed that a petroleum engineer, Frank E. Sims, who was to become a central figure in the company, joined Home-Stake that spring. Earl L. Hogard & Company, the third accounting firm to audit the books in five years, signed the accountant's letter accompanying the financial statement.

On June 1, Trippet contacted William Rosenblatt about investing in the 1960 drilling program. Rosenblatt told Trippet that he was sure the program would be successful but hadn't yet decided whether to invest. Trippet replied:

> I don't have the intention of trying to sell you on participating in this project. But naturally we will be very happy to have you join us. I value my friendship and contact with you and regardless of your decision . . . I shall keep in touch with you and look forward to seeing you when I am again in New York.

A week later Judge Frank died. Rosenblatt told Trippet at the end of the month that he might be interested in investing in the 1960 program. Trippet wrote, "We have been holding a couple of units open, so we can handle it. I hope by now some of the worst parts of the untimely passing of Judge Frank have eased and that this finds you OK in every way." Rosenblatt and his friend Dr. Lyons told Trippet on July 5 they had decided to invest $14,200—$7,100 each—in that year's drilling.

In early October 1960, Rosenblatt asked Trippet how the 1959 program was progressing and whether he expected it to pay off as spectacularly as had been projected. "I was very glad to get your letter," Trippet wrote. "I hope everything is going well for you."

> Mr. Rosenblatt, we don't make interim financial reports of our properties because of the considerable work and expense involved in our reserve evaluations. We make a . . . calculation of the financial aspects you mention . . . after the first of the year. This is an engineering job and it takes a good bit of work to do it. I wouldn't want to try to guess at this because it is important that we give you an accurate statement. . . . Just as

soon after the first of the year as possible, I will have the report for you. I am sure you understand my reluctance to just pick a bunch of numbers out of thin air. That wouldn't mean anything and it would be a disservice to you.

I can tell you in a general way that the program is moving right along and the results are . . . satisfactory.

At noon the next day—Thursday, October 6—Trippet, Plummer, and the other two members of Home-Stake's board, J. D. Metcalfe and H. Brooks Gutelius, met to hear a report on Home-Stake's financial condition. The company had changed accountants again. The new CPA firm, Frazer and Torbet, said that Home-Stake seemed to be in excellent shape. (Frazer and Torbet was the fourth accounting firm to work on Home-Stake's books in its first five and a half years of existence.)

William Rosenblatt's brother, Bernard, a lawyer and former judge, wrote Trippet a letter in the second week of December. Bernard Rosenblatt's son, David, had invested $17,600 in the 1959 drilling program, and Bernard questioned the wisdom of committing all the company's efforts to waterflooding.

Trippet's reply illuminates a crucial element of his modus operandi—personal letters to investors. Trippet wrote far more letters than the typical businessman does—and certainly more than the typical swindler. He had an extraordinary ability to bolster, through letters, his image as an astute, conscientious, and capable oil man. As effective as Trippet was in person or on the telephone, he was at his best in a letter. He could emphasize his most appealing personality traits while concealing less appealing characteristics—such as his arrogance, cynicism, and shallow knowledge of the oil-drilling business—that might emerge during a lengthy business meeting or a long social evening.

Trippet loved to summon his secretary, Helen Loop, and dictate letters to investors. Even within Home-Stake he communicated more by memorandum than by any other means. Inscribed at the top of the company's memorandum pads was: Don't Say It—Write It.

The December 15 letter to Bernard Rosenblatt was warm, articulate, somewhat rambling, but pointed where Trippet wanted it to be. It was slightly confusing in spots, but that only served to emphasize that certain aspects of the oil business *are* very complex and are best left to experts like Trippet. Moreover, the letter was so sincere and authoritative that one would have tended to accept Trippet's statements on faith without questioning them at all.

> I was glad to get your letter and to see that you are taking an interest in our oil program. I appreciate the questions you asked and they show that you are interested in analyzing the best alternatives in the oil business.
>
> The primary drilling, even if successful, would probably not have given us as good a return as the secondary work. There has been a very marked trend toward more favorable economics for secondary recovery projects for the last several years. At this time, it is costing the industry about $2.00 a barrel to develop primary oil. We can develop it somewhat cheaper, but, even so, even where we were successful in getting good prolific shallow primary production, we can't develop it for less than $1.25 per barrel. On secondary, we can develop those reserves[1] for about 60 cents a barrel out-of-pocket cash, plus about 10 cents per barrel for equipment which we finance so that the investors will not have to put out the cash and capitalize it.
>
> In 1946, 3% of Oklahoma's production was secondary. Today, waterflood production accounts for 25% of Oklahoma's total production. This is an 800% increase and it has taken the expenditure of hundreds of millions of dollars to achieve it. You don't have that dramatic an increase in favor of secondary over primary unless the economics favor it.
>
> With reference to the specific prospects in the [Home-Stake program] book, there were two specific prospects[2] and two open slots for primary. We were able to sell one of the two specific prospects and the buyer condemned it by drilling a dry hole on it. If we had done so, we would have lost better than $60,000 of the [investors'] money. The other specific primary prospect we could not sell at all and our leases have expired and Home-Stake has absorbed the loss. Had we acquired two additional primary prospects for the open slots there is no way of predicting what results they would have achieved.
>
> Balanced against the above, which could have happened but

[1] Oil in the ground commonly is known as oil reserves.

[2] A specific oil-drilling project frequently is called a prospect.

which we prevented from happening, you have the Sohoma Lake Waterflood Prospect. We know what's there. We have a very good estimate of what we can expect to make and it is very favorable as you can see from the attached notebook section.

To sum up, I would say that the chances of taking on a primary project today and hitting a great big wildcat where your return was 10 or 20 for one or better, would be in the order of one chance out of 200 or 300 and we're not interested in taking our friends' money and gambling on it with that kind of basis. We can make them a return of close to 40% per annum with waterfloods. Considering the low risk, we believe this is much more advantageous for you.

I was sorry that we didn't make connections last spring when I was in New York and had dinner with Will Rosenblatt. I had hoped that you and your son would be able to come that evening. I shall be in New York again in the next several months. I will give you a personal report on everything and will have a number of things to show you which will be interesting. Also, at that time we can have a good chance to talk about the economics of the primary vs. the secondary business. Looking forward to seeing you. Best regards.

Sincerely,
R. S. Trippet

As Trippet was solidifying his relations with the Rosenblatt group and others in the last months of 1960, he also was establishing new contacts that would prove crucial to Home-Stake's future.

With the help of New York tax lawyer William Edwards Murray, Trippet sold a $28,400 investment to Fred J. Borch, then a high-level vice-president of the General Electric Company and heir apparent to the helm of the giant corporation. Unlike the Rosenblatt group, who were known in limited circles around New York, Borch's name was familiar—or soon would be—to businessmen nationwide. By the end of the 1960s he was an internationally famous executive. Trippet managed to develop essentially the same sort of rapport with Borch and others as he had with the Rosenblatt group.

It is impossible to say exactly how much money Borch's name attracted to Home-Stake over the years, but the figure certainly is in the millions. Name-dropping had become a vital sales tool.

Even after large numbers of investors grew disenchanted, many complaints were deflected successfully by the simple statement that if Home-Stake were anything less than a blue-chip operation, prominent people such as Borch wouldn't be investing in it.

One evening in the late winter of 1961, an accountant from Frazer and Torbet was working late at the Home-Stake offices on the company's final financial report for 1960. The accountant, Elmer Kunkel, discovered records of what later were alleged to be dummy corporations that Trippet and Plummer were using to funnel money out of Home-Stake. Kunkel also found that Home-Stake had been selling more units of participation in its drilling programs than its sales literature had indicated, which meant that the company was receiving more money than it was supposed to receive. It also meant that the value of each unit was diluted, since the size of the drilling programs remained the same.

Kunkel and other Frazer and Torbet accountants confronted Trippet with the findings. Trippet claimed that the corporations purportedly serving Home-Stake actually were doing the work, and that the excess money from the oversale of units would be returned to the investors.

Frazer and Torbet prepared a report with footnotes for Home-Stake to use in its annual report to investors. Trippet didn't use the Frazer and Torbet material, however, so the CPA firm didn't sign the Home-Stake financial statement; it was signed instead by an internal Home-Stake accountant, Kermit Murdock, who was not a CPA.

Investors weren't told of Frazer and Torbet's findings. In his covering letter for the annual report, Trippet, as usual, said that Home-Stake's prospects were bright. He reported that the company had been so careful in deciding where to drill in 1961 that only three properties out of three hundred considered had met the company's high standards.

In early May 1961 Trippet visited William Rosenblatt in New York, and tentatively convinced him to buy some common stock in Home-Stake as well as an investment in the 1961 drilling venture. "It was nice to see you, but I really wish next time you

would let me reciprocate, as you are always grabbing the check,"
Trippet wrote, after returning to Tulsa. (By then it was "Dear
Will" and "Dear Bob.") "I am anxious for you to take a little
holiday and come down and inspect some of these properties. I
think you would enjoy taking a field trip with us."

In June, Will Rosenblatt, his son Richard, and Dr. Lyons decided to invest $54,880 in the 1961 drilling program. Will Rosen-
blatt visited Tulsa and came away impressed. "Let me thank
you, and through you your kind wife, for the courtesies and attention given to me during my short stay in Tulsa," he wrote to
Trippet.

> It was really delightful to be with you and meet your lovely
> family and to find out that Tulsa was such an interesting and
> attractive city. I never really realized the latter until my visit.
> ... Under separate cover I am sending a few stamps for your
> secretary. There will be more coming. [Helen Loop, Trippet's
> secretary, collected stamps.]

Trippet continued to ingratiate himself with the Rosenblatts
through the remaining months of 1961. He was invited to a
Rosenblatt family gathering on Sunday, November 12, at Will
Rosenblatt's large Fifth Avenue apartment in Manhattan. Not
one to waste a good opportunity, Trippet took the occasion to
sell some Home-Stake common stock to Rosenblatt's sister. Then
the group adjourned for the evening to the Viennese Lantern,
a restaurant and supper club.

"It certainly is a pleasure to come to New York and know that
I have a friend there like you," Trippet wrote to Rosenblatt
from Tulsa a few days later.

> It just makes the entire city seem more hospitable. We cer-
> tainly had a great day on Sunday. I enjoyed so much getting
> acquainted with everyone.
> I think you have a wonderful family there with Peter and his
> family. He's plenty sharp and he should be a big success in any-
> thing he undertakes. Those two little kids of his are about the
> cutest things I've seen in a long time. I also enjoyed so much
> getting acquainted with your sister and her son and I'm sending
> her stock to her today. I thought the entertainment at the Vien-
> nese Lantern was outstanding. I am going to buy the record
> which those Israelis made.

In the same letter Trippet began to use up some of the good will he had so carefully nurtured. He started—ever so gently—to break the news to Rosenblatt that the profits on the 1959 drilling program wouldn't be so high as originally predicted. The explanation was long and complex, but in essence Trippet said that because of certain changes in the way the program was being financed and administered, the overall return during the twelve-year-life of the oil wells would be $5,306,000 instead of $6,217,000, or 401 percent of the investors' cash outlay instead of 453 percent. For Rosenblatt, his nephew, David, and the estate of Judge Frank, it meant a projected profit of $53,060 instead of $62,170, on each $17,600 drilling unit. The figures don't take into account tax savings from the initial investment.

It was obvious from the tone of Rosenblatt's reply that he wasn't terribly concerned.

> Thanks very much for your nice letter. I want to assure you that our spending the Sunday with you was at least as enjoyable to us as you say it was to you. I also want to thank you for arranging to give my sister 100 shares of Home-Stake. Incidentally, I received a letter from her from Rome, in which she says she is having a fine time.
> I have read your explanation about [the reduction in profits]. . . . I must be stupid, but I don't understand. . . . I am certain there is an explanation but I didn't get it from the figures.

Trippet replied: "Thanks so much for your letter. I was glad to know your sister is having a good trip." He then gave another nearly incomprehensible explanation of why the profit projection had been lowered. Rosenblatt still didn't understand, but since Home-Stake was continuing to project a return of slightly more than quadruple the investors' outlay, not counting tax savings, he let the matter drop.

Meanwhile, the good word about Home-Stake was spreading through the executive suites and athletic club locker rooms of Manhattan and the New York area. By late December 1961, Home-Stake had taken in another $3,085,062 from its solicitations that year. Fred Borch, who had moved up to the presidency of the General Electric Company, contributed an additional $31,360. James H. Goss, then a vice president, invested $94,080.

(Goss, like Borch, was a client of William Murray.) Donald M. Kendall, of the Pepsi Cola Co., put in $47,040. And Ralph A. Hart, who had just moved from the executive vice-presidency of the Colgate-Palmolive Company, to the presidency of Heublein Inc.—the big Connecticut distributor of Smirnoff vodka, Black & White Scotch, and A.1. Steak Sauce—invested $15,680.

Trippet released the 1961 annual stockholders report on February 20, 1962. Again stressing the company's "high standards," he said that Home-Stake had examined 250 prospective water-flood properties before selecting only two for the 1962 drilling program. One property was in Oklahoma, the other in Kansas. The properties contained "well in excess of three million barrels of oil," Trippet said. Kermit Murdock, the internal company accountant, certified the 1961 financial statement as he had the statement for 1960.

In mid-April Trippet made his annual spring visit to New York. Whatever concern the Rosenblatts may have felt the previous autumn was no longer evident. They entertained Trippet twice, and indicated they were thinking of buying 10 percent of the 1962 drilling program. That would have meant an expenditure of nearly $200,000. When Trippet returned to Tulsa, he sent Rosenblatt a profit projection that appeared to have been prepared personally for Rosenblatt. It purported to show that he would make a 460 percent profit, including tax savings, on his investments in the 1959–61 Home-Stake drilling ventures.

On Monday, May 28, 1962, the stock market plunged 34.95 points to 576.93, as measured by the Dow Jones Industrial Average. It was the largest drop in points since the 1929 crash, and the biggest percentage decline since the day of President Eisenhower's heart attack in 1955. The May 28 slide left the market, which had been falling for several months, 21.5 percent below its level of December 1961.

Like many other investors, William Rosenblatt suffered sharp losses and was forced to reassess some of his other investments. He decided to take advantage of an offer Trippet had made to certain investors to buy back their Home-Stake drilling interests if they ever decided they wanted out. Trippet made the offer to enhance the lure of his company. He guessed correctly that few investors—at least in the early years—actually would demand their money back.

Rosenblatt asked Trippet to refund the $31,360 he had invested in the 1961 program. Trippet knew, however, that he still had the Rosenblatt group on the hook. Will Rosenblatt made it clear that he wanted to continue investing; he asked if he could have a unit in the 1962 program but delay payment until 1963. And his son Richard was thinking of buying into the 1962 program.

So Trippet decided to return Rosenblatt's 1961 investment. He used the occasion to demonstrate how agreeable and fair he was, how he always considered the investors' interests first. Dick Rosenblatt also was examining another tax shelter, Briarcliff Farms, and Trippet urged him to give Briarcliff full consideration before deciding between it and Home-Stake.

After another visit to New York, Trippet wrote to William Rosenblatt on June 21:

> It was certainly a pleasure to see you in New York. You always go to entirely too much trouble. The dinner you had was marvelous and I know it takes a lot of work to put on a big fine dinner like that. I enjoyed the chance to meet Dick's accountants and the discussion we had.
>
> I am perfectly willing to go ahead and work out anything Dick decides on, but actually I think he ought to investigate the Briarcliff Farms program first. Our tax attorney in New York is William E. Murray and he handles it. . . . We have used him for a number of years. He's first rate in every way and I know they [Briarcliff] have some very fine people in the program. . . .
>
> Concerning your own situation, I'm anxious to stress one point. I have always felt that our relationship with our participants was a two-way street. We don't want to take your tax money and then step aside if any problems arise. Consequently, I am very glad to buy back your interest in the 1961 program. . . .
>
> I don't feel it would be in your best interest to take a participation in the 1962 program. . . . My advice would be to wait and take an interest in the 1963 program. . . .
>
> Thanks again for the fine evening at your house. You certainly made a hit with the stamps and the perfume. [Rosenblatt gave

Trippet's secretary more stamps and his wife some perfume.] I want to take this opportunity to tell you how much I appreciate the opportunity to be associated with you and the many nice things you have said about us and look forward to a long and pleasant relationship in the future.

William Rosenblatt was beside himself with gratitude.

Trippet, when he sent Rosenblatt a check for his 1961 unit on July 3, wrote:

> My wife had a luncheon today and I happened to be there at noon. She gave the guest of honor a small bottle of Chanel No. 5. She said she could afford to do this because she has a friend in New York (you) who sends her free perfume. I asked her if she was giving away your perfume and she indignantly denied it.

Rosenblatt replied: "Tell [your wife] that at the moment I am short of cash but long on perfume so if she would like another bottle I would be glad to send it to her."

"I don't think you should give my wife any more perfume at the moment," Trippet answered. "She might get spoiled, so let's wait until she gets hungry again."

On July 8, 1962, P. C. Simons, Trippet's grandfather, died in Enid at the age of ninety-two, leaving an estate valued at $587,035. Trippet inherited at least $154,000.

By the summer of 1962, Home-Stake was firmly entrenched in the New York tax-shelter market. Fred Borch, the Rosenblatts, and others were telling their friends that Home-Stake seemed different from typical oil investments. Lawyer William Murray alone, directly or indirectly, had put Home-Stake in touch with fifty-seven investors. The money was flowing in, so Trippet decided it was time to introduce Home-Stake to another major region of concentrated wealth—southern California.

Harry Fitzgerald, who had been selling Home-Stake investments on a commission basis since 1959, became a salaried officer of the company. Trippet sent him to California with instructions to contact Trippet's cousin, Oscar Trippet, a Los Angeles lawyer and civic leader who had many contacts in the financial and business community.

On his way west Fitzgerald stopped in Las Vegas, where he had spent most of a year in the 1950s, drinking and spending his way through a small fortune in oil royalties. He still knew people there, and it occurred to him some might be interested in investing in Home-Stake. He dropped in on a friend, the owner of a major hotel and gambling casino. The friend referred Fitzgerald to a man who turned out to be a member of the Mafia.

The 1962 Home-Stake drilling-program circular sought to raise about $2 million from investors, and as usual, projected an eventual return of roughly three or four times the investor's outlay. To Fitzgerald's surprise, the mobster, after glancing over the circular, offered to buy the entire program and said Harry could pick up the $2 million—in cash—the following morning. Fitzgerald politely declined, explaining that Home-Stake didn't accept individual investments of more than 10 percent of a venture, and required that payment be made by check. "I had the impression that if we had accepted that man's money, and hadn't paid him the projected return, he would have sent someone around to break our legs," Fitzgerald said later.

Oscar Trippet received Fitzgerald cordially; cousin Robert had prepared the way. Oscar Trippet's prominence in business and legal circles positioned him perfectly to introduce Home-Stake to Los Angeles. He had been president of the Los Angeles Area Chamber of Commerce and the Hollywood Bowl Association. Among his clients were the Ford Motor Company and Firestone Tire & Rubber.

Oscar Trippet sent Fitzgerald to see Donald McKee, a wealthy investment banker and business consultant who, like Trippet, was a native of Los Angeles and a prominent member of the local business establishment. McKee had close ties both to the downtown Los Angeles community of bankers, lawyers, and corporate executives and to the Beverly Hills community, including lawyers who handled the affairs of entertainers. "You may feel as free to deal with Harry Fitzgerald and my cousin as you would with me," Oscar Trippet told McKee.

Fitzgerald briefed McKee on Home-Stake and told him that the company's New York clients included some high officers of corporations like General Electric and Pepsi Cola. He added that Home-Stake planned to begin drilling in California within a year or two. McKee was impressed, but Fitzgerald did nothing more than establish contacts on that first trip to California. It was Home-Stake's style to move slowly and use a very soft sell.

In New York, on Thursday, November 15, 1962, William Rosenblatt dictated a short letter to be sent to Trippet. "Is the 1959 program keeping up as well as you expected? I thought that 1962 was supposed to be a big year for this program by way of receipts. Am I correct?"

"It was certainly a nice surprise to get your letter and know that you're chugging right along," Trippet replied.

The 1959 program is coming up but it has been slower than I expected. . . . The net result of the slower than expected response (although it is going up and continues to go up) . . . is that I expect the net income for 1962 to be about $100,000. The net distributable income for the 1959 program for the calendar year 1960 was $25,000, and it doubled in 1961 to $50,000, and it is doubling again this year to $100,00. In general therefore I'd say it is going up in a satisfactory way.

Rosenblatt retorted:

If you want me to be perfectly frank, I must say I am somewhat disappointed in the 1959 program. The original figures call for a distribution of $355,000 (in 1962), while now you indicate that it will only be about $100,000. Does this mean that the entire program will be cut down, or that it will be made up in future years? This figure is less than one-third of what we were supposed to secure for 1962. Of course, I am very much concerned as to whether we will be cut down on future years as well.

Comparatively speaking, how will [the] 1960 [program] show up?

I hope this finds you and the family all in good health.

Although Rosenblatt was getting suspicious, he still was years away from fully realizing what was happening to him. It would later be alleged that by late 1962 he, his family, and his friends were ensnared in an elaborate variation on an old swindler's theme—the Ponzi fraud.

Named for Charles Ponzi, a confidence man active in Boston in 1919 and 1920, the fraud entails collecting money from investors by promising to spend it on legitimate business activity. The swindler maintains a core of legitimate operations. But instead of spending all the investments on that, he uses part of the investors' money to pay them an early return exceeding predictions. This is designed to lure more money from other investors and bigger commitments from the initial ones. After an investor has made a major commitment, payments to him are gradually reduced.

Such frauds inevitably collapse. Investors—some sooner than others—eventually discover that they have been had. But before they find out what has happened, the swindler theoretically escapes with a sizeable amount of money.

Charles Ponzi was a small, dapper Italian immigrant who, in 1919 at the age of thirty-seven, thought he had found a way to get rich. His scheme involved so-called international reply coupons, which were designed to be included with letters sent overseas as prepayment for sending a reply. The price of the coupons was fixed in each country and didn't change as currency values fluctuated.

At the time, European currencies, in relation to the U.S. dollar, were depressed. Ponzi's idea was to send U.S. currency to confederates in Europe and have them convert it into their currencies, buy international reply coupons, and send the coupons to him. He then would exchange them for U.S. stamps worth more, because of the higher relative value of the dollar, than the money he had sent abroad. The profit, Ponzi figured, could exceed 200 percent.

Ponzi offered to pay an investor $1.50 in forty-five days for every dollar invested. When word spread, crowds of investors outside Ponzi's Boston office grew so large that they blocked traffic. Ponzi found it was easier to pay off early investors with the contributions of later investors than to grapple with the mechanics of the coupon exchange, whose feasibility was questionable anyway.

Ponzi took in more than $10 million, but he didn't know when to stop. The scheme collapsed after several months under the weight of bad publicity and official investigations. Ponzi, who went to prison for fraud, was finally deported to Italy. He died a pauper in Brazil in 1949.

There have been many Ponzi-type schemes since the original. As recently as the late 1960s and early 1970s a promoter collected more than $100 million from investors by promising fat returns from a scheme to import large amounts of low-grade European wine into the United States. And in 1974 more than five hundred Montreal people invested about $2 million with a man who claimed he had an infallible system for betting on horses. Authorities labeled both schemes Ponzi frauds.

Home-Stake, however, was the largest, most elaborate, and

longest-lived Ponzi swindle in history. Robert Trippet's concept was to attract tax-shelter money by convincing investors that he was more conservative and responsible than his more flamboyant competitors, and that his drilling ventures offered a higher chance of success. Secondary recovery sounded like a sure thing. "There's no question that the oil is in the ground; we know where it is and how to get it," Home-Stake said in essence.

Trippet also portrayed his oil programs as long-lived—about twelve years. He didn't promise much in the first two or three years. The big payoff supposedly would come in the middle years. For example, Trippet one year projected that an investment of $19,000 would generate no income in the year of the investment, $430 the second year, $1,410 the third year, $5,395 the fourth year, $13,360 the fifth year, and $17,580 the sixth year. The income then would decline gradually and end after the twelfth year. Total income for the twelve years: $74,030, not counting tax savings.

Once he had an investor's money, Trippet began sending him quarterly progress reports saying the drilling was producing more oil than originally expected. The investor usually would begin getting small checks about nine months to a year after making his initial investment. Trippet made sure the checks always exceeded the extremely small amounts promised for the first two years.

Many investors were so impressed that they signed on for a second and a third year. They had no reason to be particularly suspicious until the fourth or fifth year, when payments were supposed to rise dramatically—and didn't.

This was where William Rosenblatt found himself at the end of 1962, three and a half years after making his initial investment. He, his relatives, and his friends had invested more than $90,000. Early payments had exceeded expectations. The group had grown from the first three—William Rosenblatt, his nephew, David, and Judge Frank—to include Dr. Lyons; Rosenblatt's sons, Richard and Peter; and Rosenblatt's brother, Bernard. Trippet had made a point of becoming personally acquainted with them all. They found him charming, conservative, a man of his word, and not at all like a salesman. He had become a personal friend. He not only bought back Will Rosenblatt's 1961 investment without question, but also recommended other tax-shelter programs as possibly better than Home-Stake for certain people.

By November and December of 1962, however, it had become clear to Will Rosenblatt that he was to receive a maximum of only $1,000 in 1962 instead of $3,550 projected for that year (down from a higher previous projection). He began to complain. Now Trippet had to start dealing with a dilemma that eventually confronts any Ponzi swindler: what to do when investors begin complaining about dwindling payments.

Trippet mastered this problem far more effectively than any of his predecessors. He began by making plausible excuses about why drilling wasn't going as well as expected. Most of the investors were so wealthy and had so many investments to keep track of, and Trippet had developed such rapport with them, that he managed to deflect many complaints for extended periods with nothing more than excuses.

"I've been out of town and just returned to find your letter and was glad to hear from you," Trippet answered William Rosenblatt on December 17, 1962.

Of course, I always want you to be perfectly frank. I appreciate what you had to say concerning the 1959 program because unless you tell me I have no way of knowing what I can tell you to keep you up to date about it. The original figures were predicated on several assumptions piled on assumptions. The first assumption was that we would drill four wildcat wells [1] and get oil at all of them and that would generate 12 development wells (those drilled near successful wildcats) and that the 16 primary wells would give us a big initial production which would be our main source of production while we were waiting for the waterfloods to take hold. About the time we were ready to start drilling these wells we got cold feet because success ratios had been constantly going down in wildcatting and costs going up. I wasn't interested in taking my friends' money, including yours, and pouring it down a rat hole. So, we gave up that part of the program and it turned out that we were wise in doing so as I will explain to you in more detail when I see you in New York.

[1] In early 1959 Trippet had said there would be no wildcats in the "extremely low-risk" drilling program for that year.

The results are that the entire waterflood program which remained has been much slower because it just takes waterfloods a lot longer to get going.

Since that original thinking there have been other developments which slowed down the waterfloods more than normal. In the first place, the longest steel strike in history came on and we lost six months. Immediately after that we had the worst winter we have had in 50 years and that lost us more time. The result is that the waterfloods are about a year behind what they would be normally, insofar as taking hold and increasing production.

Complaints from Rosenblatt and others were only a minor annoyance for Trippet in December 1962. He had collected another $4,195,368 from investors during the year. General Electric's Fred Borch and Pepsi Cola's Donald Kendall each chipped in an additional $42,558. James Goss of GE invested another $95,755. A newcomer in 1962 was Stuart Saunders, chairman of the board of Penn Central Railroad; he invested $21,279. Claude Kirk, Jr., an investment banker and later governor of Florida, put in $10,640.

It was later alleged that Trippet's thefts from the Home-Stake treasury were going smoothly, too. In December 1962, he had Home-Stake buy an oil lease in New Mexico from one of his dummy businesses, the Secondary Recovery Operating Corporation, for $187,000. Trippet, through Secondary Recovery, had bought the lease five months earlier for $163, its true value. He pocketed most of the profit. (From 1962 through 1968 Trippet caused Home-Stake to pay to Secondary Recovery additional amounts of $142,100, $41,489, and $248,490.)

Not all members of the Rosenblatt family were finding fault with Trippet as 1963 began. Richard Rosenblatt bought additional common stock in the company on February 4. Two days later Trippet wrote:

We're delighted to have you make this additional stock investment. We plan to raise the dividend. . . . Naturally this will be reflected in increased value for the stock.

The 1961 [drilling] program is getting alone fine. The original projection of income for 1962 was $13,500. However, it actually ran about $31,000, since the program promises to be somewhat more successful than originally projected. [Dick Rosenblatt would therefore receive $310 instead of $135 as the 1962 return on his investment of $15,600—not much to be sure, but more than twice what Trippet had promised originally for 1962.]

William Rosenblatt's irritation over the 1959 program was growing, however. On March 1, 1963, after receiving a February payment to investors, he wrote to Trippet:

Certainly the returns for 1959 are disappointing. It is amazing to find that the income on a percentage basis is higher for 1960 than it is for 1959, even though you started a year earlier. Of course, every estimate of 1959 has been a little worse than the previous one, and I hope that this doesn't continue any further. How much of our investment do you estimate we will get out of the 1959 program? Here are some stamps for your secretary.

"It was nice of you to send the stamps along for Mrs. Loop," Trippet replied. "The net distributable income [from the 1959 drilling] has doubled each year. It is true that it hasn't come along nearly as fast as we had hoped, but there are many reasons for it which you already know."

A month later William Rosenblatt told Trippet that he wanted to sell his interests in the 1959 drilling program. Trippet previously had bought back Rosenblatt's 1961 investment but he balked at this request.

I really wouldn't recommend that you sell the 1959 program just at this time. While I can't guarantee that it will be successful or that the income will increase, I believe it will and I think there is always a time to buy and a time to sell. I think the time to sell is after the program gets going good and the income gets up higher. Then you probably wouldn't want to sell anyway.

I was glad to know that you plan to go to Europe again this summer and I know it will be a pleasant time and that you'll enjoy seeing all your old friends again.

"I must say I am very disappointed with the 1959 program," Rosenblatt responded. "It is very well to say that you don't recommend that I sell my interest. I had counted on much more substantial income, as evidenced by the original prospectus."

The same month, Bernard Rosenblatt began what was to become a heated exchange of letters with Trippet.

My son, David, has asked me to ascertain the status of his [1959] investment. In examining the 1959 program as presented by you in your booklet, there appears that there should have been a more substantial payment than the small sum allotted in the early part of [1963]. I would appreciate hearing, not because we have any interest in withdrawing, but to have some assurance from you that the program is proceeding satisfactorily as seems to be indicated in your periodic reports.

Trippet replied:

The original projection of income on the 1959 program was based entirely on assumption. . . . I cannot guarantee you that the program is proceeding satisfactorily. I can tell you that my engineers say that the properties are proceeding normally and that we can expect increased income in the future. The proof of the pudding will be in the eating.

In response, Rosenblatt wrote:

I didn't realize that "the original projection of income on the 1959 program was based entirely on assumption." My brother, Will, told me last week before he left for Europe that in a conversation with you in New York you seemed optimistic and, indeed, all reports received by my son up to now from your office were that everything is proceeding according to program.

Frankly, I was contemplating to follow my son's investment should real progress in his participation warrant it—at least that the principal seemed safe and secure—but now you leave me with little hope and much misgiving.

William Rosenblatt returned from Europe in September, conferred with his brother and wrote Trippet:

To put it mildly this whole business is a terrible disappointment. It is all so far away from the original portrayal that it is extremely disappointing. It is not only a question of my interest and that of my nephew, but I also got Judge Frank involved in this matter and I originally guaranteed Judge Frank against loss. I must say that I differ very strongly with you as far as your correspondence with my brother is concerned, insofar as I must insist that positive statements were made and not merely estimates. I shall wait until our report in February and then we can take it up further.

In late October Trippet agreed to buy back William Rosenblatt's and Albert Lyons' $14,200 investment in the 1960 drilling program. They accepted $8,000 cash, the rest in installments. Trippet still refused to budge on 1959, in which the group had $52,800 at stake. It was a typical tactic of his to drag complaints out as long as possible, then grudgingly make partial restitution. And the settlement for 1960 was a simple refund; it didn't take into account the original projections, or what the investors might have earned on the money if they had invested it elsewhere during the three years Trippet had it.

In December 1963 Trippet brought another important tactic to bear. He wrote Richard Rosenblatt:

> About a month ago I called you regarding the possibility of your dad, Mrs. Frank and David Rosenblatt giving portions of the 1959 program to charity. A number of the participants will be doing this. . . . I would certainly appreciate it if you would let me know immediately."

The suggestion that an investor give Home-Stake interests to charity was an option devised specifically to placate disgruntled investors. Home-Stake prepared reports that set an artificially high value on the company's drilling shares. Then it proposed that the investor donate his shares to a university, hospital, or other charitable organization and take a second tax write-off (the first having been taken for the initial investment). The evaluation report was given to the investor to show to the IRS if it raised questions about the value of the second deduction. It rarely did in the early years. Among certain General Electric officers, donating Home-Stake units to charity came to be known as leaving Home-Stake by the "back door."

Giving shares to charity effectively silenced many 1959 investors and others who had been complaining. And since the charities hadn't paid anything for the shares, they were much less likely to sue. Home-Stake, therefore, routinely eliminated payments on interests that were given to charity.

William Rosenblatt, however, would not be placated. He wrote Trippet:

> My son, Richard, has indicated that you would like to have a decision from our 1959 group regarding the possibility of donat-

ing part of our 1959 commitment for charity purposes, so as to take advantage of certain tax opportunities. This is impossible.

To be perfectly frank, as I have indicated heretofore, we are unequivocally opposed to the entire situation with respect to the 1959 program. Representations have been made to us which are totally contrary to actual fact, and our attorneys have advised us to await your February report before deciding on what position we will take. Under the circumstances we will do nothing to alter our position. I am sorry I must write to you in this manner.

One night in January 1963, a twenty-year-old singer named Barbra Streisand opened an engagement at the Blue Angel, a nightclub on Manhattan's East Side. Streisand had become moderately well known the previous year in the role of Miss Marmelstein in the Broadway musical *I Can Get It for You Wholesale*. She didn't become nationally famous, however, untill 1963, when she released her first record album and appeared on the "Ed Sullivan Show."

That same year another young performer gained a lot of attention starring in *Best Foot Forward*, an off-Broadway show. She was Liza Minnelli, Judy Garland's daughter.

In the succeeding decade Streisand and Minnelli would become superstars and millionaires. They would need tax shelter. They would find Home-Stake.

Managing Home-Stake was getting more complicated for Trippet. The company's growth posed an increasing number of problems as well as opportunities. There was more money available to steal, but the chance of discovery was greater. The increasing number of investors made it more likely that one of them would become disgruntled enough to sue. Each time a CPA firm found irregularities and another firm took its place, the risk of exposure grew.

A key test of any company president is his ability to deal not only with problems he can anticipate, but also with the large number of random difficulties—and the occasional unexpected crisis—that inevitably arise. If the company is fraudulent, extra skill is required. For the time being, at least, Trippet was the master of every challenge.

In the summer of 1963 a Roanoke, Virginia, man received a sales circular from Home-Stake. It appeared from the circular that the drilling program was being offered to the public at large, instead of to only a few people. If it was, the man knew that the company probably was required by law to register the offering with the Securities and Exchange Commission. So he sent the circular to the agency.

The SEC contacted Home-Stake, asking for information on its solicitations. Trippet turned the matter over to Harry Fitzgerald, who consulted Lyle O'Rourke, a New York lawyer and friend. O'Rourke, who had met Fitzgerald a few years earlier, recommended Home-Stake to a few clients.

O'Rourke referred Fitzgerald to William Blum, Jr., a Washington, D.C., lawyer with long experience dealing with the SEC. Blum in turn enlisted the aid of Harry Heller, another securities lawyer, who had recently left a position as assistant director of the SEC's corporate finance division, the branch of the agency that passes on companies' offering circulars. Heller was a close friend of the head of the SEC's oil and gas regulation section, Tell T. White.

After leaving the SEC, Harry Heller had become associated with the Washington office of Simpson Thacher & Bartlett, the renowned Wall Street law firm. He later became the firm's senior partner in Washington. (Simpson Thacher's partners have included Secretary of State Cyrus Vance and Whitney North Seymour, Jr., the former United States Attorney in Manhattan. They had nothing to do with Home-Stake.)

Heller and Blum traveled to Tulsa, conferred with Trippet and other Home-Stake officers, and advised them to register their 1964 program with the SEC. Trippet took the occasion to drop a note to the SEC's Tell White.

> I am sure you don't remember me, as you see so many people and this has been a long time ago, but I got acquainted with you

in Washington in 1955. You were very courteous and hospitable and I appreciated it at that time and still do. Best wishes.

Two months later, on October 23, Home-Stake vice-presidents Frank Sims and David Davies had a meeting with Tell White concerning Home-Stake's sales circulars. The discussion was general and inconclusive, but White told Sims and Davies that the SEC had serious reservations about the reliability and propriety of estimates of future income by oil-drilling companies. Sims reported to Fitzgerald that the meeting with White was "comfortable and cordial."

We admitted that there are people who dupe the public under the guise of engineers. Our effort for the most part was to remove ourselves in his mind from this category. In this phase of our effort I think we were probably successful—at least in part anyway.

In addition to ensuring that Home-Stake would register its 1964 offering, the SEC formally asked the Washington headquarters of the IRS for guidance on the viability of the tax deductions that Home-Stake was promising its investors.

As 1963 ended, deteriorating relationships with the Rosenblatt group and other early investors, and the prospect of having to register with the SEC, didn't loom as particularly serious problems to Trippet. Home-Stake had raised $9,477,154 in new money during the year, bringing its total for eight annual drilling programs to roughly $24 million.

Certainly Home-Stake spent part of that money legitimately; it drilled some oil wells in Kansas and Oklahoma and produced some oil. But production and payment to investors didn't nearly reach the amounts projected. Apart from the money that Trippet and Plummer were stealing, much of the investments that weren't spent for drilling were consumed by company overhead and the high cost of selling each year's program. Trippet, Plummer, and Fitzgerald were spending a lot of time in New York and other cities, where they stayed in expensive hotels and lavishly entertained prospective investors.

It also cost money to keep the Ponzi scheme afloat and growing. The company had to inflate its negligible oil revenues with other money in order to pay investors enough to induce a major commitment in the third, fourth, or fifth year. A few favored investors like General Electric's Fred Borch and Pepsi's Donald Kendall—those whose names Home-Stake could use to advantage—generally received higher payments than the Rosenblatts and other lesser-known people.

Trippet and Plummer allegedly were continuing to siphon money from the company, and at the end of 1963 they included William Edwards Murray, the New York tax lawyer who had spoken favorably about Home-Stake to his clients. In December 1963, at Trippet's instigation, Home-Stake paid Trippet $40,138, Plummer $4,168, and Murray $30,035 for oil and gas leases in South Dakota and Arkansas that purportedly were worth much less than Home-Stake paid.

Murray by then had become a close associate and confidant of Trippet and "actively participated and conspired with Trippet to defraud Home-Stake for his own personal gain in connection with the sale of his lease to Home-Stake," according to a suit filed against Murray by Home-Stake's bankruptcy trustee eleven years later. Murray denied all wrongdoing. He subsequently said his share of the money from the oil leases was "in lieu of fees" Trippet owed him.

In discussing Home-Stake with his clients, Murray was careful to hedge his recommendations with a few mild warnings about the risks of oil investment. But a letter he wrote to a client in 1963 shows that the thrust of his comments clearly was favorable toward Home-Stake. Murray told the client, a high executive of a major corporation, that even though Home-Stake projected a return of more than three times the investor's outlay, he would advise being conservative and basing his financial planning on only a 200 percent return.

I have to point out to you that I am acting in this matter purely as your lawyer, not as an investment counsel, and that there are risks in connection with oil investments. I believe the risks in connection with waterflooding are minimal, but, again, my experiences in this field are limited. However, even on a two for one basis the return looks pretty good.

The soft sell. The client made a major investment in Home-Stake the next year.

The 1963 Home-Stake annual report, distributed February 24, 1964, indicated that the CPA firm of Kunkel & Company had taken over the auditing of Home-Stake's books. It was the fifth firm to audit Home-Stake in seven years. Kunkel was Elmer Kunkel, the accountant who formerly had been employed by the firm of Frazer and Torbet and had discovered irregularities in Home-Stake's books in early 1961. During preparation of the 1963 financial report, Kunkel again confronted Trippet with Home-Stake's practice of selling an excess of drilling units, thus taking in more money than it was supposed to and diluting the value of each unit. As he had three years earlier, Trippet said the extra money would be returned to the participants and there would be no dilution. Kunkel signed the accountant's letter accompanying the financial statement.

Another meager payment to 1959 investors was distributed in February 1964, and it wasn't long before the Trippet-Rosenblatt correspondence heated up again. William Rosenblatt said that he had talked further with his lawyers.

They and we feel there have been some very unfortunate misrepresentations in connection with this program. It is not merely evident in the original estimate book, but in all the subsequent correspondence, and particularly in the letters which I received telling me how much I could expect from my 1959 investment. . . . Personally I shrink from litigation, and if some method could be worked out to settle this matter I would prefer it. If you have any concrete suggestions I would be ready to listen.

Trippet's reply to Rosenblatt was another classic. Many former Home-Stake investors around the country have similar letters in their files. Instead of trying to perpetuate a cordial relationship, Trippet lashed out at Rosenblatt, attempting to put him on the defensive.

I received your letter of March 5 and first off I want to point out a few errors you've made.

1. First you say there have been misrepresentations in connection with the 1959 program. You are wrong.

2. You imply that there is something peculiar about the fact that we purchased your interest in the 1961 program but not in the 1959 program, as if we had taken the initiative about it. The fact is that you are the one who took the initiative. In the spring of 1962 I saw you in New York and the stock market had plummeted. You were worried and asked if I would buy your interest back in the 1961 program because it was the newest one. I didn't have to do this but to do you a favor I did. That favor cost us over $31,000.

You also don't bother to mention that we bought back your interest and Dr. Lyons's interest in the 1960 program.

You also don't bother to mention that all of the purchases were made for your gross cost, which gave you a huge profit, due to your tax savings.[1]

You say you shrink from litigation. I don't blame you for that because your position is unjustified and you would lose.

Frankly, I don't shrink from litigation when I know I'm right.

However, not as a matter of settlement but simply as a matter of the fact that I would like to terminate our relationship completely, I would be willing to make the following offer. (I'm quite aware that you probably will be just as glad as I will to complete the severance.)

Your nephew, David, is in only the one program. I presume your brother paid for it and made substantial tax savings. I am not willing to take him out at a profit. However, I will buy the interest back for his net after-tax cost. In order to figure this you will have to ascertain what tax bracket he was in at the time he spent the money in 1959 and 1960. Then you will have to deduct what payments he had already received, as they have been practically tax-free.

With reference to your own situation, I would be willing to settle on the basis of considering your entire situation. You seem to be willing to take the profits on the 1960 and 1961 programs without any thought about those, but I'm not. In other words, I would be willing for you to take the net cost after considering

---

[1] Trippet frequently cited tax savings in trying to minimize the significance of investor losses and to negotiate refunds. He didn't mention, however, that if an investor had chosen a legitimate and profitable tax shelter, he might have made money from the investment, as well as saving the same amount of taxes he did with Home-Stake.

your tax savings to you on the 1959, 1960, and 1961 programs Again you would have to figure what tax bracket you were in to arrive at that. I will take your word for it.

Then you would deduct from that the purchase price of the 1960 and 1961 programs [which Trippet bought back] and also deduct the [oil revenue] payments you have received. I don't know if that would leave you with much coming, but if it did I would be glad to pay it.

To complete the divorce, I would also want to buy back your stock and that of your family, except the stock Dick owns personally. He is in the 1961 program and hasn't made any complaint and as far as I'm concerned he can stay just as is, if he wishes to do so.

I want to make one thing crystal clear. The above is not a trading offer. You asked me to make a concrete proposal and I am responding to your request. If you don't approve of my proposal, feel free to go ahead and file your lawsuit.

Trippet correctly reasoned that an aggressive thrust would scare off some investors in Rosenblatt's position; they would simply accept his offer and go away. Rosenblatt didn't. Trippet's letter was forwarded to him at the Boca Raton Hotel and Club in Boca Raton, Florida. Rosenblatt replied immediately.

Your letter is most unusual, for throughout it seems to be predicated on the principle that all benefits allowed by the U.S. Government in tax deductions belong to you and your company, and not to the recipients. This is so contradictory to your original estimates, and more specifically your letters to me in which you pointed out that the investor would receive four or five times his original investment even besides any tax benefits. . . .

You state that I am wrong with regard to alleged misrepresentations and unilateral change of plan in the 1959 program. I contend that you are absolutely wrong. We shall see who is in the right. . . .

Your proposition is wholly unacceptable. Your statement that I shrink from litigation because my position is "unjustified" is purely self-serving and gratuitous. If the challenge is tossed to me, I accept.

Since aggressiveness hadn't worked, Trippet became somewhat more conciliatory in his next letter. He tried the "nothing-personal" approach.

I received your letter of March 18 and first off, I want to say something I should have said before. I know you have been most upset and distressed about the 1959 program. I want you to know I am sorry you have had this difficulty and mental anguish. I have no personal animosity toward you whatsoever and, quite to the contrary, insofar as the personal relationship is concerned, I am still your friend and I hope you are mine.

I know you are entirely sincere in your position, but I do hope you will realize that I am too, and we simply have a disagreement on a business matter. While I know you are sincere, I think your trouble is you're just a poor loser, if indeed you had any loss. In other words, I don't know that you are going to lose a dime on the 1959 program. You may make money. But let's just assume that you do lose some money. You're a poor loser because you let that fact obscure everything else and don't bear in mind the fact that you won on the 1960 and 1961 programs. . . .

I have another idea. Dick is smart and he certainly is interested solely in what is best for you. Why don't you submit my previous letter and this letter to him and then submit to him any papers on your side you want to submit to him. Then let him analyze the situation and make a recommendation to you.

I don't say that you should be bound by his recommendation, but I think he can be helpful to you.

Rosenblatt replied:

I have your letter of March 24. Thanks for your kind expression of friendship. In that same spirit, may I suggest arbitration of our difficulties, as my attorneys do not see any basis of settlement as per your letter of the 24th. I would be prepared to name my friend, Judge Rifkind, as my arbitrator [former Judge Simon Rifkind, now a senior partner in the prominent New York law firm of Paul Weiss, Rifkind, Wharton & Garrison, and a key figure in combatting New York's current financial problems], and you could name one, and the two arbitrators could appoint a third impartial arbitrator.

I do resent your reference to my being a "poor loser." I would like to know what reasonable man would not be a "poor loser" if he had received letter after letter, and had been told in person, how much money he was going to make out of a deal and then it turned out to be a "flop." Your references to my profits on the 1960 and 1961 programs are conjectures; how do you know what my tax status was in those years?

Trippet rejected Rosenblatt's arbitration proposal.

Intense as the Trippet-Rosenblatt dispute had become by the spring of 1964, it hadn't yet become public. Home-Stake's Washington lawyers, Harry Heller and William Blum, presumably knew nothing of the tussel over the Rosenblatt investments as they shepherded Home-Stake's first public offering prospectus smoothly through the SEC. The prospectus was written by Fitzgerald, rewritten by Trippet, and again rewritten under the direction of Heller, who, according to Fitzgerald, said the first two drafts "weren't worth a shit."

One might have thought that going public would have been the end of Home-Stake—that it would have had to reveal so much information that its various frauds inevitably would be exposed. The system works that way in theory but rarely in practice.

The securities laws operate on the presumption that most companies tell the truth in their prospectuses. The law prescribes penalties for false statements, but it is clear to all—government and companies alike—that the SEC has only enough manpower to enforce the law in relatively few cases. It has to depend on voluntary compliance, much as the IRS has to assume that most people will file honest income-tax returns.

Therefore, aside from the minimum deterrence stemming from the possibility of someday getting caught, there isn't any way to stop a determined and skillful swindler from lying in a prospectus. The SEC doesn't check a prospectus for accuracy; it merely ensures that the company reports the required amount of information about its operations and finances.

In some ways, then, a prospectus that has been passed upon by the SEC is a more effective swindling device than a totally unregulated piece of sales literature. A prospectus looks more official; it carries certain warnings if the SEC feels the investment is in a speculative field; it is signed by both a lawyer and an accountant.

Home-Stake's first prospectus said that the 1964 drilling program proposed to raise $7,552,000 by selling four hundred drilling interests at $18,800 each. It warned that the offering was being made only to people in high tax brackets because secondary recovery of oil by waterflooding is speculative. "It must be emphasized," the prospectus stated, "that there can be no assurance or certainty that in fact any of the projects will be successful."

The prospectus listed drilling projects in Seminole and Lincoln counties, in Oklahoma, and in Harvey, Russell, Stafford, and Sedgwick counties, in Kansas. It contained the statement that "legal matters in connection with this offering, except where otherwise indicated, have been passed upon by Harry Heller, Esq., Washington, D.C., and William Blum, Esq., Washington, D.C., special counsel to Home-Stake." The accountant's letter was signed by Kunkel & Company.

Naturally, the prospectus said nothing about Home-Stake's projections of 400 percent profits, its meager payments to investors, its deepening dispute with the Rosenblatt group and others, repeated discoveries of irregularities and frequent changes in CPA firms, and Trippet's alleged thefts from the company. (Home-Stake continued to circulate separate sales literature containing the 400 percent profit projections.)

Technically, Home-Stake's prospectuses covered only the subsidiary corporations it organized each year ostensibly to operate its annual drilling ventures. Harry Fitzgerald said later that one reason Trippet decided to form subsidiaries and have them issue the prospectuses was to avoid including the parent company's financial statement with the material submitted to the SEC. The subsidiaries served virtually no other purpose. Each year's investments were mingled with those of previous years, and the drilling was done by Home-Stake itself. The parent company's financial statement was included in its annual report to stockholders, of course. But according to John Lenoir, Home-Stake's treasurer and later financial vice-president, Trippet considered the stockholders a "bunch of dummies" who wouldn't raise questions as long as the company paid good dividends on its common stock. Trippet made sure dividends were increased regularly.

Armed with preliminary copies of the 1964 prospectus and sales circulars, Harry Fitzgerald returned to California to see Donald McKee, the business consultant to whom Oscar Trippet had referred Fitzgerald in the summer of 1962. Since then, McKee had conferred personally with Robert Trippet. He asked Trippet what made his company different from others and why other companies weren't getting into waterflooding if it was so lucrative. Trippet told McKee that it was a new field, with plenty of unexploited properties for everyone, and that Home-Stake's above-average salaries had attracted some good men from major companies.

"It was a not implausible story," McKee recalled later. "And it was all the more convincing because I was given to understand that the investors included senior officers—groups of senior officers, in fact—of some of the biggest corporations, banks, law firms of the greatest prominence—senior partners in those law firms."

Donald McKee was a cautious man, so when Harry Fitzgerald arrived in 1964, McKee introduced him to a man he considered to be the shrewdest, most astute investor in southern California, Matthew Kanin. Among other things, Kanin managed the investments of Peter S. Bing, an extremely wealthy physician and a member of the well-known New York Bing family that controls large real-estate interests. McKee knew that Kanin was familiar with every tax-shelter prospectus of any consequence, and thought that if anyone could spot a flaw in Home-Stake Kanin could. Somewhat to McKee's surprise, Kanin said that Home-Stake appeared on the surface at least to be the best thing of its kind he had seen in years.

Kanin's reaction bolstered McKee's confidence, and he arranged for Fitzgerald to see Marvin Meyer, a senior partner in the Beverly Hills law firm of Rosenfeld, Meyer & Susman. This leading southern California firm has handled the legal and financial affairs of some of the nation's best-known entertainers, including Jack Benny, Andy Williams, Marlon Brando, and Tony Curtis. It also has represented some top movie studios and talent agencies and their executives—for example, Warner Brothers' president Frank Wells and vice-chairman John Calley; and Creative Management Associates Inc. and its former president, Freddie Fields.

Marvin Meyer and his law partner Donald Rosenfeld also were impressed with Home-Stake and Harry Fitzgerald. Fitzgerald left a copy of the preliminary 1964 prospectus, and made sure that Meyer and Rosenfeld knew that Home-Stake's investors included people like Fred Borch and Donald Kendall.

Fitzgerald also established contact with the Los Angeles partners of two big CPA firms, Arthur Young & Company and Arthur Andersen & Company. He met officers of Santa Anita Consolidated, a diversified company that owns the Santa Anita racetrack among other things, and was introduced to Benno Bechhold, a wealthy businessman with interests in shipping and banking. When he returned to Los Angeles two months later, Fitzgerald signed up several of these people, including Marvin Meyer and Don Rosenfeld, as Home-Stake investors.

As Home-Stake was making its first significant penetration of southern California in mid-1964, its sales in the East soared, showing the potency of Trippet's carefully nurtured word-of-mouth network.

General Electric's Fred Borch made his largest investment yet—$132,160; and a large number of his colleagues joined him. John D. Lockton, the company treasurer, invested $56,640; Reginald H. Jones, vice-president and the man who in 1971 would succeed Borch as head of the company, $28,200; S. Wellford Corbin, vice-president, $18,800; Virgil B. Day, vice-president and later a member of President Nixon's Pay Board during the wage-price control period, $38,300; William Dennler, vice-president, $18,800; J. Stanford Smith, vice-president and later chairman of the board of the International Paper Company, $66,080; Jack S. Parker, vice-president and future vice-chairman, $75,200; Charles E. Reed, vice-president, $28,200; Herman Weiss, vice-president and later vice-chairman, $47,000; James H. Goss, vice-president, $37,600; and Donald D. Scarff, vice-president, $37,760.

William Edwards Murray had spoken well of Home-Stake to several of these executives, and they had discussed Home-Stake among themselves. "All of the executives were very clubby, and what one did the others did," Murray said later. Trippet wrote to Borch: "Thanks to you and Jim Goss, we really have a big, top-notch group at General Electric."

The GE group was joined in 1964 by two members of the

high command of the First National City Bank of New York (now known as Citibank), the second largest bank in the United States. The investors were George S. Moore, president and later board chairman ($56,400); and Walter B. Wriston, vice-president and future chairman ($18,800). Moore was friendly with some of the GE officers and talked about Home-Stake with them.

The 1964 group also included Thomas S. Gates, who was secretary of defense under President Eisenhower and by 1964 had become board chairman of the Morgan Guaranty Trust Company of New York. The amount of his 1964 investment isn't known. John G. Martin, chairman of Heublein Inc., the big Connecticut liquor and food-products concern, invested $56,640. Ralph A. Hart, a Heublein executive, put in another $56,640 in 1964. Henry Roberts, president of the Connecticut General Life Insurance Company, and Charles R. Walgreen, Jr., of the drug-store chain, each committed $18,800.

Investment analysts at Morgan Guaranty had examined Home-Stake, and their appraisal was "luke warm." "But they didn't tell me *not* to invest," Gates said later. "Home-Stake was supposed to be more conservative than the others."

Another notable 1964 investor was former South Carolina governor Ernest Hollings who put in $18,800. (Hollings was elected to the U.S. Senate in 1966.)

Home-Stake also invaded the Wall Street legal community. Robert J. McDonald and Richard S. Storrs, partners in Sullivan & Cromwell, each invested $18,800. "I was introduced to Trippet by William Murray," McDonald said. "I had been on various tax lawyer panels with Murray and he suggested, over lunch in '62 or '63, that Home-Stake was a good program. I called some people and they said 'Yes, I'm in it. Seems okay to me.' So I got in. In the future people would call me and I would say 'Yes, I'm in it. Seems okay to me.' So they got in. I was told there were a great number of GE people, Pepsi and so on. It was like the Blue Book, and seemed to get bluer."

During Barbra Streisand's engagement at the Blue Angel in January 1963, her manager, Martin Erlichman, invited a friend, Martin Bregman, to hear her. Bregman, formerly an insurance

salesman, had started an agency that managed money for entertainers. Like many others in those days, he correctly anticipated that Streisand would become a big star. He got to know
her through Erlichman, and later that winter, in a Massachusetts
motel room near a nightclub where Streisand was performing,
Bregman, Erlichman, and Streisand orally agreed that Bregman
would become Streisand's financial manager.

Over the next decade Marty Bregman's clientele would grow
to include some of the country's most eminent entertainers.
Bregman himself would produce such successful films as
Serpico and *Dog Day Afternoon*. But he was just getting started
during that winter of 1963, and one of his initial contacts in
financial management was a young Manhattan tax lawyer, Kent
M. Klineman, whom he had met at a poker game.

After graduating from Harvard law school in 1959, Klineman
began practice as a junior associate at the Wall Street firm
of Jackson, Nash, Brophy, Barringer & Brooks, where William
Edwards Murray was a partner. Through Murray, he came to
know Robert Trippet and Home-Stake.

Klineman was a slender, curly haired man, always fashionably
dressed and coiffed. He was exceptionally bright and didn't
hesitate to show it. (An associate described him as "the kind
of man you can imagine playing three-dimensional chess.")
Klineman maintained his contact with Home-Stake and put
Trippet in touch with Marty Bregman. At Klineman's suggestion,
Barbra Streisand and Elliott Gould, her husband at the time,
contacted Home-Stake and invested $28,200 in the 1964 drilling
program. (Streisand had starred that year in the Broadway
show *Funny Girl*; signed a lucrative contract with CBS; rented
a nine-room duplex apartment on Central Park West; and been
the subject of a *Newsweek* profile entitled "Money Girl.")

Of course, Home-Stake's new 1964 investors knew nothing of
Trippet's continuing war of nerves with William Rosenblatt
and other investors of the late 1950s.

On Thursday, June 18, 1964, Trippet received a letter from
Martin D. Eile of the Wall Street law firm of Stroock & Stroock
& Lavan, William Rosenblatt's legal counsel. "We would ap-
preciate your advising us of your intentions . . . so that we

may advise our clients and govern our own actions in accordance therewith," the lawyer wrote.

Trippet replied: "I would appreciate it if you would inspect the correspondence I've had with Mr. William Rosenblatt earlier this year. I believe that will answer your questions as what our intentions are."

Meanwhile, Bernard Rosenblatt had assumed a conciliatory stance.

> My son, David, has recently been appointed to a most important scientific post in the United States Government. Accordingly, I am reluctant to see him involved in any litigation. Therefore, if you are inclined to make some fair and reasonable settlement, he will be prepared to consider it. Perhaps you would be ready to offer him Home-Stake Production Co. (common) stock for his interest in the 1959 program. If not, would you object to have me substituted for my son in the litigation?

Trippet took the opportunity to stroke Bernard Rosenblatt's ego and to try to nudge him away from his brother's point of view while at the same time refusing his request. He wrote:

> I was glad to know that David has a fine new appointment. I hope that it works out well for him. As you know, I regret very much that this whole matter of litigation has arisen. I've tried to make a fair offer to Will. If you'll go back and read the correspondence, you'll see that I've already offered your net-out-of-pocket cost after considering your tax savings. I believe this is fair and reasonable.
>
> I wouldn't be interested in putting out more stock in exchange for the interest in the 1959 program.
>
> I wouldn't advise you to substitute for your son in the litigation. If we have to go that far, it will be very nerve wracking and will drag on for years and I don't think you ought to put yourself in the position of becoming exhausted over a small matter like this.

Rosenblatt responded:

> I am convinced, as a lawyer, that we have a good cause of action. . . . On the other hand I must agree with your last paragraph that this may prove a long and unpleasant dispute, and therefore [we] should . . . avoid suit if possible. May I ask you to please redefine what you are willing to do for an agreed settlement, bearing in mind that if we had invested the funds in

low income tax-free bonds, we would still have our capital intact, after collecting over $3,000 without any tax charges.

Trippet offered to pay David Rosenblatt $7,434 and permit him to keep his interest in the 1959 program, for which he paid $17,600. Trippet figured that the $7,434 represented David's out-of-pocket cost, considering tax savings, minus payments Home-Stake already had made to the 1959 investors, plus interest on the out-of-pocket cost. Bernard Rosenblatt accepted the settlement.

Over the next three months, William Rosenblatt's lawyers negotiated a partial buy-back for him similar to that which Trippet had arranged for Bernard and David. But the deal with William was never completed.

Trippet's thefts from Home-Stake allegedly continued in late 1964. On November 1 he organized a dummy partnership, the Oil Field Operating Company, listing his three daughters as partners. Trippet saw to it that Home-Stake paid Oil Field Operating $38,000 in 1964 and 1965. The company constituted a "fraudulent scheme to obtain money and property illegally," a bankruptcy trustee would allege ten years later. The trustee ultimately would conclude that Trippet also misused Home-Stake funds in other ways. For instance, he made a practice of using Home-Stake credit cards and cash to buy automobiles, food, and other personal items for himself and his family.

The Trippet family lived expensively but not ostentatiously. In the 1950s Trippet bought a large white two-story house in one of Tulsa's most exclusive residential neighborhoods. The house, then about twenty years old, was worth $150,000 to $200,000 by the mid-1970s. Trippet drove new Cadillacs, trading them in frequently, but he complained that they were "gas guzzlers." He drank Scotch whisky, though he rarely ordered by brand and hardly ever showed any effect from drinking. Most of his suits were bought off the rack at a fashionable Tulsa men's store.

The family belonged to all the "right" clubs, including the Tulsa Club downtown and the Southern Hills Country Club on the city's outskirts. Helen Grey Trippet was a member of the Junior League; and the three daughters—Virginia, Constance, and Mary Susan ("Sudie")—were active in school affairs. But the Trippets were never social lions. Bob and Helen Grey preferred to entertain small groups of friends with dinner-bridge parties at home.

Trippet wasn't enthusiastic about recreation. He played neither golf nor tennis, preferring to watch sports, especially golf, on television. He owned a part interest in a boat at nearby Grand Lake but didn't use it often. Although he occasionally attended the ballet or symphony concerts and had a player piano at home, none of these interests excited him or held his attention for very long. When he wasn't working or traveling, he usually was sitting at home reading on financial, investment, and legal matters. "He read stock market advisory letters by the pound," one friend said.

Business acquaintances and social friends both considered Bob Trippet bland company. He didn't often mix socially with his Home-Stake colleagues; and he rarely discussed Home-Stake with his social friends in Tulsa, and virtually never tried to sell any of them a Home-Stake drilling investment.

On March 3, 1965, Home-Stake issued its annual shareholders report for 1964. Stating that 1964 had "witnessed record highs in all categories," the report noted that in addition to its Kansas and Oklahoma drilling, the company had begun operations near Santa Maria, California, a coastal town of thirty-three thousand three hours north of Los Angeles by car. Home-Stake's Santa Maria properties were to become the company's showcase in the mid- and late 1960s.

The Securities and Exchange Commission cleared Home-Stake's second publicly registered prospectus on May 21. Similar in format to the 1964 version, the 1965 prospectus offered 465 drilling units at $19,000 each, for a total of $8,835,000.

In July the Rosenblatts resurfaced, and Trippet again displayed his skill at protracting a dispute. William's son Richard wrote to Trippet concerning his $15,680 investment in the 1961 drilling venture.

I am a little disappointed in the 1961 program. . . . When I heard this one was so great I really expected some bigger returns by the summer of 1965. . . . Could you let me have your ideas about this and also whatever information you have of a non-technical nature. I am afraid I will have to leave the technical stuff to experts.

"It was a pleasant surprise to hear from you," Trippet replied. "I've often thought of you and wondered how you were getting along. I know well, because you have the ability."

I, too, am disappointed in the 1961 program. It hasn't come along nearly as well as I thought it would. The accumulated return up to this time is about 90% of original projection, but at this time it is considerably below what we thought it would be. Frankly, I doubt if it's going to make as much money as we originally expected.

Rosenblatt responded:

I was completely shocked with your last letter. I have a rather extensive file going back many years covering the 1961 program. At the outset I was led to believe that the income plus return on investment would amount to over 70 thousand dollars in the final analysis. This was before the excellent news which came in during the course of the drilling and the commencement of the [water] flooding. It would be an understatement to say that I am disappointed.

I have checked with a number of people who have been in various of your programs and every single one has given me exactly the same experience. Most of them have gotten out of the program very much disillusioned. They have advised me to do the same.

I would like to sell back the interest I have in the 1961 program at a figure approximating the projections which were given me. I would also like to sell my stock back at a figure commensurate to that which you are paying others at the present time.

If 1961 is as you stated, the best year of all the programs, then the other participants must be in a sorry state.

Trippet answered:

I'm sorry that you are disappointed in the 1961 program. On the other hand, I know of no obligation on Home-Stake's part to repurchase it from you. Despite the fact that Home-Stake has no obligation to repurchase it, we will try to accommodate you by buying it back. I know full well that we would never be able to agree on a price by correspondence or negotiation. Consequently, I would suggest that an impartial appraiser be employed to appraise the value of your interest.

"I am very unhappy with your reply," Rosenblatt responded:

The original representations and estimates gave such an encouraging glow to this investment, and subsequent news was so great, that I had reason to believe I had splendid prospects. . . . With the present amount of information I have, I would not be willing to submit this to an appraiser; I would, however, be willing to submit it to arbitration at which time all issues could be examined and determined.

For the next several months, Trippet and Richard Rosenblatt debated the possibilities of appraisal and arbitration. They couldn't agree. Finally Trippet offered to pay Rosenblatt $8,354, computed as the amount of the original income projection through 1965, minus amounts actually paid. Rosenblatt retorted that he computed a higher figure when using the same formula. "This is just the very best I can do, Dick," Trippet replied.

The informal, genteel sales network that Robert Trippet, Harry Fitzgerald, and Charlie Plummer had fashioned by the end of 1965 was effective in part because many of Home-Stake's key salesmen weren't called salesmen and, in fact, weren't salesmen in the usual sense. For the most part they were lawyers, CPAs, or financial advisers whose clients depended on them to be objective in assessing investment possibilities, and free from conflicts of interest.

Trippet began a major effort to develop a market for Home-Stake investment in Washington, D.C. He was aided by William Blum, the Washington securities lawyer who represented Home-Stake at the SEC; Lyle O'Rourke, the New York attorney who had put Home-Stake in touch with Blum in 1963; and a rather unlikely third person, a British economist named Redvers Opie.

Opie, sixty-four years old in 1965, had taught economics at Oxford and Harvard; served as economic adviser to the British embassy in Washington during World War II; been a senior staff member at the Brookings Institution; and by the 1960s was an independent businessman dividing his time between Washington and Mexico City.

Most of the lawyers, accountants, and others who in any way aided Home-Stake's sales efforts were directly or indirectly compensated by the company when their clients invested. Payments came in various forms, and often the attorneys and CPAs disclaimed any connection between the compensation and

84

the investments, and denied conflicts of interests. The payments were called "consulting fees," "finder's fees," "fees for business advice," or even "legal fees." Occasionally a lawyer whose client was investing in Home-Stake also gave the company a little legal advice on the side.

But whatever the euphemism, and however the recipients interpreted the payments, there can be no doubt that Home-Stake looked upon much of the money it paid to these lawyers and accountants over the years simply as sales commissions.

New York lawyers William Murray and Kent Klineman obtained sizeable loans from Home-Stake under varying circumstances and were compensated in other ways. Money manager Martin Bregman's agency accepted loans, although Bregman later said their only purpose was to finance his and his clients' investments in Home-Stake. The firm of Rosenfeld, Meyer & Susman in Beverly Hills refused to accept money on the grounds that it wouldn't be ethical.

Blum, Opie and others were paid directly, however. They received sales commissions of three-to-five percent of the price of the drilling interests they were responsible for selling.

Redvers Opie collected $16,625 for selling $332,500 in Home-Stake interests—seventeen and a half units—in 1965. "You really broke the sonic barrier this year," Trippet told Opie. "Next year I know you'll go to 25 units."

Opie's 1965 clients included Betty Beale, then the leading society columnist in Washington; Frances A. Hufty, a grande dame of Washington society; Harold Leventhal, a judge on the U.S. Court of Appeals for the District of Columbia; and Blanche S. Dickinson, a well-traveled economist and consultant to the World Bank and the International Monetary Fund. Blanche Dickinson was a close friend of Redvers Opie (they were once engaged to be married) and relied heavily on him for financial advice.

"Delighted to have you join us," Trippet wrote to Blanche Dickinson in December 1965.

We recently enjoyed so much having Mr. Opie stop by Tulsa on his way from Mexico to Washington. He told me of your fascinating career. Having just returned from a trip to the Far East it's all the more interesting to me. One thing I shall try to avoid is copying the people who go somewhere for 10 days and come back experts. I must say, though, that I was sorry to see Japan swallowing Western ways in such big gulps, but of course that's just a personal opinion.

I have every confidence that the South Cat Canyon property [one of Home-Stake's California drilling sites] is going to be a dandy and make us all some good money. . . . I'm certainly looking forward to the privilege and pleasure of getting acquainted with you personally. I'll be in Washington in the next several months and will call you before leaving Tulsa.

Home-Stake had no trouble raising the $8,835,000 it sought in 1965. In fact, it collected $9,499,430. Senator Jacob K. Javits of New York invested $28,500. Another newcomer was William H. Morton, then head of the investment house of W. H. Morton & Company and later president of the American Express Company and chairman of the executive committee of the Singer Company. He put in $19,000. Morton's experience again demonstrated that corporate executives, bankers, and lawyers were influenced more by what their peers in the business world invested in than by conventional sources of advice, such as investment analysts and stockbrokers.

"I first heard about Home-Stake when I walked into the locker room of my country club one Sunday morning to play golf," Morton said. "I ran into two friends of mine. One of them heads one of the biggest banks in the world. They said, 'Bill, you should be in this.' I said, 'What is it?' They told me about Home-Stake. I said, 'Send him [Trippet] around to see me.' I guess I'm stupid and just don't understand oil people. I went along. He [Trippet] is the biggest flim flam man ever to hit Wall Street. Years later somebody said to me, 'Haven't you given it to charity yet?' But I didn't believe it was worth what they said. Thank God I didn't give mine to the Museum of Modern Art or Dartmouth [his alma mater]."

Victor Holt, Jr., president of the Goodyear Tire & Rubber Company, invested $19,000 in 1965. Jack I. Straus, chairman of R. H Macy & Company, committed $38,000.

There were a number of repeat investors, too. Barbra Streisand put in another $38,000, bringing her stake to $66,200. Streisand and husband Elliott Gould became so enthusiastic about Home-

Stake that they quarreled in Martin Bregman's Lexington Avenue office over how much to invest and in whose name the shares would be. (They were put in Streisand's name.)

General Electric's Fred Borch took his biggest plunge yet —$209,000—bringing his total to $600,787. Several of his GE colleagues also invested again, as did George Moore ($256,500) and Walter Wriston ($38,000) of First National City Bank, and many other important businessmen.

Former Defense Secretary Gates, still unmoved by the Morgan Guaranty analysts' mixed appraisal, invested $152,000 in 1965. At the United States Trust Company of New York, internationally known for its estate-planning expertise, the analysts' view of Home-Stake wasn't mixed; it was negative. But the bank's board chairman, Hoyt Ammidon, invested $85,500 anyway. "It was brought to my attention by William Murray, the estate-planning lawyer at Jackson Nash," Ammidon said. "He introduced Trippet. I checked it out and found it was heavily invested in by people at City Bank and GE. Because these two organizations liked it, including the head of the oil department at City Bank, it seemed to me to have merit. The people in our own oil department were against it from the beginning. Had I been smarter, I would have listened to them." (The head of First National City Bank's oil department then was William I. Spencer, a Home-Stake investor himself. By 1975 he was the bank's president.)

Neil McElroy, chairman of the Procter & Gamble Company, invested $19,000. Dean P. Fite, a Procter & Gamble group vice-president put in $10,000. "Bob Trippet and Bill Murray talked to me. I listened to the presentation. The explanation made sense. Later the problems made sense as to why they weren't paying very much."

In December 1965 William Edwards Murray was invited to conduct a seminar on trusts and estates for several bankers and lawyers in Fall River, Massachusetts. The seminar was organized by Durfee Trust Company of Fall River, with which Murray had had business dealings. The meeting also was attended by several representatives of Southeastern Massachusetts University, a small commuter school in nearby North Dartmouth.

At a dinner following the seminar, the university president

told Murray that the school needed a means of raising additional funds. Murray proposed that a foundation be formed to raise money. He volunteered to be president of the foundation, and even donated his $100 fee for conducting the seminar as the foundation's first gift.

Although the president and others were impressed with Murray's seeming grasp of the school's needs, there were other things that the university people didn't find out until much later. Had they known about them in 1965, they would not have accepted Murray's aid, for the new foundation was destined to play an entirely different role from the one envisioned by the university group on that December evening in 1965.

During this same period, and later, Home-Stake made two loans to Murray totaling between $200,000 and $300,000. He used part of the money to pay off a loan from the First National City Bank of New York and the rest to purchase Home-Stake common stock. He used the Home-Stake stock, whose market value rose, as partial collateral for a subsequent $300,000 loan from the Chase Manhattan Bank.

Trippet had Home-Stake pay $39,500 in late 1965 to another of his allegedly dummy companies, Petroleum Properties, Inc. The bankruptcy trustee later would call it part of his "fraudulent scheme to obtain money and property" for his own benefit.

Home-Stake's feud with the Rosenblatt group, still unknown to newer investors, climaxed in 1966. After Trippet reached a tentative settlement on the 1961 program with Richard Rosenblatt in February, Albert Lyons, who had invested $7,840 in 1961, requested the same terms. Trippet refused. There followed a protracted and angry exchange of letters, marked by what had become typical twists and turns by Trippet. They couldn't agree on a settlement, so Lyons, together with William, Bernard, and Richard Rosenblatt, hired the Tulsa law firm of Houston, Klein & Davidson.

Unaware of Home-Stake's frauds and feuds with investors, the SEC passed the company's 1966 prospectus without a fuss. On May 9 William Blum wrote a note to Harry Fitzgerald, who was on a selling trip to New York. "The SEC's only suggestion was that dollar signs be put in front of the figures at the top of each column on page 44."

The prospectus was approved for distribution two days later. It differed little from those for 1964 and 1965. The prospectus disclosed nothing about Home-Stake's drilling prior to 1963. Buried deep in a section where the company was required to disclose its meager payments thus far to 1963, 1964, and 1965 investors, it said that the figures "should be considered in the light of the fact that a two to two-and-one-half year development period . . . is involved in the case of each program." In other words, the investor shouldn't expect much until at least the third year. As in the past, investors weren't deterred. Home-Stake sold $10,468,000 worth of interests in 1966 with little difficulty.

Before Home-Stake registered its drilling programs publicly in 1964, it had sold investments partly through the use of sales brochures. The brochures described the programs and predicted profits exceeding 400 percent of the investor's outlay. Home-Stake wasn't allowed to make such claims in its registered prospectus. In addition to prohibiting profits forecasts in prospectuses, the SEC bars companies from making profit projections, orally or in writing, while a prospectus is being circulated.

The rules didn't stop Home-Stake. Elmer Kunkel, the CPA, warned Trippet as early as 1964 that the sales brochures were fraudulent, and Washington lawyer Harry Heller tried to convince Fitzgerald not to use the brochures. But the company continued to circulate them in 1964, and later, in a black vinyl loose-leaf binder that came to be known as the Black Book. The company gave each investor a Black Book with his name embossed on the front in gold letters.

The 1966 Black Book contained none of the high-risk warnings included in the prospectus. Of the California steamflooding the book said:

> Steamflooding there is without doubt the most important development in the secondary recovery industry in many years.

Success ratios are good, and outstanding results are being achieved.

From four specific projects we calculate that we will be able to recover 18,863,100 barrels of oil allocable to the interests of our participants at an excellent profit for them. The engineering sections of this book show . . . exact profit we expect to make for our participants.

The book projected a profit of 290 percent, before tax breaks were considered, and 569 percent for investors in the 53-percent tax bracket, with tax savings counted. The profit was broken down year-by-year over a twelve-year period, rising from $430 per $19,000 interest in 1967 to $17,580 in 1971—then dropping to $60 in 1978.

The only warning the Black Book contained was vague, heavily qualified, and buried in a section entitled "Factors in Evaluating a Prospective Secondary Recovery Property."

It must be emphasized that, although the properties in the 1966 program have been selected and acquired by Home-Stake . . . on the basis of expert engineering judgment applied to empirical and scientific data, . . . there can be no assurance or certainty that in fact any of the projects will be successful. The possibilities of failure are very real. These risks may be to a degree mitigated by the principle of the law of averages that the probability of several projects all failing of economic recovery of oil is substantially less than the possibility that a sole project will fail.

It was hardly a credible warning, when measured against the glowing and exact profit projections that the Black Book featured.

In a number of instances, Home-Stake showed investors the Black Book without showing them the prospectus. But even when an investor was shown both, Home-Stake pandered to his supposed financial sophistication. Many investors, for example, the corporate executives and lawyers, knew how formalized and uniformative prospectuses frequently are, and tended to view them with a detached condescension. To these people, prospectuses are documents prepared to the specifications of rather dull-witted SEC bureaucrats whose job it is to force compliance with a huge and tiresome jumble of securities laws and rules enacted mainly to protect the masses from dishonest stock touts.

Home-Stake portrayed its Black Book, on the other hand, as a confidential, personal peek at what the company was really doing—even though it couldn't say so in the prospectus. The Black Book was intended to appeal to a wealthy investor's sense of himself as a member of a small, exclusive society of financial super-sophisticates—a realm above such mundane encumbrances as prospectuses.

On June 21, 1966, William Blum, the Washington attorney, asked Trippet and Fitzgerald to send prospectuses and copies of the Black Book to "my friends" Earl Kintner and Henry Fox, senior partners of the law firm of Arent, Fox, Kintner, Plotkin & Kahn, one of the largest law firms in the capital. (Kintner is a former Federal Trade Commission official and author of a book on how to spot deceptive business practices.) "You will recall, Harry, that we had a nice talk with Earl Kintner last year," Blum wrote.

> I talked yesterday with Earl's partner, Henry Fox, and it occurred to me that several of his firm . . . would find [Home-Stake] a desirable and interesting medium of investment. Perhaps the next time you are here, we can catch the two of them, plus others they feel would be interested, and tell your interesting story.

That same week, Blum received a letter from Lyle O'Rourke, the New York lawyer who introduced him to Home-Stake:

> I am hopful we can be of service in developing increased participation for Home-Stake in the Washington area. I think the Covington office is certainly fertile grounds and that every effort should be made for Bob Trippet to make contacts there when he is in Washington.

The "Covington office" refers to the law firm of Covington & Burling, the leading law firm in Washington and one of the most highly respected in the nation. O'Rourke wrote to Graham Claytor, a partner in the firm:

> During a recent visit to Washington, Bill Blum and I tried to contact you concerning a client of ours, Home-Stake Production Co. of Tulsa, Oklahoma. I believe that you, Joel Barlow, Eddie

Burling and several others in your office were introduced to Home-Stake's program last year. . . . Home-Stake's 1966 program, consisting largely of steamflooding in California, promises to be exceptionally good. . . . Among Washington participants for the past several years in Home-Stake is our good friend, Corky Thom of Riggs National Bank.

Home-Stake signed up several partners at Arent, Fox, Kintner, Plotkin & Kahn that year. On September 16, Harry Fitzgerald sent William Blum a check for $2,865—his "finder's fee" for initiating the sales. The obvious conflict of interest that can arise when a lawyer or CPA accepts money for selling an investment while purporting to give objective advice to both the investors and the company offering the investment is routinely ignored by a surprisingly large number of attorneys and accountants across the country. (In addition to sales compensation, Blum was receiving legal fees from Home-Stake for his work on its prospectuses.)

When Simpson Thacher & Bartlett's Harry Heller learned that Blum was "bird-dogging" for Home-Stake—that is, finding and referring investors and collecting commissions—Heller warned him against it. But Blum didn't stop, and in subsequent years continued to accept payments for investors whom he had steered to Home-Stake before Heller's warning and who had reinvested.

(Home-Stake wasn't the first investment Blum touted that later turned out to be questionable. In 1961 he solicited investments from Washington acquaintances in a company called the Zipper Corporation of America, or Zipco. At the time he was selling Zipco stock, Blum also was acting as legal counsel for the securities firm that was underwriting the stock, and was attempting to get it registered with the SEC. A federal court in New York City subsequently said that Blum had consciously misled investors into believing they were part of a select "few key people" getting a pre-public offering of the stock. In fact, Blum knew that the stock was being sold to a much larger group, thus nullifying any advantage to his people. Zipco ultimately went bankrupt. Whether Home-Stake knew of Blum's prior activities when it hired him isn't clear.)

In July 1966, Trippet renewed his contact with economist Blanche Dickinson, the World Bank and International Monetary Fund consultant. After visiting her in Washington with Redvers Opie, Trippet wrote:

It was certainly a pleasure to have the opportunity to get acquainted with you personally. Redvers had been telling me about your very interesting life, and I can see you expect to continue it for a long time. I was just anxious to tell you something about our operations and bring you up to date. Naturally we all like to report good news, so I was glad to be able to tell you that the South Cat Canyon Project [near Santa Maria, California] is developing well. Glad to have you aboard again for the new 1966 program. I have every confidence it's going to be a dandy and make us all some good money. . . . Drop me a line whenever you get a chance and, in the meantime, have a nice summer.

In the months after the Rosenblatt group retained the Tulsa law firm of Houston, Klein & Davidson, the firm tried to negotiate a settlement with Trippet. Talks weren't productive. So on September 26, 1966, Richard T. Sonberg, the lawyer handling the case, filed a suit against Home-Stake and Trippet in the federal district court in Tulsa. It is indicative of the various manipulative skills of Robert Trippet that the Rosenblatt lawsuit was the first broad-based fraud action to be brought against Home-Stake and didn't come until eleven years and five months after the founding of the company.

The suit charged Home-Stake and Trippet with fraud dating back to 1958, when the company first contacted Rosenblatt and his fellow New York investors. Recounting how Trippet had projected profits of 400 percent to 500 percent from "low-risk" drilling, the suit alleged that he had compounded the fraud by issuing periodic reports that were misleading and by making plausible-sounding excuses for reduced production. It also said that Trippet had diverted funds to his own use. The suit was on public file in the federal courthouse, but it attracted little attention in Tulsa and elsewhere.

The $10,468,000 that Home-Stake raised in 1966 brought the

company's total for eleven annual ventures to more than $51 million. By deducting that amount on their income-tax returns over the years, the investors had avoided paying, and deprived the U.S. Treasury of, roughly $35.7 million in taxes, assuming the average investor was in the 70-percent bracket.

Martin Bregman's money management agency arranged for Barbra Streisand to invest $95,000 in 1966, raising her total exposure to $161,200. At Bregman's request Streisand also signed a contract giving the Bregman firm 5 percent of any money received from Home-Stake in excess of her "net-after-tax-benefit cost," defined as the cost of the investment after the tax saving is subtracted. Thus, for an investor in the 70-percent bracket, the net-after-tax-benefit cost of a fully deductible $10,000 investment would be $3,000. The investor saved $7,000 in taxes by making the $10,000 investment. Hypothetically applied to Streisand, this formula would earn for the Bregman firm 5 percent of everything the entertainer received from Home-Stake in excess of that $3,000.

Bregman's firm also suggested that Liza Minnelli invest $28,500 in 1966, her first year in Home-Stake (Her career and wealth were developing somewhat more slowly than Streisand's.)

In Los Angeles, Tony Curtis and Andy Williams, clients of Rosenfeld, Meyer & Susman, each put $38,000 into Home-Stake's 1966 program. Other Hollywood figures investing that year were Delmer Daves, who wrote, directed, or produced *A Summer Place, An Affair to Remember,* and many other films; Jennings Lang, executive vice-president in charge of production at Universal Pictures; Saul Chaplin, producer of *That's Entertainment, Part Two* and other musical films; and John Guedel, producer of the Groucho Marx "You Bet Your Life" and Art Linkletter "House Party" radio and television shows. They each invested $19,000.

John Guedel: "I got into this through my accountant, Ralph Jones. Ralph Jones is the most conservative man I ever met. Home-Stake had the General Electric stamp of approval. There were no earmarks of flashiness. It didn't appear to be a suede shoe thing. They all wore suits and ties and gave an air of eastern conservatism. They had the independent geologists' report saying the oil was there, the only problem was getting it.

Looking back, it's clear they spent too much money putting out those fine-looking Black Books."

Los Angeles CPA Ralph M. Jones: "A vice president of Warner-Lambert told me about Home-Stake. The chairman of Warner-Lambert was investing. I checked it out through banks and it looked good. I arranged for three or four of my clients to meet Harry Fitzgerald for lunch. Home-Stake had a lot of repeat investors—especially the GE officers. I told my clients I was buying, but they should listen to Harry, and then make up their own minds. Each of the clients at the lunch bought."

Among businessmen, one of the biggest 1966 investors was Benno M. Bechhold of Los Angeles, with an outlay of $190,000. Bechhold had wanted to invest $1,000,000, but Harry Fitzgerald told him that the company wouldn't accept more than $200,000 from any individual.

Russell W. McFall, chairman of the Western Union Corporation, made his first Home-Stake investment in 1966—$38,000. A Western Union director, John F. Rich, board chairman of New England Gas and Electric, put in $19,000. Other newcomers were James R. Shepley, president of Time Inc. ($19,000); Chester W. Nimitz, Jr., chairman of a big Connecticut scientific-instruments company and son of the World War II naval hero ($19,000); and Harry J. Volk, chairman of the Union Bank of Los Angeles ($19,000).

"William Murray really pushed it," Nimitz said later. "Bob Trippet was referred to me by U.S. Trust chairman Hoyt Ammidon, who also referred Murray. There wasn't much return. I gave one interest to Woods Hole [Oceanographic Institution, Woods Hole, Massachusetts] and another to St. Lawrence University [in upstate New York]."

Another important New Yorker who signed up in 1966 was Judson L. Streicher, a successful Wall Street stockbroker. Streicher, along with several family members and business associates, invested $200,000 on Trippet's promise that he would drill three wells just for them in Santa Barbara, San Luis Obispo, and Los Angeles counties. Trippet contacted Streicher through Philip P. Goodkin, a Wall Street CPA who referred a number of investors to Home-Stake.

The legal community continued to be well represented in 1966. Robert McDonald and Richard Storrs of Sullivan & Cromwell each invested $19,000. William Shea, the New York lawyer and Democratic party figure for whom Shea Stadium is named, contributed the same amount. At Redver Opie's suggestion, James Rowe, a Washington attorney and former high White House aide under Franklin D. Roosevelt, bought a $19,000 investment.

Redvers Opie sold $380,000 in Home-Stake units in 1966, earning a commission of $19,000. Meanwhile, Blanche Dickinson, his friend and client, was getting mildly concerned about the first check she was supposed to receive from the 1965 Home-Stake program. On October 28 she wrote Trippet:

> As an ungrateful female when I saw your letter I rather thought it would contain a check as your letter of September 16 said October 20 was the usual date for sending first payments. Did I misunderstand or has something gone wrong? Since Redvers is in Mexico I have to bother you with this question. Hope you will be in Washington soon again.

Dickinson's letter gave Trippet an opportunity for another virtuoso performance—this time with a relatively unsophisticated investor. Mixing free tax advice, folksy chitchat and eagerness to tailor the investment to her unique needs—and avoiding any hint of condescension—Trippet built up enough good will with Blanche Dickinson to last for years.

Trippet:

> The checks on South Cat Canyon went out just shortly before your letter so I assume you received yours very shortly after that. The property is developing well and we're pleased with it. Even more pleasing will be the time when you go to Los Angeles so we can take you up [to Santa Maria] and show you what we're doing, so be sure to get in touch with me any time you're going that way.

Dickinson, December 14:

> Returned from New Hampshire last night and found your

invoice for second installment ($4,750).[1] Would payment in
early January be too late? I could pay before the end of this
month but it would mean drawing out from my savings account
this amount before the quarterly interest payment is made.
Redvers suggested a few weeks delay would be acceptable but I
prefer hearing you confirm this. Would this affect tax deductions for this year?

Trippet, December 19:

I was glad to hear from you. I didn't know you went to New
Hampshire occasionally. I wouldn't go up there in December
for all the tea in China. I just heard from Redvers. He was on
his way to Bermuda to a Business International meeting and
then expected to be in Washington for a few days around
Christmastime.

Blanche, we're just here to serve your best interests, so feel
perfectly free to write your own ticket about your payments. The
main point is to get you some mileage out of your tax money.
You will have to pay $4,750 before December 31 if you need
the [tax] charge-off this year. If you do need the charge-off this
year, I would suggest mailing it on December 31. That way it
won't clear until about January 7 or 8 or even perhaps January
10. If it comes in before you want to make a withdrawal you
could just borrow the money for a couple of days.

In other words, the key to your decision is not the interest.
It's which year will serve you best for tax purposes and you have
to make the cash payment in that year to get the deduction in
that year. However, all you have to do is put the check in the
mail. It doesn't have to be cashed by us.

Dickinson, December 22:

New Hampshire was warm and snowless when I returned to
D.C. via Penn R.R. because a blizzard cancelled all planes to
my beloved city.

Redvers spent last evening with me (he looks great) and,
while discussing my income tax position for 1966, suggested I
pay three of the four installments this year. Will send you a
check for $9,500 on Dec. 31. I need that much tax deduction
for this year. Will deposit on Jan. 2 or 3 the money to cover
payment in my checking account.

---

[1] Many Home-Stake investors paid for their units in quarterly installments.

Trippet, December 26:

I was delighted to hear from you. I'm sure Redvers tried to pump you full of the Mexican bug, but I'll bet it didn't take!

You don't need to make a deposit on Jan. 2 or 3 to cover payment on the check. We won't be depositing your check until Jan. 3 here in Tulsa and it probably won't clear in Washington until Jan. 10.

We've been busy here with our children and also the first grandchild, who is four months old. Also, the first snow and sleet of the year arrived Dec. 22, but it's warmed up and all disappeared now.

Hope 1967 brings the best of everything to you, Blanche.

On January 30, 1967, New York lawyer Lyle O'Rourke dictated a letter to the dean of the Georgetown University law school, in Washington, Paul R. Dean. The letter demonstrates the tone and texture of Home-Stake's sales approach in the mid-1960s:

Dear Paul:

It was certainly good to have a chance to visit with you at some length at the Georgetown Alumni Dinner here in New York.

As I told you that evening, it struck me, as we were talking, that the annual program of Home-Stake Production Co. of Tulsa, Oklahoma, might help provide a way to encourage certain potential contributors to the new Georgetown Law Center, especially, those in a high tax bracket. Thus, in support of that thought, I am having mailed to you, under separate cover, a copy of this company's 1966 program so that you can get some idea of what it is all about, and how it works.

By way of background, may I point out that several years ago, I became associated with this company, as legal counsel for the New York area, and consequently, I have had an opportunity to follow the progress of the company quite closely. From where I sit, I believe it to provide one of the best investments that I have run across, especially for a man with a tax dollar. Basically, Paul, what Home-Stake has been successful in doing is to convert a tax dollar into an oil equity on a low-risk basis and, at the same time, achieve a substantial profit for the investor.

The company is closely held, and I have become well acquainted with management. I have visited at company headquarters in Tulsa, and have spent some time in the oil fields observing actual operations.

Its yearly participants include top people in the world of business and finance, particularly in New York and California, where the program has received more exposure.

The company doesn't employ salesmen [italics added], and relies largely on word of mouth of satisfied participants in reaching new people. In the booklet, under the heading, "Budget, Income and Taxes," you can readily see the many attractive features of the program.

Anyone interested in checking on the company can do so through the National Bank of Tulsa, Oklahoma, the First National Bank of Tulsa, Oklahoma, the Bank of California, Los Angeles, and the First National City Bank of New York. Incidentally, several of the key officers of some of these banks are yearly participants in this program.

Basically, where the new Georgetown Law Center would fit in, would be by a participant transferring a portion of his purchase to the Center, and taking advantage taxwise of the gift. A number of charities and educational institutions have been benefited by this method, while the donor has found it a most attractive way to make a gift.

While I could ramble on for pages trying to explain how this works, I believe the better way to do it would be to have either the president of the company, Robert Trippet, or the vice president, Harry Fitzgerald, contact you when either is next in Washington, as they have all the facts and figures at their fingertips.

In the meantime, if you are interested, I would have your accountant or tax man take a look at the 1966 program, and I am sure he would be able to enlighten you as to the many possibilities as far as the Georgetown Law Center is concerned.

The yearly program of Home-Stake Production Co. is very limited, as there is a great yearly demand for it from old participants. However, each year finds some changes in participation, and I am in a good position to be helpful in that area. After you have examined the program, and have discussed it with your tax man or accountant, will you let me know if you are at all interested.

Redvers Opie wrote to Trippet February 20:

I received a note from Parker Van Zandt [a Washington, D.C., investor]. . . . Parker is disturbed about the results of the 1963

program, the final 1966 quarterly payment having just arrived.
Instead of the projected $2,570 before taxes he received $980.65
—or 32.2% of projected. He goes on to say that the projected
income for 1967 is $14,715 and adds that a "60% shortfall will
really hurt!" What shall I say to him if he brings this up when
he sees me?

There is no record of Trippet's reply.

By the fall of 1966, George S. Moore, Chairman of the First
National City Bank, had been a Home-Stake investor for only
a little more than two years. Although he had $312,900 at
stake, he hadn't yet become concerned about the fate of the
money because of Home-Stake's low projections for the early
years of its programs. But he was disturbed by Home-Stake's
use of local Tulsa CPA firms for auditing its annual financial
statements. He discussed the matter with General Electric's
treasurer John Lockton and other GE investors. They were
concerned, too. Earlier that year, the Internal Revenue Service
had audited GE chairman Fred Borch's income tax returns for
1963 and 1964 and pared the value of the Home-Stake drilling
units he had contributed to charity. Borch paid the IRS a modest
sum without a fight. But the experience sparked doubts about
Home-Stake, which he discussed with some of his GE colleagues
over the next few months. They summoned Trippet to a meeting
in the General Electric board room in New York City on
Tuesday, October 25. Borch, Goss, and other GE officers attended, as did City Bank representatives. After hearing their
complaints, Trippet agreed to begin using the Tulsa office of
a national CPA firm, Arthur Andersen & Company, to audit
Home-Stake's books. Based in Chicago, Andersen is one of the
largest and most respected accounting firms in the nation.
   The GE and City Bank officers took comfort in knowing
that Home-Stake's finances at last were being audited by a
CPA firm with which they were familiar. Little did they suspect
that their reassurance was ill-founded and stemmed from
ignorance of what Arthur Andersen & Company was really
finding on the tenth floor of the Philtower Building in Tulsa.

As it happened, the firm came exquisitely close to exposing some of Home-Stake's irregularities in the early months of 1967.

The auditors at Arthur Andersen immediately spotted Home-Stake's practice of selling a greater number of drilling units than its Black Books and prospectuses indicated it would sell, thus bringing in excess money and diluting the value of each unit. Tulsa CPA Elmer Kunkel had raised that matter with Trippet as early as 1961. Trippet assured Arthur Andersen, as he had Kunkel, that the excess was returned to the investors.

Arthur Andersen & Company didn't mention the oversales directly when it certified the financial statement in Home-Stake's 1966 annual report, issued March 17, 1967, but the firm's certification statement was heavily qualified. Although Home-Stake wasn't accused of any irregularities, a number of technical questions were raised about the company's past accounting practices. Arthur Andersen said that some of these questions remained, and that certain parts of the financial statement might change depending on the answers given.

Andersen's work wasn't limited to the annual report, however. The firm also was called upon to examine the financial statement in the prospectus for Home-Stake's 1967 drilling offering, and—at the insistence of the GE-City Bank group—to audit the income, expenses and payments to investors of the 1964, 1965 and 1966 programs as well. On Saturday, April 15, an Arthur Andersen employee wrote a memorandum to another employee stating that Home-Stake was misleading investors into believing that all the money being paid to them came from oil production when, in fact, only a small portion of the payments came from oil. "Home-Stake has misrepresented the facts," the memorandum said. "We mayn't be required to point out this misrepresentation in the 1967 prospectus. However, it seems to me that we should prepare our statement in a format that the [investors] could recognize this error if they wanted to look that closely."

The memorandum indicates that employees of Arthur Andersen & Company were close to discovering a crucial element of the Ponzi scheme—the payment of money to investors under the guise of legitimate oil profits as an inducement for further investment. But the 1967 prospectus, passed upon by the SEC on April 28, stopped far short of revealing their findings clearly.

Arthur Andersen was growing very uneasy, however, and it hadn't yet completed its audits of the 1964 through 1966 programs. In addition to oversales and payments masquerading as oil profits, the CPAs had uncovered some of Home-Stake's payments to what later would be termed dummy corporations, including one owned by Trippet's daughters. At a meeting on Thursday, May 11, the auditors told Trippet that any report issued must include the oversales and the firm's other discoveries. Trippet said he could not permit any such disclosures. He asserted that if the investors learned what Andersen knew, it would be impossible to sell the 1967 offering, and Home-Stake ultimately would collapse. One of the accountants replied that Arthur Andersen "would be subject to severe criticism if we did not make the disclosures of which we had full knowledge." Trippet refused. But he assured Andersen that he would pay its fee for the audits. So the firm sent its final report only to Trippet and enclosed a letter saying that, at his request, the report would not be sent to the investors. The fraud was secure.

Arthur Andersen and Home-Stake had had enough of each other, however. Trippet knew it had been a narrow escape; and the CPA firm didn't want to continue the relationship. So they quietly parted company in May. (Arthur Andersen later denied any wrongdoing or liability in the matter.)

The General Electric and City Bank groups learned of the falling-out almost immediately and demanded that Trippet explain. He simply said that Arthur Andersen's work hadn't been satisfactory. The investors asked to see Andersen's audit records, but Trippet refused. Andersen also declined; accountant-client relationships generally are confidential unless the client agrees to release information.

City Bank's George Moore was worried. He remarked to GE treasurer Lockton that Home-Stake's operations "may have deteriorated into a Ponzi-like situation in which current dividends are being paid out of new investment money." Moore told Gerald Sherrod, an oil-investment analyst at City Bank (and a native of Tulsa, Oklahoma), to investigate the situation. Sherrod asked Home-Stake for information to substantiate the evaluation reports that Home-Stake had circulated, concerning the California properties. The reports, which had been prepared to

Home-Stake's specifications by the Bakersfield, California, engineering firm of Lewis & Ganong, set dollar values on Home-Stake's California drilling ventures. Home-Stake engineer Conrad Greer was opposed to giving Sherrod any additional information: "Any elucidation of the reports would tend to weaken our position in the eyes of most engineers," he told Trippet. "I would strongly recommend that we quit while we are ahead and not embellish the existing reports to our detriment." Greer essentially said that bank engineers were too conservative to appreciate Home-Stake's and Lewis & Ganong's advanced methods of evaluating the properties.

Trippet asked that the Lewis & Ganong reports be expanded anyway. "The problem I have is simply that Gerry Sherrod keeps demanding them and I have no choice. . . . Several of the bank's officers and clients have invested with us. I imagine he will use the reports in an attempt to get them to quit, but I don't know any way to avoid sending them."

Trippet rejected a suggestion from J. B. McKitterick, a General Electric vice-president, that Home-Stake employ a second, more conservative engineering firm to evaluate the California properties. The GE officer was told that his suggestion would consume too much time and might compromise confidential Home-Stake production techniques.

Home-Stake's drilling in California, of course, had not achieved the results that investors had been led to anticipate, and Trippet later told Greer to keep any discussion of the company's production problems "completely tight with reference to anyone outside the company, including participants or any other outsiders."

On June 1 Trippet agreed to buy back several of George Moore's Home-Stake units. But, displaying his nimblest footwork yet, Trippet managed to convince most of the skeptics over the next several months that the production problems were being solved and that Home-Stake's financial statements and audits were sound. Many of the City Bank and GE officers—including George Moore—invested again in Home-Stake in late 1967 and in subsequent years.

At the same time he was tussling with GE, City Bank and Arthur Andersen & Company in the spring of 1967, Trippet found himself facing an increasing number of inquiries from other investors. Ten days before the 1967 prospectus was cleared by the SEC, Heublein chairman John G. Martin, who had invested $284,640 in Home-Stake, received a memorandum from an adviser pointing out that a 1967 Home-Stake estimate of the amount of oil in one of its California properties differed from a 1966 estimate. Martin forwarded the memorandum to Trippet, who relayed it to Conrad Greer in California. Greer sent Trippet an extremely complex answer to Martin's query, giving only part of the information requested. Trippet told Greer: "I'm just going to photocopy it and send it on to them. It will set them back on their heels and that's what they deserve for asking silly questions any way."

Two days after the 1967 prospectus was approved for distribution, Blanche Dickinson again wrote to Trippet.

Just back from the Dominican Republic on a consulting job. Will be going to Grenoble, France, in early June for a few weeks to finish the work. When does my next installment come due? And, by the way, I have had no "quarterly checks" from you thus far in 1967. Since I'm a relative newcomer in this oil business and Redvers is in Mexico, have to bother you with these questions.

"You didn't tell me where you were going and I didn't ask because I thought it might be a big secret," Trippet replied.

Any way, it was interesting to know where you've been. I guess everything is peaceful in the Dominican Republic now and they have a chance to pay for the chaos. This must be quite an undertaking, since you'll now be going to France to finish the work.

. . . I'll save a slot in the 1967 program for you. I think it's going to be a dandy and a money maker for us all. It will be all in Southern California again. . . . Your letter undoubtedly crossed your last quarterly check as it went out the latter part of April and undoubtedly you have it by now.

The following Wednesday, May 10, Trippet filed a response in court to the Rosenblatt-Lyons suit. The litigation had been delayed partly because a group of Memphis investors—some of whom had been sold their interests by Charlie Plummer—had joined the lawsuit. A revised complaint had to be drafted. In addition to repeating the original charges of fraud, the revised suit alleged that Trippet had paid differing amounts of money to investors who had made identical investments in the same drilling programs.

Trippet denied any wrongdoing. He said that his statements to investors had been honest, based on "reliable information," and that none of the statements, as far as he knew, were false or misleading. He characterized the 400-percent profit projections as "mere sales talk." Trippet also said that if there had been losses, they had been the U.S. government's rather than the investors', because most of their investments were tax-deductible.

Neither the suit, which was on public file at the federal court house, nor Arthur Andersen & Company's hedged auditing opinion affected the continued expansion of Home-Stake's investment sales. Few if any potential investors checked the court house for suits against Home-Stake—a routine investigative procedure—or bothered to read the Arthur Andersen statement carefully. On the contrary, many still accepted without challenge the optimistic statements in Home-Stake's Black Books. The 1967 Black Book projected a 636-percent after-tax profit from that year's drilling program. It further said that "since most of the people reading this will already have participated with us in previous programs, they will already be familiar with the general income tax principles involved in an oil program of this kind." This statement was designed to nurture the idea that Home-Stake investors were a stable, exclusive group who invested year after year, and that only a few new investors were admitted each year.

Blanche Dickinson wrote to Trippet from Grenoble, France, on June 12: "Am interested in what you anticipate for the returns on my present investment (believe to date they are somewhat under estimates or am I wrong) and whether I could go in for a $10,000 unit for next year."

In Tulsa late the next afternoon, Charlie Plummer, a top

Home-Stake officer since the company had been founded, attached one end of a hose to the exhaust pipe of his car in the closed garage of his home, ran the other end into the car through a back window, entered the vehicle, and started the engine. His wife found his body about 5:45 P.M. Plummer left a note saying he was "tired of living."

Trippet named Harry Fitzgerald as executive vice-president to replace Plummer, and lawyer Thomas A. Landrith, Jr., a law-school classmate of Trippet's and a former Tulsa city attorney, to take Plummer's place on the Home-Stake board of directors. Landrith previously had done legal work for Home-Stake and was handling the company's response to the Rosenblatt-Lyons suit.

Harry Fitzgerald's main responsibility continued to be sales. The company, whose sales staff was expanding, opened a sales office at 445 Park Avenue in New York and hired a number of former stockbrokers and business executives with good financial and social connections. Although these men functioned as salesmen, they resented the label and therefore were called vice-presidents. Known as "hired guns," they were "the kind of guys you find hanging around the bar of 21 at 11:30 in the morning," says a New York businessman who knew many of the Home-Stake salesmen.

Home-Stake also established a sales office on Wilshire Boulevard in Los Angeles.

Judson Streicher, the New York stockbroker who, along with his family and associates, had invested $200,000 in 1966, put in another $365,750 in 1967. The Streicher group had been very impressed with some quicker-than-promised returns Trippet had paid them. They didn't know that much of the money was coming from Home-Stake's general pool of investments and little if any of the money they had invested in 1966 had been used for drilling the promised wells.

As a group, the 1967 investors contributed $11,605,394 in new money to Home-Stake. They included many from past years—several officers of the General Electric Company, the Western Union Corporation, and the First National City Bank of New York, and Wall Street and Washington lawyers. Among new faces were Howard D. Brundage, executive vice-president of the J. Walter Thompson Company, the giant advertising agency; Donald B. Smiley and Ernest Molloy, top officers of the R. H. Macy & Company department store chain; Eaton W. Ballard executive vice-president of the Broadway-Hale stores (now known as Carter-Hawley-Hale) in California; L. R. Breslin, Jr., a partner in the Wall Street law firm of Cravath, Swaine & Moore; and Curtis Berger and Michael I. Sovern, professors at Columbia University law school.

According to Donald Smiley: "If you're looking for tax-shelter, the word gets around the fast. Home-Stake had a strong sales organization. I checked it with the Chemical Bank investment trust department. They didn't say it was Triple-A, but there was that whole crowd from GE investing."

The number of show-business investors also continued to rise, led by the clients of Martin Bregman and Kent Klineman. Barbra Streisand added $105,545 to her past stake of $161,200 for a total of $266,745; Liza Minnelli put in another $19,000, bringing her to $47,500. (Liza Minnelli was close to Bregman personally at that point; the reception following her marriage to Peter Allen on March 3, 1967, was held at Bregman's Central Park West apartment.) Three other Bregman clients invested in 1967 for the first time: the "Today" show hostess Barbara Walters ($19,000); designer Oleg Cassini ($19,000); and Richard Adler, musical composer for *Pajama Game* and *Damn Yankees* ($38,950).

In California the Rosenfeld, Meyer & Susman group was represented by Andy Williams, with an unknown amount, and Ed Ames and Bobbie Gentry, who each invested $19,000. John Guedel invested $19,000, Phyllis Diller, $9,500. "I had it checked out by my Harvard-educated New York lawyer, the fastest brain in the East, and I knew that anything Andy Williams was into had to be pure gold," Diller said later.

Home-Stake continued to aid financially many of the lawyers who were putting it in touch with potential investors. In 1967 it loaned New York lawyer Kent Klineman $15,118 at 6 percent interest, with repayment due December 31, 1968. He didn't repay the loan by that date.

To other lawyers, Home-Stake continued to pay commissions. Lyle O'Rourke wrote to William Blum: "I am most anxious to know what results were obtained with reference to Home-Stake sales in the Washington area in which I may have an interest." Blum sent O'Rourke a check.

Blum monitored his own commissions closely, too. He wrote a letter to salesman Alan Pope in New York saying he wanted to go over the 1967 investor list with a "fine-toothed comb" to make claim for those to whom he had introduced Home-Stake. Harry Fitzgerald sent Blum a check for $3,420, covering investments by Washington lawyers Earl Kintner, Henry Fox, and others.

During the summer of 1967, Barbra Streisand made a concert tour of the United States arranged for her by Alan King, the comedian, and Walter Hyman, a former textile executive then engaged in show-business production. On becoming acquainted with Streisand during the tour, Hyman learned that she had very little knowledge of her financial affairs, which he felt was particularly dangerous because of her rapidly rising income. He advised her to have her financial picture reviewed by a firm of CPAs independent of Martin Bregman's firm. Hyman sent Streisand to Michael and Donald Hecht, accountants who had worked previously for him. One of their first recommendations was that she sell the bulk of her Home-Stake interests back to Home-Stake. The Hechts knew nothing specifically negative about Home-Stake at the time; they simply concluded that there wasn't enough reliable information available on which to base a firm judgment of its worth. In keeping with its policy of special treatment for favored investors, Home-Stake agreed in the fall to repurchase interests for which Streisand had paid $238,545, leaving her only with a 1964 investment that cost her $28,200.

In view of the millions of dollars Home-Stake was taking in, the repurchase of most of Streisand's interests was a minor blow. The use of Streisand's name had helped Home-Stake attract a lot of money from other people. Since she retained a $28,200 interest, the company could continue to claim her as an investor.

Following the Hechts' analysis of Streisand's finances, she dis-

missed the Bregman agency as her business manager. He proceeded to file suit against her, alleging breach of contract. In a
countersuit, she accused him of mishandling her funds. Streisand's lawyer filed an affidavit accusing Bregman's firm of
fraudulently procuring her signature on the contract the previous
year, giving him 5 percent of her Home-Stake payments in excess of her "net-after-tax-benefit cost." The firm denied the
allegations.

The suits were settled out of court. Streisand made a payment
to Bregman covering what she still owed under their initial contract. The amount wasn't disclosed. Because the settlement was
private, the courts never ruled on the merits of the various
claims. The settlement encompassed not only questions relating
to the Home-Stake investments but a number of other issues
as well.

Streisand wasn't the only prominent investor to withdraw in
1967. In early July, Trippet visited Betty Beale, the nationally
syndicated Washington society columnist, at her home in northwest Washington. Beale was becoming concerned about the
returns on her 1965 and 1966 investments. Trippet agreed to
repurchase her $9,500 interest in the 1965 program, but she
agreed to buy an interest in the 1967 venture.

"It was good to see you," Trippet wrote after returning to
Tulsa.

> I was just anxious to get up to date. Your new house is really
> perfect in every way and my opinion is that you're sitting pretty.
> The only ingredient missing is to get in one of those New York
> papers and I'll bet you do that before many months have passed.
>   I believe you have made the right decision on your oil pro-
> grams. . . . The net result is that you don't have any more oil
> than you had before, but it is better distributed and with better
> tax results. The main thing I want to do is to get you the biggest
> tax leverage and the highest rate of return on your actual out-of-
> pocket cost and I believe this will do the job the best.
>   Thanks a lot for your hospitality. Keep those good columns
> rolling out in the Tulsa paper and have a nice summer.

By October, Betty Beale was even more concerned. She wrote
to Trippet asking,

Can you explain why my receipts haven't anywhere near approximated the figure Redvers [Opie] presented to me? . . . The fact is, Bob, ever since sitting down and taking a good look at my investment, receipts and exact tax gain as figured out by my accountant, I have been terribly concerned over my rashness in going into anything so speculative as a secondary recovery oil program.

I was a fool, as you are well aware, for going into the 1965 program so heavily, but Redvers was so persuasive I got all fired up. What really clinched it was his saying I could get my money out any time I wanted to. So I am writing now to say I would like to entirely withdraw from the 1965, '66 and '67 programs —in short all my money.

The whole realization of how speculative it is has made me so nervous that I can hardly get through a day. I am afraid I am simply too emotional and high-strung to be cool about something like this. I have worked so hard and so late into the night for so many years for everything I have that I should never have risked it.

Trippet agreed to the refund. As in the case of Barbra Streisand, it was a small amount relative to the huge sums Home-Stake was taking in, and he wasn't about to arouse the ire of a nationally syndicated columnist.

By late 1967 Home-Stake's practice of encouraging disgruntled investors to donate their shares to charity and take a second tax deduction had become more sophisticated. Home-Stake gave investors copies of the evaluation reports prepared by the engineering firm of Lewis & Ganong, in Bakersfield, California. The investors then could show the reports to the IRS if their charitable gift deductions were challenged.

The Lewis & Ganong reports stated that, as of late 1967, a unit in Home-Stake's 1965 drilling program was worth $69,200, a 1966 unit was worth $71,470, and a 1967 unit was worth $76,010. Investors had paid $19,000 each for the units, which meant that if an investor in a high tax bracket gave a unit to charity, he saved more in taxes than he had spent for the investment (assuming the IRS didn't challenge his deductions). A number of investors made gifts; it had become clear to many who had been investing for several years that profits on the initial investments would fall far short of projections.

A major recipient of Home-Stake gifts in late 1967 was the Southeastern Massachusetts University Educational Foundation, which tax lawyer William Edwards Murray had been instrumental in forming two years earlier. He had become president of the foundation following his meeting with university officials at the Fall River dinner in December 1965. A fancy letterhead was designed and printed for the foundation and there was talk of raising $50 million in ten years. The principal gifts in 1967, however, weren't cash or blue-chip stocks; they were Home-Stake units donated by Murray's tax clients, including General Electric vice-presidents Donald Scarff and J. Stanford Smith.

On December 29, 1967, Home-Stake made another move to thwart disclosure of the fraud. Rather than submit to a public trial the allegations in the Rosenblatt-Lyons lawsuit filed the previous year, Trippet agreed to settle out of court. He repurchased most of the Rosenblatt family's and Albert Lyons' remaining interests in Home-Stake and the suit was dropped. Richard T. Sonberg, the Tulsa lawyer who had handled the suit, reported details of the matter to the Fort Worth, Texas, regional office of the SEC, which has jurisdiction over companies in Tulsa. It seemed indifferent.

The extravaganza of speculation that swept the stock market in the U.S. in 1968 and 1969 provided an ideal environment for Home-Stake to achieve its most dramatic growth and to perpetrate its most flagrant frauds. A reckless euphoria pervaded the investment world, helping to create what John Brooks of *The New Yorker* later would term the "great garbage market." Stocks that ultimately became the focus of criminal fraud investigations still were Wall Street favorites. Vast quantities of money were made, and the number and variety of tax-shelter offerings grew to meet the soaring demand for protection from taxation. Tax-shelter prospectuses seeking to raise $1.7 billion were registered with the SEC in 1969, up from $85 million in 1964.

Home-Stake continued to expand its sales network. It raised more money than in any previous period—$17,122,205 in 1968 and $19,620,266 in 1969. Yet Home-Stake drilled fewer oil wells and produced less oil from its 1968 and 1969 programs, relative to what was projected, than ever before. A rising number of investors in previous programs were complaining.

Trippet knew the swindle couldn't grow and last indefinitely. But he was far from finished. He became more calculating, more brazen, and his swindling skills—for the time being at least—were equal to the task.

On January 1, 1968, Trippet arranged for payment of $2,000 a month to a company controlled by William Edwards Murray, whose extensive contacts with prominent businessmen had been so important to Home-Stake's early growth. Home-Stake already had paid Murray's company $36,000 in 1964 and $66,000 in 1966. The payments ostensibly were for "legal and business advice," but Home-Stake considered the money compensation for Murray's role in selling Home-Stake investments.

A month later, Richard Sonberg, the Tulsa lawyer who in late December had negotiated an out-of-court settlement of the Rosenblatt-Lyons lawsuit, filed another complaint against Home-Stake and Trippet in Tulsa federal court. The plaintiff was George H. McFadden, a Memphis businessman to whom Trippet and Charlie Plummer had sold interests in the 1960 and 1961 Home-Stake ventures. The lawsuit alleged fraud and asked $364,000 in damages.

As Home-Stake's drilling declined, its sales literature became more optimistic. The 1967 annual report, issued March 22, 1968, was a model of Trippet's ingratiating informality. It began:

> This is going to be a good report, both concerning results for 1967 and concerning results for the entire decade, and an optimistic report for the future of your company. So we solicit you to settle back, relax and enjoy yourself. (Not being a big "public company," we hope that the foregoing wee bit of levity will not shock anyone unduly.)

"Our steamflooding operations in Southern California moved right ahead in 1967," the report said. It emphasized that the company had developed a "stainless-steel wire-wrap liner" to keep sand out of the oil. The liner would enable the company "to produce many millions of barrels of oil in a very economical way." The report also claimed that Home-Stake had acquired two "excellent properties" in Argentina that were "already producing at a profit."

The 1967 annual report was notable because its financial statement wasn't signed by any independent accounting firm. After parting with the Arthur Andersen & Company because it had qualified its certification of the 1966 annual report and had nearly uncovered the swindle in the spring of 1967, Trippet turned again to Elmer Kunkel, the Tulsa CPA who previously had worked for Home-Stake. By 1967 Kunkel had joined the Tulsa accounting firm of McKee, Atkins & Schuler. Kunkel discussed Home-Stake's finances with his colleagues at McKee Atkins and with Arthur Andersen people familiar with the preceding year's audit. McKee Atkins decided the financial statement should disclose Home-Stake's practice of selling more drilling units than it purported, and of inflating payments to investors with money that didn't come from oil revenues. McKee Atkins also felt compelled to disclose a stock transaction in which Trippet had made a windfall profit with the apparently unwitting aid of Thomas Landrith, the Tulsa lawyer who had defended Home-Stake against several lawsuits.

In mid-1967 Trippet had offered to sell 9,720 shares of his Home-Stake common stock to Landrith for around $12 a share—a total purchase price of $116,640. Trippet didn't tell Landrith that he had originally paid only about half that amount for the stock. He promised to find another buyer to take the stock off Landrith's hands after a few months, and assured him that not only wouldn't he lose any money on the deal, but he might even make a modest profit. Landrith didn't even have to put up any cash; Trippet accepted an IOU for the purchase price and gave Landrith the stock. A few months later Trippet saw to it that Home-Stake bought the stock from Landrith for about $2,500 more than the amount of the IOU. Landrith kept his profit and used the rest of the money to pay off the IOU to Trippet. The entire deal amounted to nothing more than a circuitous means for Trippet to pocket a $60,000 profit on stock in a company whose underlying value was deteriorating daily.

There is no indication that McKee Atkins knew the full implications of the stock deal when the firm drafted footnotes for the Home-Stake financial statement outlining the transaction and the other irregularities. When Elmer Kunkel presented the firm's report to Trippet at his Home-Stake office, Trippet angrily rejected it. He said most of the disclosures were unnecessary, and that he and no one else would decide what would be disclosed about his company. Kunkel asked him to think it over. A week later Trippet's secretary phoned Kunkel and told him to pick up the report; it wouldn't be needed.

Trippet retained a footnote indicating that Home-Stake was making some "voluntary" payments to participants, but he didn't define "voluntary." He published the financial statement without most of the other McKee Atkins disclosures and without the firm's signature. The report merely carried the words "certified correct" and was signed by Trippet; Fitzgerald; John Lenoir, the financial vice-president; and Kermit Murdock, the company employee who had signed previous annual reports.

Trippet took the calculated risk that few investors would bother to question the lack of independent accounting certification. Again, his cynical and benignly derisive view of the investors proved apt.

The same attitude was reflected in the new prospectus, filed with the SEC, and in the Black Book. Never before had there been so much contrast between the two documents. The 1968 prospectus contained the usual vague and formal language about the risks of oil investment. Buried in the middle of the prospectus, however, was the disclosure that none of the steamflood projects undertaken to date had generated sufficient income to return the investors' outlays. Steamflooding in 1963 had returned 20 percent; in 1964, 10 percent; in 1965, none; in 1966, 3 percent; and in 1967, none. The prospectus emphasized that eighteen months to three years are required to "completely develop and equip previously undertaken steamflood projects."

Many investors, however, were shown the Black Book instead of the prospectus. (They could have obtained the prospectus from the SEC but few did.) The Black Book said little about past programs. It estimated that profits from the 1968 properties would reach 302 percent before tax breaks and 712 percent after tax deductions. Again, it projected the exact number of barrels of oil the company claimed it could extract and began with the familiar words: "Since most of the people reading this program book will already have participated with us in previous programs. . . ." The 1968 Black Book also claimed that Home-Stake owned several leases which it allegedly didn't own.

Although most investors remained complaisant in the spring of 1968, the small number of skeptics was growing. Grant T. Anderson, a prominent attorney in Portland, Oregon, had first invested in Home-Stake in 1963. He had heard of the company through friends who had been sold interests by Charlie Plummer a few years earlier. The big New York names were mentioned, particularly Thomas E. Dewey and the General Electric officers. Grant Anderson invested in Home-Stake programs again in 1964, 1965, and 1966, and also bought $50,000 worth of common stock. Payments were slower than projected but that didn't concern Anderson at first; progress reports from the company were uniformly positive.

In late May 1967, Anderson flew in his private plane to attend his son's graduation from Army helicopter school at Fort Rucker, Alabama. On a whim, he stopped in Tulsa on the way home and dropped in at Home-Stake. Never having met Trippet or seen the company, he was curious. He planned to stay only a few hours, but Trippet insisted on showing Anderson around the Home-Stake offices; giving him a tour of Tulsa; serving him cocktails at the Trippet home; and taking him to dinner at the Tulsa Club. He expressed his appreciation but felt a bit uneasy. Somewhere in Trippet's effusiveness, he thought he detected a false note: The display of hospitality seemed excessive; Trippet, a little shallow. It was nothing specific, just a feeling. Anderson didn't dwell on it.

A little more than a month later, while on a cruise in the South Pacific, Grant Anderson and his wife became acquainted with another couple on the ship—an executive of Standard Oil of California and his wife. Anderson told him about Home-Stake, specifically mentioning that the company was engaged in steam-flooding work near Santa Maria, California. The executive advised him to be cautious; apparently Standard Oil had tried steamflooding in the same region and found it unproductive. Anderson was concerned enough to ask his new friend to refer him to a competent consulting geologist in Los Angeles. But he did nothing further for the time being. Then, in early December, Anderson received a letter from Harry Fitzgerald, saying that the 1963 drilling program wasn't producing oil as fast as had been expected and that the company was recommending that investors give their units to charity. Home-Stake provided an evaluation report placing a high value on the drilling units, based on projected future production, to be shown to the IRS if charitable deductions were challenged.

Anderson donated his 1963 interests and decided that it was time he looked more closely at his investments in the subsequent programs. He phoned Trippet and said he planned to be in southern California for the Christmas holidays and asked whether he could stop and have a look at the Santa Maria properties. By all means, Trippet said. Home-Stake would arrange to fly him to Santa Maria from the Los Angeles airport in a private plane. Anderson asked if it would be all right if he brought along a geologist friend. There was a pause at the other end of the line. Trippet said that Anderson was welcome to bring anyone he chose.

The geologist retained by Anderson didn't like what he saw. Anderson then decided to have an accountant examine Home-Stake's books in Tulsa. Months of increasingly acrimonious correspondence and negotiation followed. On Thursday, March 21, Anderson wrote to Harry Fitzgerald.

> From what I have already learned, there is little doubt that [Home-Stake] has breached its contracts with participants with impunity and without explanation or disclosure. . . . I am personally aware of instances where the company has willfully and deliberately withheld and concealed from participants pertinent information, and has placed in their hands other information which . . . conveyed a false and misleading impression. . . . There is even a hint that your practices when completely unveiled may reveal one of the greatest swindles perpetrated upon American investors since Ponzi went to jail for mail fraud half a century ago.

Anderson threatened to "talk to friends of mine on the staff of the SEC," consult other investors, and, if further inquiry confirmed his suspicions, file suit. Home-Stake promptly repurchased Anderson's interests. He didn't sue.

Los Angeles business consultant Donald McKee, who had put Home-Stake in touch with several potential investors four years earlier, was having second thoughts. Trippet asked McKee to help find some non-petroleum investments for Home-Stake.

McKee was told that Home-Stake was having technical problems in the Santa Maria oil fields and wasn't spending all the investors' money there. He was worried because he knew that Home-Stake's contract with investors committed it to spend their funds on oil drilling. So he retained a Los Angeles CPA, Justin Kimball, to visit Home-Stake's headquarters in Tulsa and try to determine what was being done with the money. McKee hoped to produce, with Trippet's cooperation, a candid report on Home-Stake's problems for investors.

Kimball periodically reported to McKee that he wasn't getting much help from Trippet or the Home-Stake staff. In one instance he asked Trippet to define an item in the 1967 financial statement: "reclassification of program operating expenses and payments to participants of $1,332,297."

"Justin, there are lots of borderline cases," Trippet said. "I'm the participants' watchdog. I go through and find, each year, that our accountants have been overzealous. They have classified a lot of [costs incorrectly], in effect charging the participants twice. I re-classify."

It was still unclear years later what the item in the financial statement really signified. If the money in question actually was paid to the participants, it likely was part of Home-Stake's overall plan to pay at least some of them enough to keep them from complaining. Justin Kimball eventually returned to Los Angeles and told Donald McKee that he "hadn't gotten anything accomplished."

More and more New York people who were close to Home-Stake were growing uneasy, too. In November Lyle O'Rourke wrote William Blum: "I certainly hope Home-Stake improves its production and payout, as those who have participated due to introduction by me have been complaining. None of my people repeated this year."

That same month, Trippet bought back interests from two more investors who had threatened to sue. Meanwhile, Home-Stake purchased an apartment complex in Santa Barbara, California, for $2.5 million. The company's investors had been told that all their money would be spent for drilling.

Trippet's alleged thievery continued. In addition to diverting thousands of dollars in cash into his pocket, he spent $6,020.79 of Home-Stake's money in December 1968 on two automobiles and furniture through one of his dummy companies.

Although Home-Stake's fraud and the pressure from disgruntled investors rose markedly in 1968, the dangers went largely unnoticed by potential clients. The heady investment climate of the times caused many of the old investors to ignore the evident signs of trouble as well.

The Judson Streicher group in New York, which had invested $200,000 in 1966 and $365,750 in 1967, had been getting favorable reports from Trippet. In 1968 the Streicher group invested $2,156,500. (By this time Home-Stake had discarded its policy of turning down investments of more than $200,000 to $300,000 from one investor or small group.)

Most of the General Electric, Western Union, and First National City Bank officers invested again, including Reginald H. Jones, who succeeded Fred Borch in 1971 as chairman of the board of GE. Jones bought a $19,000 unit in the 1968 program. The Wall Street and Washington lawyers came back for more, too. (William Blum was paid a commission of $3,135 for his Washington group.)

The 1968 investor list also included some impressive newcomers. Nathaniel Goldstein, a New York lawyer-CPA and former attorney general of New York, invested $19,000, as did Murray I. Gurfein, Goldstein's law partner. (Gurfein later was named a federal judge in New York City and wrote the original Pentagon Papers decision.) Louis Singer, a partner in Troster, Singer & Company, a Wall Street investment house, put in $285,000.

"It was a terrible error," Singer said later. "I had the impression that it was on the up and up. Not being too well versed in oil matters, I took the advice of others. Sixty-eight and '69 was a weird period in the investment business. Guards were down. Everybody was looking for tax shelter. It was the usual con game. Nobody's immune. You think you're a sophisticated man. You find you're a boob [sic] in the woods. You know the best tax shelter? Don't make any money!"

Another new investor in 1968 was Norris Darrell, Jr., a partner
in Sullivan & Cromwell. He invested $38,000 and later was
reticent to discuss the matter. "I knew other people in it . . .
various friends. I assumed it was all right." Two of Darrell's
law partners, Robert McDonald and Richard Storrs, who had invested previously, increased their total stakes in 1968 to more
than $90,000 each.

Actor Walter Matthau invested $200,000 at the end of the
year. At one time an avid gambler, Matthau was steered to
Home-Stake by his New York lawyer, Arnold Krakower. Kra-
kower's principal contact with Home-Stake was New York CPA
Philip Goodkin, who also had introduced Home-Stake to the
Judson Streicher group.

One reason Matthau invested was that he was able to obtain
a $150,000 loan to pay for three-quarters of his units. Home-
Stake told Matthau that his loan came from the First National
Bank & Trust Company of Tulsa, one of the largest banks in
Oklahoma. The bank's seeming willingness to finance investments
in Home-Stake increased Matthau's and his lawyer's confidence
in the oil company. They felt that the bank wouldn't be willing
to make such loans if it hadn't investigated Home-Stake and
found it legitimate. Matthau didn't discover until much later
that the loan actually came from Home-Stake and not the bank.
(He paid off the loan in full by January 1970.) Eventually
Matthau sued the bank for aiding the Home-Stake fraud by
"fronting the loan," thus enhancing the company's respectability.

The Tulsa bank allegedly "fronted" about $4.9 million in loans
for Home-Stake. In addition to Matthau, the borrowers included Jack Benny, Andy Williams, Alan Alda, designer Bill
Blass, and director Mike Nichols. Most of the loans were repaid
in full before the swindle was revealed. Trippet handled the
loan arrangements personally through William E. Bender, a
senior vice-president of the bank who by mid-1976 had become
chairman of its credit-policy committee. Trippet and Bender had
been friends since college. Trippet would simply send Bender a
note on a Home-Stake interoffice memorandum form saying: "I
would appreciate it if you would front the following loans for
me." Home-Stake would deposit the money with the bank; the

bank would lend it to the investor; and repayments to the bank were forwarded to Home-Stake.

Another 1968 investor from the entertainment world was Candice Bergen, who contributed $9,500. That is ironic in retrospect because at the time she was living with Terry Melcher, Doris Day's son. In the summer and fall of 1968, Melcher was in the midst of bringing suit on behalf of his mother against a Beverly Hills lawyer, Jerome B. Rosenthal, who allegedly had mismanaged Doris Day's funds over a period of eighteen years. Among other things, Rosenthal was accused of putting Day's money into risky and sometimes illegitimate tax shelters that didn't include Home-Stake but resembled it. Doris Day ultimately obtained a judgment against Rosenthal in a California state court of more than $22 million in damages. He denied her allegations and, at this writing, is appealing.

Candice Bergen's investment was arranged by Martin Bregman's firm. His other clients buying 1968 investments were Liza Minnelli and Oleg Cassini, who each chipped in $38,000, double their 1967 outlays; Faye Dunaway ($40,375); Sandy Dennis ($9,500); Joseph Bologna and Renee Taylor, the actor-screen writers responsible for the films *Lovers and Other Strangers* and *Made for Each Other* ($19,000); Barbara Walters ($9,500); and Bill Blass ($19,000).

The Rosenfeld, Meyer & Susman investors in 1968 included Ed Ames ($28,500); Bobbie Gentry ($19,000); and Andy Williams (amount unknown). Other show-business investors were Bob Dylan ($38,000); Jennings Lang, executive vice-president in charge of production at Universal Pictures ($19,000); Ozzie Nelson ($38,000); and Buddy Hackett ($38,000).

When asked later why he invested in Home-Stake, Hackett replied, "I haven't the vaguest idea. I just tell jokes. My lawyers and accountants look into these things and explain them to me in baby talk. If it sounds okay we go ahead." An attitude of casual helplessness toward handling money isn't uncommon among entertainers. A Los Angeles lawyer who manages millions of dollars for show-business people says a typical client hands over his money and says, "We're children about this. Just keep the sheriff and the IRS away from the door."

Thurman Munson, who had just signed a contract with the

New York Yankees, put $19,000 of his bonus money into the 1968 Home-Stake program.

Redvers Opie and Robert Trippet sipped drinks at the Harvard Club in Manhattan one day in mid-December. They were checking off Opie's 1968 clients. He had sold $275,500 in Home-Stake interests, earning a commission of $13,775. The investors included World Bank consultant Blanche Dickinson, who, despite her doubts, chipped in another $9,500; Washington attorney James Rowe ($19,000); E. T. Collinsworth, Jr., a vice-chairman of Armour & Company, the Chicago meat-packing firm ($19,-000); and Helen B. Taussig, M.D., an eminent physician and professor at Johns Hopkins University medical school ($19,000).

An important reason why so many 1968 investors were shown only the Black Book and not the prospectus was that Trippet discouraged the sales staff from distributing the prospectus. Unfavorable information in the prospectus was largely buried, but a diligent investor could have spotted it.

The senior New York City sales vice-president, Alan Pope, knew that failing to distribute the prospectus could be a violation of law. In late 1968, after repeated attempts to get Trippet to release the prospectus, Pope resigned and consulted a lawyer, who reported the matter to the SEC in Washington. M. David Hyman, then the SEC's chief enforcement attorney, referred it to the agency's regional office in Fort Worth, Texas, which had been informed a year earlier of the Rosenblatt lawsuit. The Fort Worth office again did nothing.

On December 31, 1968, the $364,000 fraud suit filed against Home-Stake eleven months earlier by George McFadden of Memphis was certified as a "class action" by the Tulsa federal court. That is, it was deemed to have been filed on behalf of all those who invested in the years McFadden did, 1960 and 1961. But the lawsuit was settled out of court a month later for $141,000. The class-action certification was withdrawn, and no other investors were informed of the settlement, the class-action designation, or the suit itself. For Home-Stake it was another close call. Had word of the class-action suit gotten around, the company might have been flooded with demands for payment.

In January 1969, again under the threat of lawsuits, Trippet repurchased the interests of six investors, dating back as far as the 1961 program.

As dissatisfaction spread among investors, Trippet tightened his personal control over how salesmen dealt with them, what they were told, and which ones were used as references. He dispatched a memorandum to the New York salesmen.

> I want to stress . . . that these lists [of investors or potential investors] are totally confidential and shouldn't be shown to anyone. . . . Many of these people do not wish their names released to anyone and still others of them are not particularly good references. Therefore, please do not use the list wholesale for references. Instead, if you want some references, please ask me which one and I will tell you which are the best ones.

By the late 1960s, Trippet had become very friendly with Kent Klineman, the New York tax lawyer who had arranged Barbra Streisand's first Home-Stake investment and steered Martin Bregman and his clients to Home-Stake. Trippet gave Klineman a wedding present (a rug) in early 1967, and Trippet and his wife dined with the Klinemans in New York on numerous occasions. By 1969 Bob Trippet and Kent Klineman were engaging in business deals together, apart from the sale of Home-Stake drilling interests. Klineman by then had stopped practicing tax law and had become a partner in a New York stock-brokerage firm, J. M. Dryfoos & Company.[1]

Trippet and Klineman weren't natural friends; their personalities, ages, and life-styles were very different. The two were drawn to each other, however, by a single, crucial calculation: Each was uniquely situated to help the other make a lot of money.

In late January 1969, Klineman arranged a luncheon meeting for Trippet in Beverly Hills with Stanley Goldblum, chairman of the board of Equity Funding Corporation of America. Equity Funding, an insurance and mutual-fund conglomerate, was growing fast, and its stock eventually was to become popular on Wall Street. Of course, no one at the 1969 luncheon knew that a little more than four years later, Equity Funding would

[1] Unrelated to the Dreyfus Corporation or any of its affiliates.

become the focus of the biggest insurance scandal in history, and that Stanley Goldblum would be sentenced to eight years in prison.

Klineman had proposed to Trippet and Goldblum separately that Equity Funding, which was rapidly expanding the number of investment packages it offered, might want to acquire Home-Stake or certain of its properties. Trippet, knowing his scheme couldn't last forever, had begun to ponder the possibility of making a few million dollars by selling his company while its true nature still was largely camouflaged. Trippet and Goldblum discussed acquisition possibilities in general terms, but nothing came of the talk. Trippet wasn't in a hurry to sell. Besides, he didn't like Stanley Goldblum; he was offended by the way Goldblum isolated himself at one end of a big conference table, and positioned Trippet and the others in a cluster around the other end.

American investors are probably fortunate that contact between two of the most notorious swindlers of the twentieth century ended with one lunch in a Beverly Hills executive dining room. Still, one can't resist speculating on what might have happened if Trippet and Goldblum had struck a deal. Would either man have discovered the fraud in the other's company before completing an acquisition? What would have happened if either had made such a discovery? Blackmail? An alliance toward more and bigger fraud? If neither had discovered the other's fraud, would Goldblum have purchased Home-Stake with Equity Funding stock, which would have been worthless four years later? Would Trippet have insisted on a large portion of the purchase price in cash?

Equity Funding in early 1969 also was considering purchasing a cattle-breeding business owned by three of Kent Klineman's clients: Leland Leachman; his brother, Lester; and Leland's son, James. Klineman was a partner in the Leachmans' company, known as Ankony Angus, and tax-sheltered investments in the company had been sold to a number of people. (The tax laws favored the cattle business and other farm-related activities, making them attractive as tax shelters in some of the ways that oil was.) Klineman also had proposed that Eastman

Dillon Union Securities, a big Wall Street investment house, might underwrite a purchase by a holding company of both Home-Stake and Ankony Angus. (At least one Eastman Dillon partner had invested in Home-Stake's drilling.) The Eastman Dillon deal didn't work out, but Equity Funding decided it would acquire Ankony Angus. The price was $1 million cash, plus Equity Funding stock then worth $8.5 million and an additional sum depending on Ankony Angus's earnings in the subsequent three years. Klineman's share was $350,000 in cash and a block of Equity Funding stock with a market value of $350,000.

Meanwhile, Klineman, Trippet, and the Leachmans were dabbling in another venture. In February 1969, they formed a partnership to buy twelve acres of land on the Pacific Coast of Mexico eight miles south of Puerto Vallarta. The film *The Night of the Iguana,* starring Ava Gardner and Richard Burton, was made on the site in the early 1960s. Trippet paid $20,000 of Home-Stake's money for a 13-percent share of the property. Its value increased later.

Separately, Trippet loaned Kent Klineman $500,000 in Home-Stake funds, part of which Klineman invested in his brokerage firm, J. M. Dryfoos & Company. Klineman ostensibly put up some security for the loan—a block of stock in a company that he and William Murray had been instrumental in forming. But the real security wasn't the stock; it was Trippet's knowledge that Klineman would be selling increasing numbers of Home-Stake drilling units. Trippet opened a brokerage account at Dryfoos and turned over $25,000 to Klineman to invest at Klineman's discretion. In addition, Trippet began paying Dryfoos a retainer of $2,000 a month.

In March, Blanche Dickinson told Trippet that she wanted to invest in the 1969 Home-Stake drilling program. "Am working again (at the World Bank) as a consultant which makes my income tax too much.

"Isn't the stock market and the economy as a whole a thing of beauty and a joy forever!"

Dickinson also said that the woman with whom she shared an apartment, Dolly Yoshida, a $16,000-a-year Pentagon civil servant, had become interested in investing in Home-Stake "when she saw my tax reductions." Dickinson asked if Yoshida could invest as little as $5,000.

"The size of her investment doesn't make any difference—any friend of yours is a friend of ours, Blanche," Trippet answered. "I was in California about a month ago and our production is moving up every quarter. We had a lot of interruptions due to the very rainy season, but no substantial damage."

The annual report for 1968, distributed on March 18, 1969, again portrayed Home-Stake as a healthy, profitable company. The accountant's letter accompanying the financial statement was signed by Norman C. Cross, Jr., a Tulsa CPA. Cross, who was recommended to Trippet by Home-Stake financial vice-president John Lenoir, was the company's eighth outside auditor in fourteen years. Lenoir later testified that he had heard (although he was unable to substantiate it) that Cross had lost two sizeable accounting customers and might be more amenable to Trippet-style accounting than others had been.

"I need an audit," Trippet told Cross. "I am going to pay $15,000 for it. You don't need to do any work, if you will just sign the [auditor's] letter." Cross didn't make any promises, but Trippet felt that he at last had found an accountant who wouldn't insist that all those embarrassing footnotes accompany Home-Stake's financial statements. (Cross later said that he would not have considered signing an auditor's letter without performing a legitimate audit; he said he didn't take Trippet's offer literally.)

Trippet also hired Elmer Kunkel as Home-Stake's treasurer. Kunkel, the lawyer-CPA who had audited the company's books several times as an outside accountant, had found a number of irregularities over the years. But Trippet told Kunkel he "trusted and respected" him and blamed John Lenoir for most of Home-Stake's accounting "problems."

The annual report for 1968 said that Home-Stake's profits were $890,000, or $2.79 per share of common stock (unrelated to drilling units), up from $746,000, or $2.47 per share in 1967. What the report didn't say was that the 1968 earnings figure was "backed into." Instead of computing earnings from the true results of Home-Stake's operations, Trippet simply selected a profit figure he wanted to show for the year and gave that figure to Elmer Kunkel. To produce the profit figure, Kunkel first had to have financial and oil-production records to manipulate. These numbers could come only from Trippet or Frank Sims, the vice-president of operations. Kunkel pressured both men to give him the information. Noncommittal memoranda and oral statements bounced back and forth for days between Trippet and Sims and Sims and Kunkel. Kunkel warned Trippet that he was going to "end up like Billy Sol Estes." Trippet became angry and said that he was "a lot smarter than Billy Sol Estes." [2] Finally Kunkel got the information and Trippet got his profit figure. (There is no evidence that Norman Cross was aware of any of these events at the time.)

Through the mid- and late 1960s, Home-Stake's California drilling properties became the company's showcase. About two hundred corporate executives, lawyers, stockbrokers, and others, many from New York or Los Angeles, flew to Santa Maria and toured the properties, which were situated a few miles outside of town. The visitors included Fred Borch of General Electric; Chester Nimitz; actor Elliott Gould; John Martin of Heublein; Marvin Meyer of Rosenfeld, Meyer & Susman, in Beverly Hills; New York CPA Wallace Sheft, Buddy Hackett's financial manager; Kent Klineman; Judson Streicher; and Redvers Opie.

At least some of these people left Santa Maria convinced that Home-Stake was a legitimate company making solid progress in extracting the thick, sandy oil that was said to lie in abundance beneath the scrubby hills and fertile valleys of the region. "If it was a fraud it was a good one," a Santa Barbara businessman said later. "The stress seemed to be on operations rather than sales and promotion."

Typically, Home-Stake would arrange to have investors flown to Santa Maria from the Los Angeles airport in private planes. If they were important enough, Trippet or Fitzgerald would fly out from Tulsa and accompany them. The visitors were met at the Santa Maria airport by either Harvey Garland, operations

[2] The Texas con man convicted of fraud in the early 1960s.

manager for the Santa Maria facility, or Conrad Greer, the chief engineer. They were taken first to Home-Stake's offices on the second floor of a modern building in a shopping center at the edge of town. There, with the aid of elaborate scale models and bright, colored maps and charts, Conrad Greer, a trim, articulate man of about forty, briefed the visitors on what Home-Stake claimed to be doing in the oil fields. Most of the investors had heard about the sand and how difficult it was to separate from the oil. The scale models made it appear that Home-Stake had developed equipment capable of doing the job successfully.

Then visitors and hosts would pile into one or two station wagons and drive to the oil fields. From 1965 through 1967, Home-Stake drilled in hills and shallow canyons about ten miles southeast of Santa Maria. The projects had names like the Victory Steamflood Project and the South Cat Canyon Steam Injection Project. Other oil companies were drilling in the same hills, and the entire area had the look and feel of a productive oil field: derricks were visible, pumping units were operating, and pipe was stacked here and there.

In such a setting it was easy for Home-Stake to exploit most visitors' ignorance of oil drilling. The company seemed to think that if it put on a showy display, few visitors would ask incisive questions about production. That assumption generally proved correct. Many of the visitors were men with large egos who talked mainly about themselves and their activities, and looked upon their oil investments as a somewhat boring sideline. Fred Borch told Harvey Garland about his occasional meetings with President Lyndon Johnson. Kent Klineman talked about Barbra Streisand.

Visitors sometimes were driven to a particular well that appeared to be pumping oil from the ground. Expensively tailored men, sometimes accompanied by their mink-wrapped wives, would step from the station wagon, taking care to avoid getting too close to the greasy equipment or field workers. On cue, a roustabout would turn a valve at the base of the well, and what appeared to be oil would ooze forth into a jar. The valve would be closed. The jar would be taken over and shown to the investors. They would look at each other, smile, nod, and mumble how impressive it all was. What they weren't told was that that particular well had malfunctioned and was rigged so that it would appear to be pumping oil from the ground when it really wasn't. What they were seeing wasn't oil; it was kerosine distillate, a substance that was circulated through some wells to keep them free of sand.

Then the party would move on to another well—a functioning one. It was equipped with a "squirter," a nozzle-like device that, when turned on, would shoot a pressurized stream of oil against the face of a nearby bluff. Company staffers would take color photographs of the investors, standing next to the squirter as it shot the oil, so they would have a tangible souvenir of their visit. Field personnel found it necessary to have squirters at separate locations, pointed in different directions, in order to allow for the direction of the almost constant wind and make sure it didn't blow oil on the investors.

The field workers hated the squirters because after the visitors left, the workers were required to clean up the oil that had been shot against the bluff. It was an extremely messy and time-consuming task. But Trippet insisted on the demonstration and gave detailed instructions on how the photographs of investors were to be taken.

"I got the picture you took," Trippet told Harvey Garland. "You are a top engineer, but I wouldn't call you the Leonardo da Vinci of the oil fields. You have to put the stream of oil between you and the subject and also you have to crouch down. I'm enclosing one of my masterpieces which will give you an idea of what I'm talking about."

Garland, never comfortable in his public-relations role, sometimes chose not to take pictures. Trippet reprimanded him. "Apparently you have quit taking pictures," Trippet said on one such occasion. "I believe this is the loss of the most valuable propaganda tool you have. . . . Please be sure to always take a picture where you get on one side of a pumping well with a squirter on it and put the participants on the other side. They should point at the stream of fluid as it squirts out, as though they were staking claim to it, and you snap the picture so that you get the stream of fluid and the participants in the picture.

. . . These pictures should be enlarged to 8″ by 10″ size and *several* copies sent to them so they can spread them around to their friends."

For its 1968 and 1969 drilling programs, Home-Stake chose a large plot of flat, plowed farmland about three miles directly east of Santa Maria. No other companies were drilling there, and it turned out that Home-Stake didn't do much drilling either, so the area never looked nearly as much like an oil field as the hills did.

Ever conscious of appearances, Trippet fretted for months about how to give the farmland the appearance of a working oil facility. He discussed it with Garland and Greer, and with Frank Sims, the Tulsa-based vice-president of operations. In early April of 1969, Red Malkin, a field foreman, was told to install tall oil derricks at the corners of one of the farmer's fields to mark it as an oil-producing area. Malkin resisted because the derricks would be hazardous to low-flying crop-duster planes in the vicinity. So the company decided on another tack.

Home-Stake obtained permission from Owen Rice, the farmer who owned the land, to paint the verticle concrete pipes that handled overflow water from his crop-irrigation system. The pipes were eight- to ten-feet tall and a foot to a foot and a half in diameter, and were spaced every few hundred feet along the edges of the fields. A Santa Maria painting contractor, with the help of several Home-Stake field workers, painted the irrigation pipes bright pink. To the top of each pipe. Home-Stake attached a foot-square piece of dark sheet metal bearing a white X or O.

The painting and coding were intended to make the pipes look as if they were part of Home-Stake's oil facility. Ostensibly, the pipes were the above-ground portion of a subterranean oil-pipeline network and marked spots where oil wells had been drilled—the X-pipes signifying production wells, the O-pipes marking steam-injection wells. In fact, of course, wells hadn't been drilled at those locations.

The painted pipes embarrassed most of the Santa Maria staff, and whenever possible they avoided showing visitors the farmland. Instead of seeing their own properties, investors in the

1968 and 1969 programs often were shown the visually more impressive properties in the hills that were part of the 1965–1967 ventures.

From 1964 through mid-1973, Home-Stake drilled approximately 110 holes in the ground at its Santa Maria properties, mostly in the hills. How many of the holes could accurately be called oil wells is questionable. Statistics on file with the California state government indicate that on the average, there were never more than forty-nine wells producing oil in any year; much of the time the number was under forty. "Home-Stake has, as a matter of unwritten policy, committed itself to the commercialization of submarginal properties," Conrad Greer complained to Trippet in 1969.

It's known that Home-Stake drilled at least three five-hundred-foot holes and gave the impression they were oil wells when the company knew there wasn't any oil at five hundred feet.

(While Home-Stake was reporting many false production figures to investors, its Santa Maria staff was reporting fairly accurate figures to the California state government's division of oil and gas and to the Conservation Committee of California Oil Producers, a private research group. The latter figures were available at the Los Angeles Public Library. Had an investor known of the second set of figures and been willing to devote the time to analyze them, Home-Stake's low oil production might have been exposed sooner.)

Some former Home-Stake employees say that the company might have been able to produce more oil at Santa Maria, but never was willing to spend as much money on people and equipment as would have been necessary. Others say Home-Stake bought some expensive equipment but didn't use it properly or at full capacity. There is little doubt, however, that Harvey Garland and Conrad Greer made a legitimate effort to produce as much oil as they could under the circumstances.

After visitors had seen the oil fields, many of them were whisked to the airport and flown back to Los Angeles. But some stayed for dinner and even overnight, which posed problems. Trippet worried that some of his less loyal employees might say the wrong thing after a few drinks with investors or with

Home-Stake's own relatively naive salesmen. He tried to ensure loyalty by paying premium salaries and providing an array of fringe benefits to the Santa Maria supervisors, including unlimited personal use of company cars, elaborate medical insurance coverage, and country-club memberships. Trippet even permitted Garland and Greer to take their wives on business trips at company expense.

But Trippet and Garland never got along well. Garland, a large-featured, bear-like man in his forties who formerly supervised Texaco's oil production in several midwestern states, was a simple, straightforward person and considered Trippet somewhat artificial—"one of the original backslappers." Garland also had growing misgivings about the way Home-Stake conducted its Santa Maria operations. Generally he kept his doubts to himself when investors were around, but Trippet was always afraid Garland might have too many martinis some night and spill the beans.

Apart from concern about loyalty in Santa Maria, Home-Stake found it difficult to entertain people there. The town offered not a single restaurant, private club, or night spot comparable to those the visitors were used to in New York or Los Angeles. Santa Maria is near Vandenberg Air Force Base, and the town's night life is tailored more to the desires of young servicemen than to Gucci-shoed Wall Street and Wilshire Boulevard financiers. Most of the restaurants are informal steak houses with cellophane-wrapped saltine crackers on every table and a loud rock or country music combo blaring in the bar. One place in the area had a bordello on the second floor staffed by Mexican prostitutes.

Fortunately for those who didn't like dining and drinking in Santa Maria, Home-Stake executives discovered the Madonna Inn, a sprawling 110-room motel, restaurant, and gift shop complex thirty miles up the coast on the south edge of San Luis Obispo. Whether one considers the Madonna Inn beautiful or garish, it is unique by even the most exotic standards. The architecture is quasi-Swiss and the decor features stained-glass windows, open fireplaces, interior fountains and waterfalls, trees strung with Christmas-style colored lights, and stone-

and-clamshell lavatories and urinals in the restrooms. The prinicpal interior color, dark pink, is used everywhere, even in the food. The bread is pink, as is the foil on the baked potatoes.

Home-Stake entertained a number of people at the Madonna Inn's dining room. The Santa Maria staff opened a charge account there after Trippet ran up a big tab entertaining a large group one night when he was low on cash.

In the autumn of 1969 Trippet told an increasingly apprehensive Conrad Greer that he wanted the engineering firm of Lewis & Ganong to endorse Home-Stake's future oil production and income projections without being given as much documentation as Home-Stake had provided in the past. The deteriorating quality of the company's already meager operations made it more and more difficult to provide plausible documentation for the millions of barrels of oil production it was predicting.

"Heretofore," Greer told Trippet, "we have gotten Lewis & Ganong to endorse our [production] and cash flow projections because we were able to offer a logical basis for the projection along with our assurance that the necessary work would be performed to realize the results being predicted. Needless to say the work hasn't been performed, nor have the results been achieved. . . . I don't believe [Lewis & Ganong] are sufficiently destitute that they would care to professionally perjure themselves for the relatively small amount we are accustomed to paying. . . . However, I may be over-estimating the integrity of these people. Shall we find out?"

Blanche Dickinson wrote to Trippet again on September 15 to ask if she could delay paying her September quarterly installment until October 2.

"Glad to hear from you," Trippet responded.

If I had nothing more to worry about than your credit, I'd be out fishing. Payment on the 2nd of October is pretty fast compared to a lot of people with whom we do business. Never worry about a few weeks on paying us.

Hope you had a beautiful harvest all summer and this fall. Are you still getting goodies from the garden?

Dickinson, November 6:

Some preliminary estimates of my 1969 income tax make it look possible that I will need another $5–$10,000 purchase of Home-Stake. Will you let me know how you can fit this in and how late in December I can confirm this? Oh yes, garden huge success, still getting Chinese cabbage, lettuce and turnips. Raspberries until two weeks ago were perfect.

Trippet:

Good news that the garden has been prolific right along. Next thing I know you'll be building a hot house. I'll be glad to make another piece of the 1969 program available for whatever you need. . . . However, I have a better suggestion. This is a one-shot deal. As you know, gifts of appreciated property (property whose value has increased) are under attack and this may be the last year you can get the big leverage of making a charitable contribution. You do this with no charitable motives, just to make money. . . .

When you know how much deduction you need, let me know and I'll send you the necessary instructions, which are quite simple.

Dickinson:

Occasionally I am told I am intelligent. At other times I know I am little sister to an ass! The gift of property you suggest—I am utterly confused. Could you spell it out for me? Say on the 1965 program I choose to give $6,000 to Wellesley College. How much would that reduce my quarterly dividends? [Your statement that] "you do this with no charitable motives, just to *make* money" is possibly the source of my confusion. Has the value of each $10,000 unit increased to $14,000—and why if so? Now that you know the degree of my stupidity, I will just beg for your forbearance. PS. Still picking lettuce and Chinese cabbage.

Dickinson, December 7:

If it isn't too late I'd like to take you up on your "charitable" suggestion. I would like to give $5,000 from either the 1965 or 1966 program, whichever you think preferable, to The Wilderness Society, 729 Fifteenth Street, N.W., Washington, D.C. If I understand you correctly the entire amount can be deducted from my income for 1969. Please let me know at once how to go about this high finance.

Dickinson, December 17:

The Wilderness Society has given me the letter of acceptance with the proviso that their accountant approves. I think they are suspicious of all oil companies—especially since the leak off California. I assured them none of our holdings are off shore—correct?

Dickinson, December 22:

It's been rough to get The Wilderness Society to accept my gift. They have been worried that they might be subject to assessment should losses be established. Perhaps by this time they have reached you by phone. At any rate today I was informed they have accepted [the gift].

There is no record of Trippet's replies to these four letters.

In December 1969, sensing that the collapse of the swindle wasn't more than a few years away, Trippet secretly began an intricate series of maneuvers that were to constitute his biggest known theft from Home-Stake. He and Harry Fitzgerald called the plan "The Great Train Robbery" at a luncheon conversation at the Tulsa Club.[1]

Under Trippet's management contract with Home-Stake, which he drew up when he founded the company in 1955, he claimed to own half of a 20-percent "reversionary interest" in profits Home-Stake theoretically received from certain of its oil programs after the participants had recouped their full investments. That is, 20 percent of such income "reverted" to the company (the other 80 percent going to the participants), and Trippet received half of the 20 percent, as he interpreted his contract. Of course, Home-Stake's oil programs generally hadn't come close to repaying investors their full outlays, so there had been little if any legitimate extra income from which Home-Stake could take 20 percent and Trippet could take his half. Thus there was a serious question in late 1969 whether the reversionary interest had any value. Trippet himself had told financial vice-president John Lenoir that the 1968 and 1969 drilling properties weren't worth "spending too much money

<hr>

[1] Eight years later Trippet and Fitzgerald said that the term "Great Train Robbery" had been used in jest and that there was nothing "sinister" about it or the plan to which it referred.

on." Furthermore, it later would be questioned whether Trippet's 1955 contract really entitled him to half of the reversionary interest in the first place.

Nevertheless, in late 1969 Trippet had Lewis & Ganong, the California engineering firm which prepared evaluation reports for Home-Stake investors, assess the value of his half of the interest, based on estimated future income from Home-Stake drilling. After allowing for the fact that the income was future income, subject to risk and difficult to predict with precision, Lewis & Ganong set the value at $2,564,131.

Trippet then transferred his interest to a corporation he had formed, T & F Oil and Realty Company. The T was Trippet, the F was Fitzgerald. Trippet owned more than 99 percent of the stock in the company; Fitzgerald, less than 1 percent. Trippet also transferred to the corporation a number of parcels of real estate, including some land near Enid, Oklahoma, which he had inherited from his grandfather. Trippet estimated the total value of T & F Oil and Realty at about $2,650,000.

Next Trippet induced New York lawyer-stockbroker Kent Klineman, to whom Home-Stake had made a $500,000 loan earlier in the year, to buy T & F Oil and Realty for $2,650,000. Showing Klineman the Lewis & Ganong evaluation of the reversionary interest, Trippet said that he wanted to sell the interest before the end of 1969 because he would treat his profit as a capital gain, and it appeared that the federal capital-gains tax would rise in 1970.

Klineman borrowed the money for the purchase from a bank in the Bahamas, paying about $2,635,000 to Trippet and $15,000 to Fitzgerald. Actually, Klineman borrowed $3.2 million, and used $2,650,000 to pay for T & F Oil and Realty, $500,000 to repay Home-Stake's loan to him, and $50,000 for "personal purposes." Klineman borrowed the money in the Bahamas after at least two New York banks refused to loan him the money. But Klineman couldn't have swung the deal at all without Trippet's help. Trippet facilitated the loan by placing $3.2 million in U.S. Treasury notes, purchased with Home-Stake funds, on deposit at the Bahamas bank as security for its loan to Klineman. He also agreed to make further loans to Klineman to aid him in paying interest on the Bahamas bank loan.

In short, Trippet had tied up $3.2 million in Home-Stake corporate funds as security for a loan to Klineman, and he had promised to make further loans to him, so that Klineman could pay Trippet and Fitzgerald $2,650,000 in cash for a company whose principal asset was a reversionary oil interest that would prove to be worthless.

There is no evidence that anyone other than Trippet knew the full ramifications of the deal at the time. Fitzgerald has said that when Trippet gave him Klineman's check for $15,000, Trippet claimed that the money was "part of the Great Train Robbery" and that the less Fitzgerald knew about it the better. The $3.2 million of Home-Stake funds was transferred, on Trippet's instructions, to the Bahamas bank by company treasurer Elmer Kunkel, but Kunkel wasn't told the purpose of the move.

As for Klineman, he later denied knowing that the reversionary interest was worthless and that Trippet might not legally own it. Klineman said that he had hoped to sell the interest at a profit after it had begun to accumulate the anticipated income. But there is reason to doubt that he really expected any reversionary income in the near future. Since 1966 Home-Stake had sent Klineman quarterly reports on his clients' income from their Home-Stake investments. Thus he knew or had reason to know that the income was falling short of projections and wasn't approaching the total payout necessary to trigger payment of reversionary income.

Still, the deal appeared lucrative for Klineman. Trippet had enabled him to finance the transaction with minimal personal risk. In addition, the loans that Trippet had promised Klineman to help him pay interest on the $3.2 million loan gave Klineman, at least temporarily, what amounted to free tax shelter; his interest payments on the Bahamas bank loan would be tax-deductible, as all interest payments are. Separately, Trippet intended to make additional loans to Klineman's New York brokerage firm.

The implicit *quid pro quo* for all these transactions was that Trippet expected Klineman to sell a substantial number of Home-Stake drilling interests in 1970. Klineman didn't disappoint him.

Trippet deposited the $2,635,000 check from Klineman in the Trippets' personal checking account at the First National Bank of Tulsa. The deposit brought the total in the account to well over $4 million, and during the next month, Trippet spent and invested actively. In addition to investing $2,739,055 in corporate bonds and debt obligations, he loaned $131,000 to Harry Fitzgerald and made a gift of $6,000 to Fitzgerald's wife, Mary Anne.[2] He also loaned another $500,000 to Kent Klineman's brokerage firm. And he paid $150,000 for a partial interest in a luxury cooperative apartment at 75 East End Avenue, New York.

Most of the corporate executives and lawyers in New York, Washington, and Los Angeles who had invested in 1968 were back again in 1969 with even more money. There were also two notable newcomers, both New York City physicians: William S. Howland, second-in-command at the Memorial Sloan-Kettering Cancer Center ($20,000); and Arthur Sackler, another eminent doctor ($200,000).

Dr. Howland was wooed at two dinner parties given by Home-Stake in private dining rooms at 21 and at The Brussels, another plush restaurant just off Park Avenue. Arthur Sackler invested at the suggestion of his accountants, the Manhattan CPA firm of Siegel & Goldburt. The doctor and Siegel & Goldburt's other clients didn't find out until much later that the firm accepted more than $100,000 as compensation from Home-Stake for referring investors to it.

Asked later about the payments, Louis Goldburt, of Siegel & Goldburt, said: "Mr. Fitzgerald offered me—'I wanted to do something for you—I would like to give you $20,000.' Well, you know, greed. I took it. In 1970 he said to me 'I will give you $42,500.' I took it. In 1971 Trippet gave me $45,000."

Another of Siegel & Goldburt's clients was Nicholas V. Marsh, a New York manufacturer and importer of artificial flowers. Marsh had invested $552,000 in Home-Stake by the end of

[2] Fitzgerald married Mary Anne Meyers, his third wife in 1960, shortly after he began selling for Home-Stake. They had met while Mary Anne, a registered nurse, was doing research on Alcoholics Anonymous in New York City and Harry was still attending AA meetings.

1969. Eventually he put a total of about $2 million into the company, the largest amount of any individual investor. Trippet decided he wanted to reward Marsh. He offered him $32,000; in effect, a small discount on his investment. Marsh asked that the money be given instead to his daughter, a divorcee with a child. Trippet complied. Marsh later said, "I assumed that maybe I deserved some sort of reward for being his largest participant." Goldburt, who witnessed the offer, was asked what he thought Trippet's purpose was. "Well, it's the usual gimmick. Why did he offer me money? To get you involved; and this was a way of getting Mr. Marsh involved more."

Another new investor in 1969 was Leopold Godowsky, a concert violinist and coinventor of Kodachrome film processing. Godowsky and his wife, Frances, sister of the late George Gershwin, committed $20,000.

Many entertainers invested again. Andy Williams, through Rosenfeld, Meyer & Susman, in Beverly Hills, put in $200,000 following a meeting at the law firm's Wilshire Boulevard offices. The meeting was attended by Williams and his father and brother; Home-Stake's Harry Fitzgerald and Conrad Greer; and Marvin Meyer and Lawrence Kartiganer, partners in the firm. Other Rosenfeld, Meyer & Susman investors in 1969 included Jack Benny, Bobbie Gentry director Mike Nichols, and Warner Bros. president Frank Wells. Several of the firm's partners also invested again.

But the 1969 Rosenfeld Meyer investments were different from those of previous years. Because of the group's favored status —its names could be dropped to attract others—Home-Stake agreed to an arrangement that partially protected the Rosenfeld Meyer clients and partners against loss. They were permitted to finance three-quarters of their investments with loans from the First National Bank of Tulsa. They also could resell their investments to Home-Stake within three years if payments didn't conform to Black Book predictions. (The group didn't know at the time that the purported bank loans—similar to the loan made to Walter Matthau in 1968—actually were coming from Home-Stake itself.)

Rosenfeld, Meyer & Susman also was the link to Home-Stake

for a young Los Angeles criminal-defense lawyer, Barry Tarlow, known for representing William Garretson, the first suspect in the Charles Manson-Sharon Tate murder case. Garretson, the caretaker, was playing his stereo in another house on the Beverly Hills property the night of the murders. (He was quickly cleared of any connection with the crimes.)

Tarlow, a former assistant U.S. attorney in Los Angeles, practiced at Rosenfeld, Meyer & Susman and subsequently established an independent practice with an office on Sunset Boulevard. He stayed in touch with several people at Rosenfeld Meyer, however, and after his income began rising in the late 1960s, Tarlow discussed several tax-shelter deals with Lawrence Kartiganer, the Rosenfeld Meyer partner coordinating the Home-Stake investments.

"I had lots of faith in Kartiganer," Tarlow said later. "I assumed they had checked both the tax and economic aspects of Home-Stake thoroughly. I didn't evaluate Home-Stake myself so much as I evaluated Rosenfeld, Meyer & Susman as a law firm. It's a desperate feeling when it gets to be December, especially if you're self-employed and you have all this money in the bank —$50,000 or $100,000—that will just go in taxes if you don't make some investment. It's like throwing it down a sewer."

(Lawrence Kartiganer says Rosenfeld, Meyer & Susman did investigate Home-Stake thoroughly. But since Barry Tarlow wasn't formally a client of the firm, he didn't get the special protection afforded the others in 1969.)

Among Martin Bregman's clients, Alan Alda put in $20,000, his first investment. Other show-business figures making initial outlays that year were Freddie Fields and David Begelman, then talent agents and later film-studio executives; Jacqueline Bisset; Diahann Carroll; producer Phil D'Antoni (*The French Connection*); and Buffy Sainte-Marie, the singer-songwriter. Candice Bergen put in another $20,000.

Kent Klineman passed the word to Marty Bregman that Home-Stake would pay him 5 percent of the price of each Home-Stake investment his clients bought in excess of $150,000. It isn't known whether Bregman reached that level or received a fee.

By early 1970 there was less and less pretense inside Home-Stake that the company was legitimate. More officers and employees knew that the company was a fraud or had reason to suspect wrongdoing. False oil-production reports were being sent to investors not only by Trippet but by others as well. One reason none of the employees resigned and reported the fraud to authorities at that time was that they knew they were being paid higher salaries than they could earn at other oil companies. A Home-Stake employee later called the company's high salaries and liberal fringe benefits the "golden handcuffs."

Mary Lou Patrick, a Home-Stake secretary and accounting clerk, went into Elmer Kunkel's office nearly in tears and complained that she was being required to send more money to some investors than to others with identical investments. Kunkel confronted Trippet, who said that it wasn't Kunkel's business how Home-Stake's money was spent. Kunkel told Patrick there was nothing he could do.

Fitzgerald said that engineer Conrad Greer and vice-president David Davies told him they calculated that between $25 million and $30 million collected by Home-Stake couldn't be accounted for.

The company's continuing practice of selling more drilling shares than it had registered, thus taking in more money than it was supposed to, was discussed one day at a meeting of Trippet, Fitzgerald, Kunkel, and Richard G. Taft, an Oklahoma City lawyer who had done some legal work for Home-Stake. "You can't resist all that money, can you, Bob," Kunkel quoted Taft as saying.

The oversales also had been noticed by Carl A. Clay, a CPA on the staff of Norman Cross, whose firm had become Home-Stake's outside auditor in 1968. Clay wrote Cross a memorandum about oversales and other problems, but left final decisions on handling the audit to Cross. During this same period, Trippet offered Carl Clay a $2,500 bonus. Clay said that he felt the payment would be "improper," so Trippet and Kunkel arranged to have the Cross firm's fee increased by $2,500 and asked Cross to pay Clay the money. Cross paid Clay about $2,000 under an agreement that Clay would get a portion of fees his work generated for the firm. Kunkel didn't feel the payment was sufficiently direct; he complained to Trippet that "we received no benefit at all from the $2,500."

Trippet also gave another of Cross's employees $400. Cross made her return it. He kept the Home-Stake account, however, and on March 4 signed the auditor's letter in the company's annual report after insisting that Home-Stake expand a footnote to say that much of the company's drilling was in an early stage and estimates of drilling costs might be revised later.

As the amount of oil produced at the Santa Maria properties declined in relation to projections, Trippet ordered that the show put on for visitors be made more elaborate than ever. Harvey Garland was balking and Trippet got angry.

"Harvey, I wish you would just follow my instructions instead of changing them without notice to me. What you were doing doesn't accomplish the objectives I have in mind at all.

"What I want you to do is as follows:

"1. Take pictures of each participant witih our own camera. They should be color film.

"2. Have 8 x 10 enlargements made and send several to the participants and send one copy of each different shot to us in Tulsa.

"3. If possible, take a picture of them with the oil squirting out of the well as a backdrop.

"4. There is no excuse for not taking pictures just because it is winter. I don't believe the excuse is valid and won't accept it."

Separately, Trippet reminded Conrad Greer: "Don't forget to use a squirting oil well as a prop for one picture where they stand and point at the stream. You put the stream between yourself and the participant, of course." Two weeks later Greer drew an elaborate diagram for foreman Red Malkin to use in arranging the photographs.

"Here goes nuisance value," Blanche Dickinson wrote to Trippet. She asked if she should deduct the appraised value of her gift to The Wilderness Society, $5,550, from her income tax due. "How the devil does one do this? Help!"

Trippet replied:

Yes, your deduction on the gift is $5,550. However, you don't deduct it from your tax. You deduct it from your taxable income. I just returned from South America. My wife and I went to Rio for a few days, just for a holiday. Then to Venezuela for a combination business and holiday trip. We have acquired a large number of excellent properties there which are only partially developed. We can make a big profit by completing the development and it's a real opportunity. I'm looking forward to telling you about it.

On Friday, March 6, H. W. ("Trip") Trippet, Robert's father, died in a Bartlesville hospital at the age of seventy-seven. The funeral, held the following Monday at St. Luke's Episcopal Church, was large. Trippet's father left his only child $434,000 in cash and property. (Robert's mother, Mary, had died in 1968.)

Home Stake on March 18 again spent a sizeable amount of money—$3.9 million—on a project unrelated to oil. It bought an apartment complex in Panorama City, California, a San Fernando Valley suburb of Los Angeles.

Don Steinmeyer, a Home-Stake petroleum engineer in Tulsa, resigned from the company in April. Trippet refused to allow Steinmeyer to exercise an option to buy Home-Stake common stock to which Steinmeyer felt entitled. So Steinmeyer drafted some notes showing the discrepancy betwen the company's actual oil production and figures given to participants. He took the notes to Harry Fitzgerald, threatening to write an article based on the notes and send it to *Newsweek* or *Business Week*. Fitzgerald conferred with Trippet and Sims, and on May 1 it was agreed to pay Steinmeyer $3,600 as a "consulting fee." Over lunch, Sims explained the terms to Steinmeyer. He didn't write the article.

Home-Stake's annual stockholders meeting was held the following Monday on the top floor of Tulsa's First National Bank building. As usual the meeting was informal, friendly, and concerned only with routine matters. Several out-of-towners attended, including Redvers Opie; Arnold Nadlman, a CPA working for Home-Stake in Los Angeles; and Leo Fialkoff, an investor from Santa Barbara. The Tulsa contingent included Trippet's personal stockbroker, Virgil Reese; Trippet's wife, Helen Grey; and Fitzgerald's wife, Mary Anne.

In the course of routine audits, the IRS by mid-1970 had begun challenging the claimed value of a few of the Home-Stake drilling units that investors had donated to charity. There was no national coordination of the audits. Rather, two local IRS offices coincidentally and independently had asked certain investors for documentation to support their charitable gift deductions.

The IRS in New York had challenged Emil Pattberg, chairman of the board of First Boston Corporation, a leading investment banking house on Wall Street. The Indianapolis IRS office had contacted Neil McElroy, Procter & Gamble's chairman in Cincinnati, as well as several other Procter & Gamble officers who had invested in Home-Stake and donated their interests. The IRS was concerned mainly with units of the 1965 Home-Stake venture.

Two Cincinnati lawyers representing the Procter & Gamble group traveled to California and conferred with Conrad Greer in Santa Maria on Sunday morning, May 24. Greer described the 1965 program to the lawyers, Henry H. Chatfield and Harold W. Walker, and gave them a tour of the drilling properties. Two IRS agents arrived the next morning and discussed the value of the properties with Greer and the Cincinnati lawyers. The agents expressed doubt that Home-Stake could produce as much oil as projected, but they deferred a final decision on the tax deductions and the meeting ended. First Boston's Emil Pattberg wasn't represented at the meeting. (His lawyer was Robert J. McDonald of Sullivan & Cromwell in New York, also a Home-Stake investor.) An IRS agent told Conrad Greer, however, that the tax agency's decision on the Cincinnati group's deductions probably would apply also to Pattberg.

During that same period Greer was complaining bitterly to Trippet that Home-Stake couldn't meet its production commitments if it didn't increase its efforts in Santa Maria. Unknown to investors, Home-Stake actually was reducing operations. The field labor staff was cut by more than a third in mid-1970, from forty-four to twenty-nine workers, and construction was nearly halted. Without the construction, "whatever predictions have been made for increased production will fall flat, and a whole new round of excuses will be necessary to ward off Home-Stake's critics," Greer told Trippet.

Trippet introduced a new concealment technique in a chart he distributed to salesmen on June 9. The first column showed the per-unit cost of each Home-Stake program from 1964 through 1969. The second column listed the "total past and future net revenue per unit" for each program. Conveniently, the figures weren't divided into their past and future components, but it made little difference since the numbers were false anyway.

On June 15 Trippet signed an operations report to investors in the 1968 program, saying that as of June 1, 1970, the program had produced 16,797 barrels of oil. The true figure was much less. On July 6 Trippet sent a note to Harvey Garland: "I have seen the production for March, April and May on the 1968 and 1969 programs and note there wasn't a single barrel of oil sold."

On July 8 Home-Stake loaned Kent Klineman $121,500, unsecured, to aid him in paying interest on the Bahamas bank loan that he had obtained in order to buy Trippet's reversionary oil interest.

Harry Fitzgerald wrote a letter in August to an investor who had agreed to buy an interest in the 1970 program if Home-Stake would agree to buy it back the following year. Such an arrangement usually jeopardizes an investor's tax deduction if the IRS learns of it; a prearranged buy-back can mean that the money isn't being invested in oil drilling, the tax-deductible activity for which it is intended. The transaction may be merely a façade erected to get the tax break. Fitzgerald wrote: "You had better put this letter in your desk drawer because I suppose the IRS would take a pretty dim view of this sort of prearrangement between us."

Although the pace of Home-Stake's fraudulent maneuverings

quickened during the spring and summer of 1970, they remained essentially invisible to most outsiders. But the seeds of the company's ultimate destruction were beginning to take root. The next eighteen months, in fact, saw a succession of major emergencies that would have broken a man less able than Trippet.

For the first time, Home-Stake was having difficulty getting its prospectus through the Securities and Exchange Commission. Although the document was filed with the SEC May 28, the commission didn't respond for more than three months. In mid-September SEC staff members requested a conference with Trippet and treasurer Elmer Kunkel in Washington. Trippet refused to go and sent Fitzgerald in his place. "I'm not gonna let those Jew s.o.b.'s tell me how to run my company," Trippet told Fitzgerald. "They can go fuck themselves."

Fitzgerald and Kunkel conferred with Harry Heller in Washington, and Kunkel and Heller went to the SEC. The commission finally permitted release of the prospectus September 30, well into the tax-shelter selling season.

Trippet wasn't deterred by the delay. He had already distributed several hundred copies of the 1970 Black Book in early June and used it as the company's principal sales tool through the summer. Home-Stake sought to raise $18,280,000 in 1970. The Black Book projected that a $20,000 investment in the 1970 program would produce a 358-percent pre-tax profit. The Book described nine specific drilling projects that Home-Stake proposed to undertake in Venezuela. Included was a letter indemnifying investors against loss if the Venezuelan government should expropriate Home-Stake's properties. (Home-Stake had purchased a majority interest in a Venezuelan oil company in 1969.)

When the prospectus finally appeared on September 30 it contained more warnings more prominently featured than any previous version.

THESE SECURITIES INVOLVE A HIGH DEGREE OF RISK AND THE EXISTENCE OF THE POSSIBILITY OF SUBSTANTIAL COMPENSATION TO THE OPERATOR [Home-Stake]. To date, none of the investors in any of the prior programs which Home-Stake and its subsidiary operators have offered to investors have recovered their entire investment.

Other risks the prospectus featured were:

Exploration, development and production of oil and gas is extremely speculative and uncertain. There is no certainty that oil will be found in commercial quantities or, if found, will yield sufficient amounts to cover the investments of investors. . . . To the extent that the projects include the use of secondary recovery methods additional risks may be encountered such as the availability of water, equipment and the uncertainties as to the question of oil that may be recoverable.
There is and may be no future market for the [investments]. Investors should contemplate that they will have to retain their investment so long as the program is in existence.

The prospectus didn't say where Home-Stake planned to drill that year, but it did say that it would present "specific projects" for approval of investors before accepting their money. The document also stressed that no one was authorized to distribute any information on the 1970 program except for what was in the prospectus.

The 1970 prospectus was essentially a meaningless formality, as far as Trippet was concerned. By September 30, when the SEC cleared the prospectus, a lot of people already had bought interests based on the Black Book and sales pitches by Home-Stake officers and salesmen.

Furthermore, many investors' attitude toward prospectuses in general was as cynical as ever. The SEC was forever making companies warn investors about the "high risk" of this or the "speculative nature" of that. What the investors wanted was something that would give them a candid, inside look at what an investment was really capable of producing. And despite all that had happened, Home-Stake retained a unique aura because of the prominence and sophistication of its clients.

Home-Stake again oversold its offering in 1970, diluting the potential value of each $20,000 unit. Instead of taking in the prescribed $18,280,000, it collected $25,106,484. The total since 1955: approximately $125 million. By paying that amount to Home-Stake, the investors had avoided turning over $75 million to the U.S. Treasury in tax revenues (assuming that the average investor was in the 60-percent tax bracket).

Blanche Dickinson wrote Trippet on October 13: "Redvers visited with me recently and was surprised I hadn't received your prospectus on Venezuelan oil. He apparently thinks it's good. Is there any reason you haven't sent me one? May I have a $10,000 interest in it?"

Trippet replied:

Delighted to receive your letter. It was quite a coincidence, as I had just mailed a 1970 program book [3] to you yesterday. This resulted from my review of correspondence from Redvers telling me of his very nice evening with you recently. I hope everything is going well with you. This has been an exceptionally busy year for me and has prevented me from having the pleasure of getting to Washington to see you. Don't think it's because I didn't want to and I hope next year will be easier so I can make it.

Dickinson invested $10,000. Her roommate, Dolly Yoshida, put in $5,000.

A few investors from the business community didn't repeat in 1970. First National City Bank's Walter Wriston made 1969 his last year, keeping his total stake at $210,000. Many participants returned, however. Western Union chairman Russell McFall invested $60,000, the same as his 1969 contribution, for a total of $234,000. Norris Darrell, Jr., of Sullivan & Cromwell, put in another $40,000. Several General Electric, Bethlehem Steel, and Heublein officers invested again. Jack Straus, of R. H. Macy, contributed another $40,000, bringing his total to $346,000. The Judson Streicher group in New York invested an additional $690,000.

The largest 1970 investment came from James, Leland, and Lester Leachman, the cattlemen who had sold their company to Equity Funding Corporation through Kent Klineman the previous year. Together they put $1,245,000 into Home-Stake's 1970

[3] Dickinson asked for the prospectus, but Trippet mailed her the Black Book. She apparently didn't know the difference.

venture on Klineman's recommendation. Trippet helped to facilitate the investment by having Home-Stake buy about $600,000 worth of the more than $6 million in Equity Funding stock that the Leachmans had received from Equity Funding when it bought their company. (The Leachmans subsequently bought the stock back from Home-Stake, well before the price of the stock collapsed.)

There were some new show-business investors and increased commitments from previous ones. Jack Benny chipped in another $200,000 in 1970, double his 1969 outlay. Buddy Hackett invested $110,000; Liza Minnelli, $40,000; Andy Williams, $300,000; Ed Ames, $45,000; Candice Bergen, $55,000; Bobbie Gentry, $30,000; Brenda Vaccaro, $12,000; John Calley, executive vice-president in charge of production at Warner Bros., $7,600; and Bob Dylan, $120,000. (Rosenfeld, Meyer & Susman made the same protective arrangements as it had the previous year for its clients—Benny, Williams, Ames, Gentry, and Calley.)

Trippet, as usual, was personally active in the 1970 sales effort. In October and November he spent several days in New York, staying at the Carlyle Hotel; and in December, several days in Los Angeles, staying at the California Club, an exclusive private retreat in downtown Los Angeles.

R. Dobie Langenkamp graduated from Tulsa Central High School, earned a bachelor's degree and Phi Beta Kappa honors at Stanford University in 1958, and received a law degree from Harvard University in 1961. After practicing law in Washington, D.C., for two years, Langenkamp returned to Tulsa and over the next decade became an active centrist in the Democrat party, a perennial finalist in the Tulsa Tennis Club's annual tournament, and a successful attorney with the firm of Doerner, Stuart, Saunders, Daniel & Langenkamp.

Dobie Langenkamp generally was well acquainted with the oil community in Tulsa, but until Tuesday, November 24, 1970, he had never heard of Home-Stake. That afternoon he got a call from a lawyer in New York City who said that one of Langenkamp's law-school classmates had recommended him. The lawyer told him that he had a client who was having difficulty with a Tulsa drilling company known as the Home-

Stake Production Company. Langenkamp asked that the client, Bernhardt Denmark, executive vice-president of Glen Alden Corporation in New York, phone him directly. When Denmark called, he told Langenkamp that the quarterly payments he was getting from Home-Stake were substantially less than the amounts a friend with an identical investment was receiving.

Denmark mailed Langenkamp his Home-Stake records, including quarterly-payment vouchers, Black Books from the 1965 and 1966 programs, and Lewis & Ganong reports. Meanwhile, Langenkamp had looked up Home-Stake in the telephone directory and found that its offices were in the Philtower Building, adjacent to the building where Langenkamp's offices were located.

He studied the material and discussed it with a Tulsa oil man more familiar with the intricacies of the business. The Black Books and other documents obviously had been drafted skillfully. They seemed on first reading to have been written with precision, but further study revealed them to be vague in key spots. It was impossible to determine definitely from the material whether Home-Stake actually had found much oil. Denmark's tax records indicated that the amount of oil was negligible; he had received very little benefit from the oil-depletion allowance. Payments to him had been divided into two parts: the smaller portion was labeled "oil and gas revenue"; the larger part, "other."

The possibilities seemed ominous to Langenkamp. It appeared that Home-Stake had raised in the range of $10 million a year for several years—perhaps $50 million to $100 million in all. Not much oil. Unequal payments. "Other." There might be valid explanations, of course. But the surface signs pointed to the possibility that Home-Stake was nothing more than a giant Ponzi fraud.

Langenkamp tried unsuccessfully to contact Trippet, who was out of town a lot and difficult to reach when he was in Tulsa. Finally, a friend in the Philtower Building in a position to observe Trippet's whereabouts agreed to tip Langenkamp when the Home-Stake executive was in his office. When the call came, Langenkamp phoned Bernhardt Denmark in New York and told him to fly to Tulsa immediately. He arrived that evening.

The next morning they went unannounced to the Home-Stake offices to see Trippet. After keeping them waiting an hour, he emerged from his office, greeted them cordially, and apologized for the delay. Langenkamp explained the reason for the visit. Trippet summoned treasurer Elmer Kunkel, and the four men went into Trippet's office. Langenkamp asked why Denmark was receiving lower payments than another person with an identical investment. And what was the meaning of "other" on the payment voucher?

Trippet said that the differing payments must have resulted from a computer error. He apologized and promised a correction. "Other," he said, was oil that was trucked instead of being moved by pipeline. Langenkamp was skeptical and hinted that he suspected fraud. Trippet got angry and asked Langenkamp to contact Elmer Kunkel in a week or so for a fuller explanation.

Denmark returned to New York. The Home-Stake men stalled for two weeks. Then Trippet told Langenkamp that Home-Stake had researched the matter and that his client actually owed Home-Stake money. He had been paid too much by mistake.

Langenkamp drafted a lawsuit accusing Home-Stake of fraud and said he would file it in federal court in two weeks if Trippet didn't refund his client's investment. The day before the deadline, Bernhardt Denmark phoned from New York. Trippet was there offering a refund if Denmark would sign a statement releasing Home-Stake from any future claims against it. Should he sign? he wanted to know. Langenkamp said that he felt Denmark had a valid claim for damages as well as for the refund. It seemed possible that Home-Stake's financial condition might be getting precarious, which could jeopardize future payment of refunds or damages. So Denmark accepted Trippet's offer as the safest alternative.

In late January 1971, another New York investor contacted Langenkamp. He obtained a refund for the second man using roughly the same tactics that he had employed for Bernhardt Denmark. Though he still lacked conclusive proof, Langenkamp emerged from the two episodes convinced that Home-Stake was a fraud.

As Dobie Langenkamp was becoming acquainted with Home-Stake for the first time in late 1970, the company was continuing to tell investors that everything was fine. Senior vice-president Frank Sims sent out a report stating that as of October 31, 1970, the 1968 drilling properties in California had produced 50,047 barrels of oil. In fact, they had produced about 3,500 barrels, and the investors' share was less than that. On January 7, 1971, Sims ordered that the steam-generating facilities on the 1968 and 1969 drilling programs be shut down, effectively ending those ventures' minimal production.

Home-Stake made another unsecured loan to Kent Klineman in December 1970 to help him pay the interest on his loan from the Bahamas bank. His total personal debt to Home-Stake, counting the loan the previous July and another in 1967, was $260,744. And Trippet and Home-Stake had loaned Klineman's firm, Dryfoos & Company, $800,000 in 1970. Furthermore, the firm was paid more than $100,000 in commissions during the year for selling $2,430,000 in Home-Stake drilling units. Siegel & Goldburt, the Manhattan accounting firm whose clients included Arthur Sackler, was paid $42,500 in commissions in 1970. Neither Klineman nor Siegel & Goldburt told their clients fully of their separate financial dealings with Home-Stake.

Home-Stake loaned Martin Bregman's firm, the financial management agency for entertainers, $40,000 at the end of the year.

The Venezuelan government enacted higher taxes on oil companies in late 1970, thus disrupting Home-Stake's financial planning. Home-Stake spent at least $75,000 in a lobbying effort to exempt the company from the higher tax. Some sources who have analyzed the lobbying say that part of the money may have been paid to individuals associated with the Venezuelan government. Furthermore, it is known that Home-Stake bankrolled thousands of dollars worth of medical treatment in the United States for an influential Venezuelan involved in the lobby. (Whether the medical treatment was part of the $75,000 or was a separate outlay hasn't been determined.) In any event, the lobbying effort was in vain; Home-Stake didn't get the tax concession.

Home-Stake also spent thousands of dollars flying potential investors or their advisers (and the investors' and advisers' wives) to Venezuela to see the oil properties. After jetting with his wife to Caracas, CPA Louis Goldburt said, "They took us out on an old DC-3 to the interior of Venezuela and showed gas flowing. For a bunch of New Yorkers it was very impressive."

Trippet's mounting problems weren't limited to complaining investors and Venezuelan taxes as 1970 drew to a close. Only six weeks after it had permitted release of Home-Stake's 1970 prospectus on September 30, the SEC's interest in Home-Stake was renewed. An employee of a competing tax-shelter drilling company obtained a copy of Home-Stake's 1970 Black Book, which he took to an acquaintance at the SEC. "If they can use a document like this, why can't we?" the employee asked.

On November 16 Richard B. Nesson, an SEC staff lawyer, asked for copies of all sales literature relating to the 1970 drilling program. Nesson and other SEC staffers questioned Harry Heller and William Blum, Home-Stake's Washington lawyers, on November 19. Three weeks later the agency subpoenaed all documents bearing on drilling projects in the 1970 ventures. Home-Stake gave the SEC the subpoenaed material on January 18, and the next day Elmer Kunkel flew to Washington to testify.

The Venezuelan oil claims made in the 1970 Black Book were analyzed by J. Lawrence Muir, the SEC's chief petroleum geologist, and his assistant, Charles R. Criss, a petroleum engineer. Muir, himself a native of Oklahoma, had worked as a geologist in Tulsa for fifteen years.

The Black Book estimated that there were 54,142,200 barrels of oil in four of the properties in the 1970 program. Muir and Criss, using what they considered to be more reliable sources, derived an estimate of only 12,990,000 barrels. Muir concluded: "It appears that the projections of income and profitability . . . listed in the Black Book are based upon unreliable, inaccurate, and uncertain data and don't have a reasonable basis in fact."

On January 22 Richard Rowe, assistant director of the SEC's

division of corporate finance, sent a letter by certified mail to Harry Heller saying that evidence indicated that Home-Stake had "willfully" violated the securities laws in soliciting 1970 investments. Any disbursement of the approximately $23 million[4] collected would "compound the willful violations," Rowe said.

The SEC filed a lawsuit against Home-Stake in the U.S. District Court for the District of Columbia on Thursday, February 11. The suit accused Home-Stake, Trippet, Fitzgerald, Kunkel, general counsel Thomas Landrith, and two other board members of violating the "registration" and "antifraud" provisions of the federal securities laws. It was noted that Home-Stake had circulated the Black Book without registering it with the SEC, a practice that can be illegal. The company also was accused of knowing or having reason to know that the oil estimates in the Black Book substantially exceeded the true amounts. The lawsuit asked the court to enjoin Trippet and the others from further violations and to take measures that would safeguard the $23 million that Home-Stake had collected from 1970 investors but hadn't yet spent.

The next day Home-Stake agreed formally in court not to communicate directly or indirectly with any 1970 investors until the SEC lawsuit was settled. (This restriction is standard during pending SEC proceedings.)

Trippet wasn't surprised by the SEC's action. In fact, he was relieved that the agency had focused only on the 1970 program and had failed to penetrate the overall fraud. But outwardly Trippet displayed a great deal of righteous indignation.

The Wall Street Journal ran a brief article on the SEC suit, quoting Trippet as saying that Home-Stake would "categorically deny the principal SEC allegations and vigorously resist the lawsuit." Trippet also went to extraordinary lengths to reassure the Home-Stake family of officers and salesmen, and through them, the investors. He distributed two memoranda that reveal his aggressive side more vividly than he ever displayed it personally to friends or business associates. (The memoranda violated the agreement not to communicate with investors.)

"Enclosed are two private Memoranda which are for your eyes

[4] The IRS eventually computed the total 1970 figure to be $25,106,484.

only. Please do not file these in your general filing systems but keep them in your own desk, under your own control. These are being sent to some of our friends only."

The first memorandum stated:

This is the tale of two cities, Washington, D.C. and Tulsa, Oklahoma. Dickens wrote his unforgettable *Tale of Two Cities* about events which occurred 180 years ago. The same conditions prevailed in France then—the tyranny of the state over the individual. His tale recites how this was rectified in full.

Now again we have the tyranny of the state over the individual. A complaint was filed against us in November for a technical violation which will be described below. The SEC thereupon proceeded to investigate it privately. They muzzled us. They absolutely forbade us to tell anyone that the investigation was being conducted and this is why I haven't contacted you. Upon completion of the investigation they filed a lawsuit and struck like lightning while we were still muzzled.

If that isn't tyranny, what is it?

Now that we are un-muzzled I can tell you that the lawsuit is without merit and we will defend it vigorously and have every confidence that it will never come to trial, but in the unlikely event it does we should win handily.

The complaint is simply for a technical violation on timing, which we admit. We sent out the [Black Books] before the effective date of the [prospectus]. The substance, however, is that the . . . prospectus did become effective and cures any substantive problem and leaves only the technical timing violation. This is what they are sore about and want to punish us for. Their punishment will consist of a settlement whereby we will make a rescission offer to each participant. Few participants will accept the offer, in my opinion, and that will be the end of the matter. Quite to the contrary, we will come out stronger than ever when this matter is completed, and we'll be held even in higher esteem by our participants.

In an attempt to put a little meat on the barebones of their technical complaint on timing, the SEC cast around for some substantive charge and decided they could always complain that we misrepresented the oil reserves. This is an old trick, because they can always get some "testifying engineer" to lower the reserves. Our answer doesn't come from any "testifying engineer." It comes from three independent sources. First, our own engineering staff. Second, Keplinger and Associates, of Tulsa,

Oklahoma, nationally known petroleum evaluation engineers. Their approval was in writing in May 1970. Third, Babson & Burns, nationally known firm, of Los Angeles. The latter firm wasn't even paid by Home-Stake but was employed by an independent investor at his sole expense to make an investigation and Babson & Burns' approval is also in writing, in December, 1970.

It is thus quite apparent as to why the SEC will never want to try their own case—it would be built on the shifting sands of a technical timing violation and the support of a "testifying engineer."

The second memorandum said:

You may have seen the word "Fraud" in connection with the SEC allegations against Home-Stake. In this memo I shall not try to be technically accurate from a legal standpoint, but instead I want to present a concept.

We all have a rather general idea of what "Fraud" means in an ordinary lawsuit. It means something very bad. The SEC language is an attempt to use this emotional semantic reaction to its own advantage to evoke Pavlovian responses in the reader and listeners when it uses the same word. The facts and the law are, however, that the use of the word "Fraud" under the Federal Securities Law does not mean the same thing as our general conception of it at all, necessarily.

There are all kinds of degrees of "Fraud" under the SEC law, and when you get down to the mildest degree the word isn't apropos. It is "the big lie" technique.

To be specific, if the SEC really meant "Fraud" in the sense in which we mean it, they would have brought a criminal suit against Home-Stake. They couldn't do it, although they would have been delighted to do so had such an opportunity presented itself.

Then you have severe civil penalties for milder "Fraud" under the Federal Securities Law. These include suspension of the right of the securities offeror to trade or engage in business for varying lengths of time, and you have seen plenty of them for one year. You have also seen civil fines of money and other kinds of punitive actions civilly. Here again, the SEC couldn't make any such action stick against us, and didn't even make any such allegations.

What they did was to accuse us of the mildest kind of "fraud," which actually couldn't possibly rise to the dignity of "Fraud" in any sense in which any of us would understand it in a general way.

Actually, what the SEC has done is make certain allegations against us (which we categorically deny, except for a couple of the parking ticket variety) to the effect that we have violated some of their technical rules. This would be properly designated as a "technical error or violation," not as "Fraud." The use of the latter word is outrageous, scurrilous, malicious and punitive.

Furthermore, they have alleged misleading statements as to our oil reserves, and I have previously written you that they can't make them stick because they would try to base them on evidence given by their own paid staff "testifying engineer." Such men are poor-as-church-mice punks making about $18,000 per year and lucky to be doing that, because they can't make anyone's team. I have already explained to you what our sources for the reserves are—the three sources I mentioned. Reserves are entirely and always a matter of expert opinion, and when we assert expert opinions based on the impeccable sources I have mentioned, it is again outrageous, ridiculous and "the big lie" to accuse us of "Fraud" in that connection. If they disagree with us, and want to so allege, they should simply have stated that our statements of oil reserves are misleading, or partially erroneous.

I just want everyone to understand that we don't have to behave like Pavlov's dogs at the cry of "Fraud," since we are human beings capable of reasoning for ourselves, and we happen to be experienced and sophisticated—everyone to whom this letter is addressed. It is just too easy to see through their Alice-in-Wonderland non sequitur going something like this: "You overparked for 15 minutes. Therefore, you are guilty of "Fraud."

In addition to distributing the two memoranda by mail, Trippet ordered Fitzgerald and other salesmen to read the *Tale of Two Cities* memorandum, as it came to be known, over the telephone to investors. "The statement should be read only to those people whom you can trust not to pass it on to the SEC," Trippet said. "In no event should it be read so slowly that the listener can take it down."

The SEC lawsuit renewed Dobie Langenkamp's interest in

Home-Stake. He sent a law clerk to the federal and county courthouses in Tulsa to determine whether Home-Stake had been sued previously. The clerk immediately discovered the thick records of the Rosenblatt-Lyons and McFadden suits. He also found that Home-Stake had been sued in 1960 by a Tulsa oil partnership, which had accused Home-Stake of overcharging and other irregularities. Home-Stake, blaming the problems on bookkeeping errors, settled the lawsuit by paying the plaintiff $12,915.

On February 23 Frank Sims wrote Trippet a memorandum on Home-Stake's California operations: "The next few months are important and 1971 is going to be a make or break year. . . . There's a time to live and a time to die and as far as ever making a profit from producing oil in California, I think we're nearer death than the unrealistic prefer to think about."

Trippet complained to Conrad Greer three days later that the Lewis & Ganong engineering firm was charging Home-Stake too much money. Greer replied:

It is important to point out that the invoices submitted by Lewis and Ganong are distinct bargains. They of course are putting their reputation, the reputation of their families, and their personal security on the line every time they place their signatures on our literature. Under the circumstances, paying these people for only the actual hours expended, without regard to the excessive risk, has got to be considered a bargain.

It wasn't long before the SEC found out about Trippet's two memoranda to salesmen and investors. Trippet quickly apologized and denied that he had intended the 1970 participants to see the memos. Affecting deep humility and shame, Trippet sent an eight-page handwritten letter to J. Lawrence Muir, chief petroleum geologist at the SEC.

Dear Mr. Muir,
I'm writing this to you long-hand because I'm so embarrassed and ashamed of myself I just can't bring myself to dictate it to anyone. I owe you a personal apology for my intemperate remarks in the two memoranda I wrote.
First, let me say that my remark about $18,000 per year punks

wasn't directed at you. I know you make more than that, and I know you aren't a punk. It was a mindless flailing out—a tilting at windmills if you will—against unknown members of the engineering staff. Well, I don't even know them—not even by name, let alone by ability. It was a calculated attempt, albeit written in the heat of passion, to evoke Pavlovian conditioned reflexes in the minds of our own men—the very thing of which I accused the SEC staff. . . .

My remark about poor-as-church-mice was ridiculous! It's a hell of a note for me, of all people, to say that. When I started this Company 16 years ago I was poor as a church mouse. Only God, my friends and good luck have brought me to the point I've reached—not my ability, which is sadly lacking.

Perhaps you will understand the heat of my passion. I had been accused of fraud—with no hearing and no warning. It embarrassed my wife and has left my Company's reputation hanging in shreds, with blood dripping down. I suppose we'll survive, but the scars will never leave. This is my life's work I'm talking about. I couldn't count the hours I've spent to bring this Company to be a sizeable factor in the oil industry. This has involved much physical pain on my part. Night after night, month after month, year after year, I've gone home actually aching from fatigue due to the endless pressure. I have to attend to 1,000 details, and also to try to get time to think big in keeping with a business which has grown from nothing to $25,000,-000 per year gross revenue. . . . This is my baby—I'm the founder. To see it suddenly—without warning—accused of fraud, was more than I could bear. I would no more consider defrauding anyone than flying to the moon. Not being able to bear it, I took refuge in pills. They don't affect my ability to work, but they do release my inhibitions. I know, because this pill deal happened once before, in 1965. I wrote several nasty letters then, so I know what they do to me.

I bear you no malice. I do think the SEC is doing a lousy job in the areas I know about. Whether this is the fault of the underlying statute, or the SEC, or both, I don't know. . . .

I just think the SEC is mired in a bog of pettifogging about nit-picking language in registration statements. It diverts your time—countless hours—from more important matters. It is also mired in a bog of enforcement proceedings, I believe. . . .

We jumped the gun with our black books. That's just the way practically all new issues are sold. It can be no other way in this fast-moving world. The broker calls the customer, makes the sale on the phone, and the prospectus is mailed with the bill. This is workable—the customer just should have the right of rescission at that point. In other words, SEC rules are being violated as a matter of course, and nothing is done about it except in rare instances like ours, where a complaint is filed.

While I'm having my say, perhaps at a most inappropriate time, I do want to make one last remark. Prospecti are mostly gobbly-de-gook. I suspect it's because everyone is afraid of his shadow—that some trivial mis-statements or silences will occur which will come back to haunt them. I don't have the time or ability to read or understand them. Now, they're just read by investment analysts, not by the public whom they're supposed to be informing.

Anyway, too much of all that. I want to apologize—sincerely —for being such an ass. I'm sending copies of this to Richard Rowe and to Richard Nathan [SEC staffers]. I want them to know how humiliated I am. But I don't suggest this be circulated to anyone else. It might be interpreted as a groveling attempt on my part to escape the consequences of my own actions. That isn't true. I'm a man and expect to try to behave like a decent one henceforth—including taking my medicine like a man.

I'd like to be your friend. It's in my heart to do so. If that isn't possible, though, from your standpoint, considering my asinine memos, I'll understand fully.

Sincerely,
Bob Trippet

To make matters worse, I've been a member of the Bar for 30 years.

I'm not sending a copy of this letter to Harry Heller, Bill Blum, our own men, or anyone else. If they saw it they might make me tear it up, and I want the catharsis of my own confession. So if it doesn't do you any good—it will have me.

In stark contrast, the tone of Trippet's private communications with Harry Heller in March, as Heller and Blum were negotiating a settlement with the SEC, was light-hearted, even jocular. At a negotiating session, an SEC staffer had referred to either Heller or Trippet as "doctor," even though neither held a doctor's degree. Trippet thought that was hilarious. In writing to Heller he addressed his memoranda to "Dr. Heller from Dr. Trippet" or "Dr. Jekyll from Mr. Hyde" or "Dr. Heller from Dr. Zhivago."

One of the people most concerned by the SEC accusations against Home-Stake was Los Angeles business consultant Donald McKee, who had put the company in touch with a major group of investors in the early and mid-1960s. After the SEC suit, McKee implored Trippet to settle it as soon as possible and make a candid statement to investors about Home-Stake's problems. McKee didn't accuse Trippet of fraud; he was too cautious and diplomatic for that. He simply said that he thought his suggestion was wise in a tactical sense and also would relieve the stress on Trippet that the SEC action must have caused.

Trippet replied:

I'm not under any stress on account of the SEC matter except my usual situation of being overworked.

The stress caused by overwork isn't anything new to me. It's been going on thirty years ever since I graduated from Law School at 23 years of age. By ten years thereafter, I suppose I was in the upper 1% of the lawyers in Tulsa from the standpoint of net income from legal fees.[5] However, I had a great many responsibilities thrust on me during that time—much more than I had the capability to absorb. I finally got sick of the stress of overwork and decided to quit and go into the oil business full-time, since that is basically what I had been doing as an attorney anyway.

I thought that entering the oil business full-time would make my load easier. How wrong I was! Instead, for the succeeding 20 years right up to the present time, I have continued unceasingly under the stress of overwork.

All of that, however, has made me plenty tough. A matter like this SEC matter runs off me like water off a duck's back.

Furthermore, knowledge is power. I am in the incomparable position of knowing both the facts and the law. As to the facts, I know that, apart from a couple of technical violations, Home-Stake's position with the SEC is unassailable. These facts are much more important than the law. Very seldom is

[5] Trippet had just told the SEC's Muir that he was "poor as a church mouse" when he started Home-Stake.

litigation controlled by tricky legal maneuvers. The facts almost always control. However, I have the added advantage of a good knowledge of the law applicable in the matter and the ability to understand it. All of this makes me double tough.

Still further, I have a mighty right arm in Harry Fitzgerald. He's a very gentle person and probably not quite as tough as I am, but he's tough enough and also he is my equal in the "knowledge is power" department.

Last, but not least, is the fact that we have a Washington SEC attorney, Harry Heller, who is an absolute genius. He's a very experienced man, has a mind like a steel trap, and gobbles up the pages of type with one great gulp, thinking as he goes. I've never seen anyone his equal. He was with the SEC quite a number of years and is now a senior partner of the prestigious New York firm of Simpson, Thacher and Bartlett and is in charge of their Washington office.

None of these matters changes the advice you gave me, which is that we should settle with the SEC. We know that perfectly well. They have all the cards. We have done just that. However, we have made a rather good settlement, I believe.

I hope you will forgive these personal remarks. I wouldn't write them to someone whom I simply regarded as a business associate but I don't regard you in that way as you well know, Don, but instead as my very good personal friend.

SEC suits such as the one filed against Home-Stake rarely go to trial. Typically, the accused company merely agrees to a court injunction against violating in the future the laws it has been accused of violating in the past. There is no penalty. This essentially is what Home-Stake did in April 1971, but it was forced to agree to an additional concession, as Trippet had predicted in the *Tale of Two Cities* memorandum. The SEC forced Home-Stake to offer to refund investors the $23 million-plus collected in 1970. The company and the SEC agreed on a draft of a rescission-offer prospectus, which in effect told investors that some of the information dispensed in 1970 was misleading or without foundation. The prospectus revised the previous descriptions of the Venezuelan drilling projects. It said that investors could have their money returned to them, but any funds left in the program would be spent as described in the rescission-offer prospectus.

The SEC hoped enough investors would demand refunds to put Home-Stake out of business. The result wasn't immediately clear, but the lawsuit and rescission offer did set off a nation-wide frenzy of telephoning. Investors called their lawyers and accountants. Lawyers and accountants called each other. Bank investment analysts were consulted. People in New York called people in Los Angeles. People in Los Angeles called people in New York. A lot of people around the country called Trippet and Fitzgerald.

Louis Goldburt, of Siegel & Goldburt, the New York CPA firm that had taken money for placing Home-Stake investments, said that Home-Stake told him the main reason for the SEC lawsuit was that the company had sold more 1970 units than it was permitted to sell. "They told me there was such a terrific demand that 'we got checks by the bushel . . . we have to [give] a few million dollars back . . . you will do us a favor if you have some of the people take back some money.' I didn't [rescind]. I fell for it. I swallowed the bait."

Goldburt's client, Nicholas Marsh, said, "I was very annoyed with Harry Fitzgerald. I thought I was being done out of something good when they made this rescission. . . . At the time I thought it [Home-Stake] was still good."

Some investors who took their money back did so hesitantly. Barry Tarlow, the Los Angeles criminal-defense lawyer, said, "Other lawyers—tax lawyers I respect—stayed in. I thought I must be making the wrong decision [to get out]."

Many people agonized over the decision for weeks. Ivan Anixter, a San Francisco businessman, informed Home-Stake that he wanted to rescind his 1970 investment of $10,000, then wired the company to "stay" the decision, then decided to keep the investment.

John Lockton of General Electric wrote to his colleague, Milton Kent: "I have a very uneasy feeling about this whole situation. . . . As you know, First National City Bank has been suspicious of this situation for some time. George [Moore] is afraid of a Ponzi-like situation where money is being taken from the new subscriptions each year to make payments purporting to be the profits from previous operations."

Neither Lockton nor Kent rescinded his 1970 investment.

From the time of the SEC's lawsuit in February until the rescission offer expired June 7, the investors' money was in an escrow account at the First National Bank of Tulsa and unavailable to the company. Having become dependent—as any Ponzi swindler does—on a constant influx of new money in growing amounts, Home-Stake ran dangerously short of funds. Without revealing the urgency of the situation, Trippet arranged a meeting with the high command of the Tulsa bank to ask for additional credit. Before the meeting, he dispatched a letter to the bank officers: Chairman Frank G. McClintock; vice-chairman Russell F. Hunt (Trippet's former law partner); senior vice-president William E. Bender (Trippet's loan-fronting contact); and another senior vice-president, K. C. Olinger. The letter again showed Trippet's aggressive self-confidence.

We have done $100,000,000 of banking with you. Now we are starting on our second $100,000,000. This conference today will determine whether we do it with you, or whether we are forced to do it in New York and California and Caracas. You have never given me any indication which would lead me to believe that you wouldn't want to do it, and I approach our conference optimistically.

Also involved is my quite considerable personal fortune. My net worth is about $3,000,000.

At the outset, I might say that the $100,000,000 of banking we have done with you has been almost entirely a one-way street, where we have been mostly a depositor and have asked for hardly any loans at all. However, it hasn't been exclusively one way—you have given excellent service and accommodated us in many ways, and we appreciate it.

The statement about our conference determining whether we continue to do most of our banking with you is not a threat, nor is it made as a matter of hostility. Quite the contrary, I regard each of you as my personal friend and I want to continue right along with you. Furthermore, it would be more convenient for us, rather than being forced to do our banking out of town.

We already have accounts in New York with City Bank. Walter Wriston, the Chairman, is one of our Participants. William I. Spencer, the President, is one of our stockholders. We also have good banking relationships and accounts with Chemical Bank and with Marine Midland. In California, our main bank would be Union Bank. Harry Volk, Chairman, is one of our Participants. We will have no trouble whatsoever in making the switch, if that is what you desire.

What I want to suggest is that you set up a $4,000,000 line of credit for us. I really don't want to pay a stand-by fee, and prefer to leave it informal, based on your general assurance which isn't legally binding.

. . . We have many millions of dollars of quick assets, and additional millions of productive properties. . . . One of our interesting assets are notes from the many prominent people about whom you know.[6]

. . . Our annual audit is nearing a close and we can furnish you with that very shortly. It will show a very fine picture indeed. This will be certified by an Independent Certified Accountant. . . .

Sincerely,
R. S. Trippet

P.S. Don't believe everything you read in the newspapers about the SEC matter. . . . It should be settled and disposed of very expeditiously. We have a right to deny, and do deny, the principal allegations of the SEC, and we are presumed innocent until proven otherwise. The only thing that will get my dander up is somebody taking an undemocratic attitude about this. By the way, I'm sure you realize this is a civil suit and not a criminal suit.

The bank approved a line of credit but required very stringent terms. Home-Stake had difficulty staying solvent through the rescission period. Trippet even found it necessary to loan the company $1.3 million from his and his wife's own funds until the investors' escrowed money was released.

In the end only a little more than $5 million was reclaimed, leaving Home-Stake more than $18 million. The result again demonstrated the remarkable persuasive powers of Robert Trippet and Harry Fitzgerald, and the cynical attitude of many businessmen toward the SEC, which dispenses wrist-slaps by the hundreds for "technical" violations of the securities laws.

On April 29 Elmer Kunkel resigned as treasurer of Home-Stake.

---

[6] A reference to the outstanding loans which the bank had fronted.

It had been ten years since his first experience with the company, and he had finally seen enough. Three weeks later, he told Conrad Greer, according to Greer's personal diary, that he:

> believed there would be no basis for anyone to go to jail if the [Home-Stake] books were audited. However, the monies had been severely manipulated. Other manipulations had taken place as well and the development funds were generally disappearing. Elmer said he wasn't leaving because he feared jail, etc., but because of the poor management.

Bruce M. Stiglitz, a Beverly Hills lawyer representing Walter Matthau,[7] wrote to Home-Stake in April 1971 asking "what the presently projected income on Mr. Matthau's program is, for 1971 especially, but also whatever 'guesstimate' you might have as to the years after 1971." When Matthau invested $200,000 in Home-Stake, the company projected he would receive $2,300 in 1970, $15,150 in 1971, $46,350 in 1972, and $58,080 in 1973. The payments were to rise to a peak of $75,900 in 1977, then decline, giving him a total return of $802,200 by 1987. Stiglitz was doubtful that the payments would meet that schedule.

"As you might guess, I am rather disturbed by the [SEC] report on your company," Blanche Dickinson wrote Trippet on May 5.

> It makes me wonder about the integrity of your reports on all the other programs in which I have participated, especially since the checks I receive are so very much less than those anticipated. It is also disturbing that as of today I haven't yet received the quarterly check. Is there a connection?
> I see in the report that you aren't permitted to communicate with participants in the 1970 program, which makes it even more difficult to evaluate. . . . I had hoped for a note from Opie, who so assured me of the outstanding qualities of the Venezuelan program. Nothing has been forthcoming to date. Am sorry to write in this manner but I am sure you can understand how disturbed I am.

Trippet replied: "I have your letter and you have correctly

[7] Arnold Krakower, the New York attorney who recommended Matthau's Home-Stake investment in 1968, had died.

stated the case. We aren't permitted to communicate with our participants during the rescission period. Your quarterly check just was mailed so you have it by now."

Through the late spring and summer of 1971 more investors were complaining and threatening to sue, and Trippet privately and grudgingly was buying them off, depending on how potent and threatening he judged a complaint to be. But publicly he continued to act as if he were running one of the world's healthiest companies and were simply being harrassed by petty tyrants in an overzealous federal bureaucracy.

He displayed both postures during the long weekend of activities surrounding the May investors meeting in Tulsa. The smooth performance at the meeting itself, in the Crystal Ballroom of the Mayo Hotel, and the bland generalities about California and Venezuela satisfied some investors but not all.

Sherman Welpton, a senior partner in the prestigious Los Angeles law firm of Gibson, Dunn & Crutcher, had heard the same stories the others had heard: Home-Stake had run into problems in Santa Maria and wasn't spending nearly all it was committed to spend on drilling. Welpton cornered Harry Fitzgerald during the evening festivities at the Fitzgerald home on Monday, May 24. He and Harry had become very friendly in the year and a half that had passed since January of 1969, when they breakfasted at the Stock Exchange Club of Los Angeles and Sherman Welpton had first become interested in Home-Stake. He had discussed the company with Fitzgerald and Trippet several times, and even had spent an entire day with Fitzgerald driving from Los Angeles to Santa Maria, touring the oil fields, and traveling back to Los Angeles. Of course, he had read the standard risk warnings in the prospectuses. But Fitzgerald and Trippet had assured him privately that he could expect to get his money back and a 300-percent profit besides. Now, on this cool May evening in 1971, Sherman Welpton was in his friend Fitzgerald's living room saying quietly but pointedly, "I am very upset about the California situation."

"Go and see Bob Trippet tomorrow morning," Harry said. "He'll probably have something to work out with you."

Trippet received Welpton and his wife cordially. He passed a few minutes telling them about a trip he and Helen Grey had made to South America. Then he said, "I understand you are disturbed about the 1969 program."

"Yes, I am. I've heard reports that the program isn't good, and I'm quite disturbed about that because I have $100,000 invested in it. I want to get out. I had been satisfied it was a fine program but apparently that isn't true."

"Well, that program has gone sour," Trippet said casually, his resonant voice quiet and steady. He took out a pencil and sheet of paper and began doing some calculations. "There are one or two or three arrangements we might work out. We can do this: we can buy a unit from you, a $20,000 unit, for $40,000. That would establish the value of that unit for tax purposes, and then you could give some of your other units away on that basis to charitable institutions and take that as a tax deduction."

"I'm not interested in any gimmickry of that nature," Welpton responded.

Trippet made a few other proposals but refused to consider any approach not based on what he assumed to have been at least a 50-percent tax saving for Welpton on his investment.

"Well, let me go back and check with my tax accountant. I'll be back in touch with you," Welpton said.

Three days later, Sherman Welpton phoned Harry Fitzgerald from Los Angeles. "I want a refund of 85 cents on the dollar, excluding tax savings," he announced. "I'm not threatening to sue, but that's a firm figure as far as I'm concerned. I'd like a response."

Fitzgerald called Welpton back the same day. Trippet had agreed to his demand. A check was sent.

Sherman Welpton got his way because Trippet knew he was one of the smartest and toughest lawyers in California, a man not to be toyed with. Trippet was managing to keep most other investors in line, however, as evidenced by the withdrawal of only $5 million out of $23 million in the 1970 program. His public confidence was evident again in June, when Home-Stake issued its annual report for 1970.

Through 1969, the company's annual reports had been modest, rather informal four-page summaries printed in simple black type on plain white paper. The 1970 report ran twelve pages and was printed on slick paper. It had a bright blue cover and was filled with color pictures and charts. There were a color photograph of Trippet and Fitzgerald; bar graphs showing the company's growth from 1961 through 1970; and color photos of a soaring oil derrick and other oil-production equipment, presumably operating.

In a section entitled "The Company in Review," the report stated that Home-Stake Oil & Gas Company had been founded in 1917; Home-Stake Royalty Corporation, in 1928; and Home-Stake Production Company, in 1955. It also said that the Home-Stake Production Company had been sponsored by the older firms. The report did not say, however, that relations had been permanently severed in 1958 after auditors brought Trippet's irregular dealings to the attention of Strother Simpson. Also excluded was any mention of the SEC action against Home-Stake's 1970 program and the rescission offer.

The report said that Home-Stake had acquired "several hundred million barrels of producible reserves in the Santa Maria, California, area and production continued to rise steadily. The work which was initiated with the 1968 program in the Santa Maria Valley field was expanded. The developments associated with these projects in the 1969 program created enlarged areas of activity." Those statements were false or at best misleading.

Norman Cross, the CPA, again signed the accountant's letter accompanying the financial statement. Earlier, Cross's assistant, Carl Clay, had approached Cross about some of the same Home-Stake accounting problems to which he had alerted his boss in previous years. "I don't want to talk about it," Cross retorted. However, he again made Home-Stake say in a footnote that much of its drilling was in an early stage and cost estimates might change.

Shortly thereafter, Clay resigned from the Norman Cross firm and joined Home-Stake as treasurer. Possibly Clay was following the same curious if-you-can't-beat-'em-join-'em logic that earlier had attracted Elmer Kunkel into Home-Stake after years of observing accounting irregularities from the outside. It is also worth noting that Trippet paid Clay an annual salary of $30,000. When Clay began working for Norman Cross three years earlier, he was making $15,000.

Trippet was able to assuage some of the concerns of Cross, Clay, and others by showing them written legal opinions, signed by Home-Stake's lawyer, Tom Landrith, which seemed to provide a legal basis for the activities that the accountants were questioning. What the accountants didn't know was that in some instances the legal opinions had been drafted by Trippet, not Landrith, and presented to Landrith for his signature. Trippet would outline for Landrith an array of hypothetical facts and circumstances to which the legal opinions ostensibly applied. Years later Tom Landrith said that he had signed each opinion "in good conscience," but, "there were occasions when I later learned that the opinion . . . had been used to justify personal and corporate conduct which I would neither have approved of nor condoned had I been advised of the use to which the opinions were to be put." [8]

Harvey Garland, the California production manager, and one of his assistants, David Hollis, were fired in June. In a personal and confidential letter, senior vice-president Sims told Garland that Home-Stake would give him an additional month's salary if he would agree to make no derogatory remarks about Home-Stake, its management, or its properties. A similar arrangement was made with Hollis, who called the additional pay hush money.

[8] The accountants continued to worry about Home-Stake's practice of selling more drilling units than it had registered with the SEC, and over the years Trippet had developed several plausible-seeming rationales to offer when asked about oversales. He said that some investors inevitably asked Home-Stake to buy back their units. In order to be able to grant such requests without reducing the advertised size of a drilling program, the company sold extra units. (He didn't add that the repurchases usually were demanded by investors who had grown suspicious.) Trippet also said that if there weren't enough repurchases to reduce a program to its proper size, the company added drilling properties so that the value of the units wouldn't be diluted. (In fact, Home-Stake rarely added properties. And since it did far less drilling than promised, the number of properties in a program frequently was academic.) In addition, Trippet occasionally claimed that excess units were sold only to small groups, apart from the regular investors, and registration with the SEC wasn't required. (The validity of this explanation still was in question years later.)

On June 23, Harold Walker, the Cincinnati lawyer representing Procter & Gamble investors, told his clients he was confident, based on another meeting with Conrad Greer and Richard Ganong, of Lewis & Ganong, that the IRS's challenge of investors' gifts to charity would be successfully rebutted.

In July Washington lawyer William Blum asked for his sales commission on 1970 investors. Trippet sent him a check for $750. Trippet also complained to Harry Heller of Simpson Thacher & Bartlett about the size of his firm's bill to Home-Stake. Heller replied that the bill ($62,000) would have been larger if the settlement with the SEC hadn't been reached. "I believe it is generally appreciated that the services performed were extremely beneficial to Home-Stake and the 1970 program and that but for the settlement which we succeeded in achieving, the bill for a long trial would have been substantially larger," Heller said.

Conrad Greer told Trippet on July 22 that Texaco had committed itself to buy two of Home-Stake's steam generators in California. Home-Stake had stopped using the generators several months earlier. "I felt it important that you be made fully aware of this situation," Greer said. "Obviously, with these moves, the East Santa Maria Field properties will no longer present even the guise of an operable oil installation."

Trippet continued to employ new salesmen in 1971, not all of whom had totally unblemished reputations. On July 29 he hired John M. Pogue as a sales vice-president for the Chicago area. In 1968 Pogue was accused in a lawsuit, along with several dozen other people, of fostering stock manipulation in the collapse of Westec Corporation, a major debacle of the mid-1960s. The following year, in March 1969, Pogue, together with two other men, was indicted for allegedly participating in a fraudulent deal related to the Westec case. Pogue pleaded innocent, and the charges against him were later dismissed. He also denied the charge in the civil lawsuit, and eventually it, too, was dismissed as it pertained to him. Whatever his role in the Westec affair may have been, however, he was well known in Chicago financial circles as a superb securities salesman.

Home-Stake's salesmen were active in the summer of 1971. Grant Hubley, a New York sales vice-president, wrote to Peter Paul Luce, a son of Time Inc. founder Henry Luce:

It was a great pleasure talking to you after so long a time. Enclosed is our 1971 preliminary prospectus. The Lewis & Ganong estimates on the 1967 program are being sent to you from Tulsa. [Luce had invested $38,000 in the 1967 program.] It just occurred to me that one of Home-Stake's long-term participants is Jim Shepley [president of Time Inc.]. Please don't hesitate to check with him on his overall thinking in regard to the company and participating in Home-Stake programs.

Peter Luce complained to Hubley that payments on the 1967 program were declining. Hubley sent the complaint to Trippet. Again taking care to avoid offending anyone with access to a major press organ, Trippet wrote personally to Luce.

I have just heard from Grant Hubley and he told me that the payments on your participation in the 1967 program had been declining substantially. I just have checked it and am hastening to send you a correction check. Also enclosed is a schedule which shows the errors which were made. I want to apologize for these errors on programming our computer. When the first error was made, it was programmed in permanently and has grown proportionately each time. There is no excuse for this. It reflects the kind of clerical help one is able to obtain these days. We now have your account under particular surveillance and will make every effort to see that no errors are made in the future.

Peter Luce put quotation marks around the word "error" in his records; he suspected there might be another explanation.

On August 3, Bruce Stiglitz, Walter Matthau's lawyer, again wrote to Trippet.

Thank you for the March, 1971, appraisal of the 1969 Home-Stake program, valuing the program at $41,710 per unit. Our client, Walter Matthau, has ten units in this program. If you know of any individuals or customers who might be interested in acquiring a portion of Mr. Matthau's interest, I would very much appreciate it if you would contact me.

Stiglitz sent a blind copy of the letter to Matthau. There is no record of a substantive reply from Home-Stake.

First National City Bank board chairman Walter Wriston phoned Grant Hubley, the New York Home-Stake salesman, on September 15 and asked if Home-Stake would buy back his $19,000 interest in the 1966 program. Hubley relayed the request to Trippet, stressing that Wriston had been very friendly and had made no demands. Trippet scrawled a reply across Hubley's memo and sent it back to him: "Not interested at this time."

The same day that Trippet hired Chicago investment salesman John Pogue—July 29, 1971—Harry Fitzgerald resigned as executive vice-president of Home-Stake. Fitzgerald, the engaging James Joyce expert and reformed alcoholic playboy whom Trippet had rescued from the gutters of Manhattan in 1959, had been trying to quit Home-Stake for some time. As the company's top salesman, his attitude always had been that of the brothel pianist who claims ignorance of what goes on upstairs. He was unavoidably aware, however, of some of the rising number of irregularities in the company, and they upset him. Trippet's $2,650,000 "Great Train Robbery" of December 1969 had bothered Fitzgerald even before he knew all its details. The SEC lawsuit and accompanying disclosures in February 1971 had disturbed him, too, despite the company's emergence in remarkably good condition. Fitzgerald complained to Donald McKee in Los Angeles that he was being asked to sign documents containing false information that Home-Stake was to submit to the SEC.

Finally, Fitzgerald found himself deeply disgusted by the public-relations blitz—the parties and other hoopla—that surrounded the 1971 shareholders meeting in May. "This is a circus," Fitzgerald told his wife, Mary Anne. "This guy [Trippet] doesn't want to run an oil company; he wants to engage in machinations."

Fitzgerald gave Trippet a handwritten letter of resignation in June.

My mental and physical condition have deteriorated to such an extent that I can't even begin to continue. . . . You have been my loyal friend and have probably done more for me than anyone I know. . . . Don't worry about me. (Remember I've been to the Winslow.) As long as I'm breathing I'll stay warm on a full stomach and so will Mary Anne and the children.

(The Winslow was the New York hotel where Trippet had found Fitzgerald unemployed and broke and had offered him work with Home-Stake.)

Trippet refused to accept the resignation. The prospect of Fitzgerald's leaving upset Trippet as much as SEC scrutiny and threats from investors. Fitzgerald was an extremely effective salesman, and he knew enough about Home-Stake's activities to make Trippet uncomfortable.

Trippet offered Fitzgerald more money—his salary was $60,000 a year at the time. Harry refused.

"Well, everybody has a price," Trippet said, according to Fitzgerald. "Suppose I could show you a way that Mary Anne could have $500,000 in her bank account and nobody would ever know where it came from?"

"Well, it wouldn't change my mind."

Increasingly distraught, Harry began drinking again for the first time since the late 1950s.

Mary Anne Fitzgerald phoned Trippet and said she had to see him. Trippet always had been warm toward Mary Anne. She was more attractive, intelligent, and articulate than some of the other Home-Stake officers' wives, and Trippet had relied on her to appear at company parties, converse with big-city investors, and make a good impression on them. Now, however, Trippet was noncommittal and rather cold. Mary Anne told him Harry would drink himself to death if his resignation weren't accepted. Trippet pried for information on how much she knew about Home-Stake's activities. She wept. They talked for two hours but reached no conclusion.

Fitzgerald finally had his doctor telephone Trippet and falsely say that Fitzgerald had a serious heart problem and that further work for Home-Stake would kill him. Trippet had little choice; he finally accepted the resignation on July 29.

Word spread fast, and Fitzgerald's departure was seen as

still another signal of serious problems within Home-Stake. "Are you sure that Harry Fitzgerald has resigned?" Lyle O'Rourke wrote to William Blum on July 30. "Do you know the circumstances? I will appreciate word from you, as I would like to know before I write him."

Within a few days after the resignation, Harry and Mary Anne Fitzgerald began receiving anonymous telephone calls. Unidentified male and female voices said, "Do you know where your children are?" (the Fitzgeralds had four school-aged children), or "We know your schedule for today and we'll be watching you."

The calls came day and night. During one two-hour period, the phone rang every five minutes. The callers didn't mention Home-Stake, although the Fitzgeralds naturally suspected a connection with the resignation. Neither the police nor the telephone company were able to help.

To escape the pressures of Tulsa, Harry Fitzgerald flew to Los Angeles and moved into an apartment at the Panorama City complex, which Home-Stake owned. After he had been there a few days, he received an anonymous letter stating that the sender had photographs of Fitzgerald engaging in sexual frolics with women other than his wife, and that the pictures would be mailed to Mary Anne Fitzgerald if Harry didn't pay $30,000. The letter said that someone would telephone Harry the next day with further instructions.

Fitzgerald rushed to Donald McKee's office with the letter. McKee phoned the office of the Los Angeles district attorney. An assistant DA arranged to have the blackmailer's call tape-recorded the following day, and instructed Fitzgerald to stall, that is, tell the caller it would take time to raise $30,000. The call was taped, Fitzgerald stalled, but nothing more was heard and no arrest was made. (There is no evidence linking anyone at Home-Stake to the anonymous calls or to the blackmail letter.)

Fitzgerald huddled with Conrad Greer in Los Angeles. According to Greer's diary:

Harry said he quit for the obvious reason of avoiding incrimination along with Bob for something he had no control over. Harry said he was never allowed to see the books or know what the financial problems were during his stay. . . . He said he wasn't ill in any way . . . but had quit irrevocably for liability reasons. Harry said Home-Stake's treasury had been dissipated. He said Carl Clay [the CPA who replaced Elmer Kunkel as treasurer] had told him that underneath the annual report facade, Home-Stake actually only had a net worth of $200,000. Carl said he had recommended to Bob that he declare voluntary bankruptcy, but Bob had refused. . . . Carl had estimated that Home-Stake wouldn't be able to make the payroll after Nov. 1, 1971 unless [Trippet] located a new source of revenue. The 1971 prospectus had been submitted to the SEC for approval but it was doubtful that approval would come, and subsequently the money (from sales to investors), in time to ward off the impending financial crises.

The fate of the 1971 prospectus indeed was in question, but SEC scrutiny wasn't Home-Stake's only problem. The company's own Washington lawyer, Harry Heller, was having serious doubts. He had been hearing many of the same rumors about Home-Stake that had circulated at the Tulsa cocktail parties in May. In particular, Heller had been told that Home-Stake might have spent drilling for oil only a small portion of the money it had raised in 1968 and 1969 for that purpose. (Home-Stake had budgeted $22,565,000 for the two annual drilling programs and actually had raised $36,742,471 from investors.)

On Thursday, August 12, Heller and his colleague, William Blum, telephoned Conrad Greer in Santa Maria and asked how much of the money had gone into drilling there. "I don't have access to the books, but in well development I would estimate an amount somewhere around $500,000," Greer said.

Heller was shocked. Other revelations also disturbed him. He and company treasurer Carl Clay, who was in Washington during August to help draft the 1971 prospectus and other official documents, knew that Home-Stake had $3.2 million in U.S. Treasury notes on deposit with a bank in the Bahamas. Trippet had told them the funds weren't restricted and could be withdrawn at any time. But in examining the transaction more closely Heller and Clay discovered that the notes were pledged as security for a loan from the Bahamas bank to Kent Klineman and therefore couldn't readily be withdrawn by Home-Stake. Heller and Clay

also learned that Klineman had used the loan to buy an unidentified company owned by Trippet.

Incensed, Heller telephoned Trippet. "You lied to me about
these [U.S. Treasury] notes. You've got to tell me the truth. I
can't work for you unless you tell me the truth."

Trippet assured Heller and Clay that the $3.2 million would be
returned to Home-Stake by the end of the year. They felt slightly
reassured, but only because they remained ignorant of several
key facts. The purpose of the entire Klineman transaction was to
facilitate a $2,650,000 theft by Trippet. The company Trippet had
sold to Klineman for that amount was T. & F. Oil and Realty.
Most of its assets were worthless, consisting largely of Trippet's
so-called reversionary interests in Home-Stake oil programs—the
interests under which a portion of Home-Stake oil income above
a certain amount was supposed to revert to Trippet. Since the
programs showed little prospect of profit, the reversionary interests probably had no value. The deal had been laughingly
called "the great train robbery."

Kent Klineman, of course, shared Heller's and Clay's ignorance
of the true significance of the transaction. But Klineman's relations with Trippet were deteriorating that summer anyway.
Trippet had asked that the $800,000 he and Home-Stake had
loaned Klineman's investment firm be repaid. Trippet didn't
tell Klineman that the real reason he needed the money was to
help assuage Home-Stake's cash shortage; he simply said that
he wanted the money back because he could get a higher rate
of interest on the funds elsewhere.

Angered by Trippet's demands, Klineman took the occasion
to insist that Trippet buy back the reversionary oil interests.
He complained that he had suffered stock-market losses in 1971
and was having difficulty meeting the interest payments on his
Bahamas loan, even with the money Home-Stake had loaned
him for that purpose. So he pressured Trippet to find a buyer
for the reversionary interest and for the real estate that had
been part of the original deal. Klineman wanted $3.5 million,
$850,000 more than he had paid Trippet two years earlier.

Trippet's choices were limited. He wasn't about to repurchase
the reversionary interest himself with the money Klineman had

paid him. And finding someone else naive enough to purchase it would have been difficult and time-consuming. So Trippet decided that he had no alternative but to have Home-Stake buy the interest with corporate funds.

That meant getting the approval of the Home-Stake board of directors—a delicate but not insurmountable problem in view of the malleability of the board. In addition to Trippet, the board consisted of Thomas Landrith, the former Tulsa city attorney who had done legal work for Home-Stake for several years, and Brooks Gutelius, Jr., and J. D. Metcalfe, both Tulsa businessmen. Landrith's, Gutelius's and Metcalfe's knowledge of Home-Stake's activities generally was limited to what Trippet told them. Board meetings usually consisted of informal luncheon conversations, with the other three directors assenting to whatever Trippet proposed.

In arranging for Home-Stake to purchase the reversionary interest, Trippet was even less candid than usual with the directors. Rather than summon them to a group meeting, he conferred with them individually, lunching with Landrith, visiting Gutelius at his home, and inviting Metcalfe to the Trippet home. To cloud the significance of the reversionary-interest deal, Trippet placed it in a broader context. He said that he was exhausted from running Home-Stake all these years, that he was going to try to find a successor as head of the company. And, oh yes, one more thing: So that he would have some financial security, he was going to try to sell his reversionary interest. It was all rather vague, and Landrith, Metcalfe, and Gutelius posed no objections.

What Trippet didn't tell them was that he had already sold the interest and pocketed $2,635,000 nearly two years earlier and that now, in the late summer of 1971, he was planning to use Home-Stake corporate funds to buy the interest back, under pressure from the initial purchaser.

Minutes were drafted, as if a formal directors meeting had been held on Thursday, August 12, the same day Harry Heller had confirmed with Conrad Greer the minimal spending on the 1968 and 1969 drilling programs. The minutes briefly stated that the board had approved Home-Stake's purchase of reversionary interests in the programs for 1965 through 1971 for

$2,991,822. Trippet had derived the dollar figure from updated Lewis & Ganong estimates, based on information Home-Stake had given the California firm. Separately, Trippet arranged for another buyer to pay $40,000 for the real estate included in the original deal. Kent Klineman accepted the terms, but the transaction wasn't completed until later in the year. Harry Heller, William Blum, Carl Clay, and most others still didn't know the full, crucial details of the Trippet-Klineman arrangements.

By September 1971 the pressures of operating Home-Stake's California properties had become too much for Conrad Greer to bear. He had been placed in charge after Harvey Garland was fired. Greer had developed ulcers and was seeing both a family doctor and a psychiatrist. On September 28 he wrote Trippet a long, emotional letter, marked it "personal and confidential," and sent it to Trippet's Tulsa home. The doctors concurred on one point, Greer said.

> The best way to rid oneself of ulcers is to get away from the problem which is causing them. Of course, I did not need to go to a doctor to identify the problem. It is ever present in my mind: . . .
> 1) I haven't been able to rationalize the morality of soliciting funds . . . such as the fifty or sixty million dollars solicited for the California Projects, and not actually devoting the appropriate fraction of this amount for the intended purpose.
> 2) In the face of overwhelming evidence indicating that the California project funds either aren't available, or aren't going to be devoted for the intended purpose, the California effort obviously can only attenuate into a dead end.
> 3) In view of the fact that I don't possess legal expertise, nor do I have access to the records, I cannot be sure that these problems aren't serious. In the event that they are, I would presume that I would sustain personal liability, as an officer of the corporation.
> The conclusion which logically proceeds from these tenets is to divorce myself from Home-Stake at the earliest opportunity.

Greer stressed that he liked his engineering work and proposed that after resigning, he be retained as a technical consultant to Home-Stake. "I am physically sick; morally depressed; fearful of uncontrollable legal liability; but enamored with my task," Greer concluded. He said he would stay on as a Home-Stake vice-president until mid-October.

On Friday, October 8, Trippet and Greer were summoned to a meeting in New York City with Frank Caponegro, an IRS agent who was auditing the tax returns of actress Faye Dunaway, U.S. Trust Company board chairman Hoyt Ammidon, and other Home-Stake investors. They all had donated drilling units to charity and had taken deductions. Caponegro, a trained engineer who specialized in evaluating oil properties, had done enough investigating to know that Home-Stake's oil production in California consistently fell far short of forecasts. The agent noticed that the company routinely supplemented meager oil payments to investors with other money. When he pressed Trippet for an explanation, Trippet was evasive. In a memorandum to his superiors, Caponegro recommended that a $47,298 gift deduction taken by Faye Dunaway be chopped to $7,898.

Home-Stake sold back most of the Equity Funding stock that it had bought from Kent Klineman's clients, the Leachmans, the previous year. The Leachmans repurchased part of it. Klineman bought the rest and then sold it to the Leachmans. Home-Stake received $524,284 for 21,658 shares, about $24.21 a share, close to what it had paid for the stock in 1970. Despite the large sum that the Leachmans had invested in the 1970 Home-Stake program—$1,245,000—they decided against accepting the refund offer in the spring of 1971.

The SEC staff and lawyers Heller and Blum dickered for weeks with Trippet over the wording of the 1971 Home-Stake prospectus. The agency didn't permit its release until November 3. The prospectus, which sought to raise $24,680,000 in new investments for more Venezuelan drilling, featured many of the same risks stressed in the 1970 prospectus. A brief account of the SEC action against Home-Stake earlier in the year wasn't high-lighted but appeared in the "management" section on page 43. More important was a footnote buried toward the end of the prospectus that was cryptic, oblique, and legalistic, but that should have raised serious questions in the mind of anyone who read and pondered it.

> Cash returned to investors includes funds derived from production and a return upon their capital contributions to the programs as payment for the use of the contributed funds by Home-Stake. . . . In the case of the 1965 to 1969 programs, inclusive, which are steamflood operations, funds derived from the latter sources have constituted virtually all of the net cash returned to investors.

In other words, most of the money paid to investors was nothing more than a small portion of their own investments being returned to them. Revenues from oil production, at least in the case of the programs from 1965 through 1969, made up only a tiny fraction of the payments, because through mid-1971, only a small amount of oil had been produced by those programs.

It was a remarkable disclosure, but was apparently either overlooked, ignored, or not understood by investors and the SEC.

The prospectus was in circulation less than two weeks when it became necessary to consider amending it. On Tuesday, November 16, Trippet strolled into Carl Clay's office and handed him a photocopy of a check for $2,991,822 that was being sent to Kent Klineman in New York. Home-Stake, Trippet said, was buying some reversionary oil interests. He told Clay that the payment would enable Home-Stake to recover the $3.2 million it had on deposit in the Bahamas. Trippet left without further explanation and caught a plane for New York.

For a few moments Carl Clay just stared at the check. The picture that had been murky for so long was becoming clearer. Clay knew that the $3.2 million in the Bahamas bank was there to secure a loan that the bank had made to Kent Klineman. Clay knew that Klineman had used the money to buy some sort of company from Trippet. Although Clay had never known the nature of the company or its assets, the necessity for Home-Stake to pay nearly $3 million to Klineman in order to release the security deposit could mean only one thing: Home-Stake corporate funds were being used to buy back whatever it was that Trippet had sold to Klineman. Trippet had mentioned reversionary oil interests. His method had been extremely circuitous, but in simplest terms, Clay surmised, Trippet had, in effect, caused Home-Stake to pay him about $3 million over a two-year period for the reversionary interests. Clay didn't know precisely what the interests were worth, but he had reason to suspect that their value might be in doubt because of Home-Stake's paltry oil production. Whatever their worth, Clay concluded that the payment from Home-Stake to Klineman would put the financial stability of cash-short Home-Stake in dire jeopardy.

Carl Clay telephoned Harry Heller in Washington and poured out his suppositions. Clay then drafted a letter of resignation from Home-Stake and dashed a block down Fifth Street to the office of company lawyer and director Thomas Landrith. Distraught with worry, Clay briefed Landrith on his findings.

Harry Heller called Landrith on Wednesday morning. Heller, too, was very upset. He said that the $2,991,822 payment to Klineman appeared to be coming from Home-Stake investors' funds that were committed to be spent for oil drilling. He also expressed deep concern about possible liability of Home-Stake's directors as well as himself and William Blum as its Washington attorneys.

Tom Landrith wrote a formal letter to Trippet saying that he felt obligated as a director of the company to investigate the reversionary-interest transaction. Landrith said that he intended to resign from the Home-Stake board as soon as the matter was resolved because he feared "civil and criminal prosecution for some damn-fool thing Home-Stake might do unknown to me."

Without informing Trippet, Heller and Blum flew to Tulsa on Friday afternoon and met secretly with Carl Clay at his home that evening. At the meeting were Tulsa lawyers John Eagleton and David James, who, in addition to Tom Landrith, had done legal work for Home-Stake. (Landrith had left town for the weekend.) Eagleton's and James's law firm, Kothe and Eagleton, had cosigned the 1971 prospectus with Heller and Blum. The Klineman transaction and its effect on Home-Stake's financial stability were discussed at length. It seemed obvious that buying the reversionary interest back from Klineman would make it difficult for Home-Stake to spend as much money drilling for oil as the company had promised investors. That fact, the lawyers knew, would have to be disclosed immediately to the SEC. The 1971 prospectus would have to be amended.

The group convened again on Saturday morning at the Eagleton law office downtown. They proceeded unannounced to the Home-Stake offices and confronted Trippet. He had returned from New York, and as usual was spending Saturday morning at his desk.

Harry Heller cursed and berated Trippet at length for lying about the substance of the Klineman deal. He demanded that Trippet return the $3 million to the Home-Stake treasury and spell out the entire transaction in a supplement to the prospectus. Eagleton and James had drafted a supplement and presented it to Trippet, along with a formal letter saying that "in the event the supplement isn't filed with the Securities and Exchange Commission, we will make our position known to the commission."

Trippet calmly refused to return the money. "This has been approved by the board of directors," he said. "Here are the minutes of the meeting." He pulled from his desk drawer the minutes from an August 12 board meeting that never occurred.

The lawyers could accomplish nothing more until they had conferred with the other directors—Landrith, who was out of town for the weekend; Metcalfe; and Gutelius. Heller and Blum returned to Washington but stayed in touch with Eagleton and James by telephone. Carl Clay agreed to delay his departure from Home-Stake until November 30 so that he could serve as a contact within the company.

Back in Tulsa from a weekend of worry, Tom Landrith phoned Trippet Monday morning. "Bob, these sons of bitches are setting me up. Both Heller and Clay are saying they are finding things wrong about Home-Stake. When someone questions them about it and someone will, they will be asked 'When did you learn of this and what did you do about it?' They will each say, 'I immediately reported it to the Board of Directors by reporting it to Tom Landrith.' This puts the whole load on my back."

Trippet said Heller's and Clay's analysis of Home-Stake's financial condition was incorrect.

John Eagleton telephoned Tom Landrith later that day to say that he and Harry Heller had learned of other "errors and omissions." The prospectus, for example, hadn't disclosed that Home-Stake had made about $2 million in loans to finance investments that participants could revoke. (The loans to the Rosenfeld, Meyer & Susman group in California were in this category.) If the investments were cancelled the loans couldn't be collected. Eagleton told Landrith that he planned to call a meeting of Home-Stake directors and demand that the 1971 prospectus be withdrawn from circulation; that Trippet's deal with Klineman be rescinded; and that Trippet declare Home-Stake insolvent.

Eagleton met with Trippet at five o'clock that day, but Trippet again refused to cancel the Klineman transaction or to withdraw the prospectus. Landrith meanwhile was phoning Brooks Gutelius and J. D. Metcalfe, the other directors in addition to Trippet and Landrith, to inform them of the latest developments.

On Tuesday Carl Clay relayed word to Landrith from Harry Fitzgerald that "rumors were flying" in California about Home-Stake. Fitzgerald reportedly said that several California investors were about to file a lawsuit against the company.

John Eagleton summoned Landrith to the Eagleton offices and showed him a draft of an amendment to the Home-Stake prospectus. Eagleton said that Trippet had refused to accept the draft, and that he had dictated his own much briefer and less revealing version on the telephone to Bill Blum's secretary in Washington. Blum had agreed to take Trippet's version to the SEC. Eagleton also told Landrith that the Eagleton firm and Harry Heller planned to resign as counsel to Home-Stake.

For the remainder of that week and most of the next, several lawyers continued to mull various drafts of a possible supplement to the Home-Stake prospectus. One draft (known as a sticker because such documents sometimes are glued to the front of prospectuses) said:

> Home-Stake's current assets have declined substantially. . . .
> In order to carry on its operations . . . it will be necessary to
> borrow money from financial institutions or others or to mort-

gage or sell its properties. Home-Stake will attempt to utilize these sources to provide funds. . . . However, there is no assurance that funds will be derived promptly from any of these sources or in amounts sufficient to enable Home-Stake to carry on its operations.

That draft also told how Home-Stake had put up the $3.2 million as security so that Klineman could buy Trippet's reversionary interest. The draft then stated that there had been no income of the type that would have reverted to Trippet, which strongly implied, without stating explicitly, that the reversionary interest was worthless. The draft said that the Home-Stake board had approved purchase of the reversionary interest from Klineman for $2,991,822, and that the $3.2 million security deposit thus would be released for Home-Stake's use. (The board of directors by this time had decided that it was too late to reverse the deal that Trippet had made with Klineman. Klineman already had cashed the $2,991,822 check that Trippet sent to him. Klineman claimed that he lost about $160,000 on the overall transaction because the large interest payments he had to make to the Bahamas bank exceeded his profit. The government later calculated, however, that Klineman made $110,269 on the deal, considering the $40,000 he received from the real-estate sale, and the unsecured loans Home-Stake made to help him with the Bahamas interest payments. He hadn't repaid those loans. The calculation of Klineman's profit, which he disputed, didn't take into account the value of the tax shelter afforded Klineman by the interest payments aided by Home-Stake.)

The early drafts of the prospectus supplement were never used. Trippet managed to convince William Blum, if not Harry Heller, that Home-Stake could raise sufficient funds to keep operating and that it wasn't necessary to disclose the full details of the Klineman transaction. Blum later claimed that he talked to an officer of the First National Bank of Tulsa who told him that Home-Stake could borrow $10 million on the signature of a top Home-Stake officer, presumably Trippet.

At Blum's request, Trippet wrote him a letter, dated Thursday, December 2, saying that "it is unnecessary to refer [in the prospectus supplement] to any suggestion of possible need to curtail or defer development of . . . programs."

The final version of the supplement, therefore, contained none of the warnings stated in the early drafts. It merely reported the level of Home-Stake's current assets and notes receivable as of November 30, 1971, without commenting on their significance.

William Blum later testified that at 3:30 on Friday afternoon, December 3, he met with Mike Valadez, a lawyer on the staff of the SEC in Washington. Blum said that he showed Valadez the proposed supplement to the prospectus, together with Trippet's letter. Valadez, according to Blum, read the documents carefully and said that he didn't "feel it was necessary or appropriate" to issue the supplement. Blum returned to his office and prepared a handwritten memorandum of the conversation for his files. (Valadez later said that he didn't recall meeting with Blum.)

The following Monday, Harry Heller, who since 1963 had been Blum's co-counsel in representing Home-Stake before the SEC, quit as the company's Washington representative; however, he continued to give informal advice to Blum. Kothe and Eagleton, John Eagleton's Tulsa firm, resigned as counsel on Tuesday.

That same day Bill Blum wrote a letter to Trippet, marked "confidential from counsel," in which he recommended that all "earlier drafts" of the supplement be "sealed or destroyed." One reason for the letter, Blum said, was that the SEC had "recently gotten supplemental appropriations," in part earmarked for continued investigation of "oil-drilling tax-shelters such as Home-Stake."

Notwithstanding the possibility of future SEC interest in Home-Stake, Blum's seal-and-destroy letter marked the end of the immediate controversy—the company's second major crisis that year. Home-Stake's treasurer and three of its lawyers were the latest to quit, and more resignations would follow. Miraculously, however, the company was still intact, and most of the investors were none the wiser.

In handling the "sticker" episode, William Blum made no investigation beyond examining Home-Stake's balance sheet and conferring with the Tulsa bank officer. In fact, he hadn't any way of determining how much money Home-Stake needed to meet its obligations. That wasn't surprising to anyone familiar with Blum's work for Home-Stake prior to 1971. He had never tried to learn how much of the investors' money Home-Stake was using for its intended purpose of oil drilling and exploration. He hadn't investigated why Arthur Andersen & Company or any of the other outside CPA firms had stopped auditing Home-Stake's books. And he hadn't inquired why Home-Stake's 1967 annual report didn't carry an independent accountant's letter certifying the report's financial statement.

The $12,670 in commissions (apart from legal fees) that Home-Stake had paid Blum for selling its investments meant, of course, that he had a financial interest in having the company portrayed in a favorable way. A number of investors later alleged that, in effect, Blum had participated in a conspiracy to defraud them.

At the same time Trippet was grappling with the controversy over the Klineman deal, he also was feeling increasing pressure from Conrad Greer, who had agreed to stay with Home-Stake temporarily. Greer was concerned about the difficulty of continuing to present the 1968 and 1969 drilling ventures in a positive light for the Lewis & Ganong firm, which Home-Stake hoped would write favorable reports about the programs.

"The romance is gone," Greer told Trippet.

It appears to me that the only way Lewis and Ganong would author a favorable evaluation report on the 1968 and 1969 programs would be if we withheld material facts and didn't apprise them of our intentions with respect to development. . . . If the land areas in question aren't subject to development, wouldn't we be acting fraudulently if we led Lewis and Ganong to believe they were?

Greer and Trippet also discussed the continuing IRS investigation of the value of Home-Stake properties. Trippet had heard again from New York IRS agent Frank Caponegro, who was auditing Faye Dunaway's income-tax returns. The IRS inquiry still wasn't coordinated nationally, but Trippet feared it might be if the agents dug much deeper.

"Goddamn Caponegro wants a complete accounting of all

production year-by-year up to the present time so he can show that we didn't achieve that production or anything close to it and I just don't know what the hell to do," Trippet said. "If we give it to him he'll just use it against us."

"Well, maybe we ought to just drag our feet on that, Bob, and see how this thing comes out with Procter & Gamble," said Greer on the phone from Santa Maria. "I think we got a much stronger situation there and it's easier to deal with Temple [the IRS agent auditing the Procter & Gamble group] than it would be with Caponegro. I know from having been exposed to both of them, you know. Then if we are anywhere near successful with Temple we could probably point to this thing and use it as a precedent."

Investor complaints kept coming in late 1971. One of those threatening Home-Stake was Robert McDonald of Sullivan & Cromwell in New York. Trippet paid McDonald $48,000 for drilling interests that had cost him $78,000.

A sizeable number of investors, however, particularly in the wake of the SEC action, chose the charitable-gift route out of Home-Stake. On December 1, 1971, Home-Stake distributed Lewis & Ganong evaluation reports claiming that units in the 1965 through 1970 programs still were worth $30,000 each or more. The claimed values were lower than they had been in prior years but still remained above the original purchase price of the units—$19,000 or $20,000.

George Moore, who had recently retired as chairman of the First National City Bank of New York and had feared since 1967 that Home-Stake might be a Ponzi scheme, donated four units—one each to Lincoln Center for the Performing Arts, the Metropolitan Opera Association, the Spanish Institute, and the Society of the New York Hospital. Walter Wriston, of City Bank, gave a unit to the Fletcher School of Law and Diplomacy at Tufts University.

On December 27, four days before the deadline for 1971 tax deductions, Martin Bregman, Candice Bergen, composer Richard Adler, and screen writers-actors Joseph Bologna and Renee Taylor gave a batch of Home-Stake interests to the Library of Congress. In a letter to librarian L. Quincy Mumford, Bregman claimed that the interests were worth $235,750 and could be expected to pay an annual return of between $11,500 and $23,000 to the library.

At Southeastern Massachusetts University in North Dartmouth, Massachusetts, however, people were becoming skeptical about the value of the Home-Stake units that William Murray's tax clients had been donating to the school's foundation since 1966. The foundation, it seemed, claimed assets of about $750,000 but hadn't made any significant gifts to the university, the purpose of the foundation's formation five years earlier. It was decided to ask a Fall River, Massachusetts, CPA firm to audit the foundation's books.

In retrospect it seems remarkable that Home-Stake raised any new money at all in 1971. But it did—nearly $14 million, which was $11 million less that it sought to raise. It was the first time that the company hadn't reached its goal for an annual drilling venture. Although many people still hadn't gotten the word, suspicions about Home-Stake's legitimacy clearly were spreading.

Another reason for the decline of investment in 1971 was the Tax Reform Act of 1969. Enacted at the end of 1969, the law was the most comprehensive tax-revision act passed in the United States since the 1954 overhaul of the Internal Revenue Code. The law didn't eliminate the deductibility of oil-drilling investments or charitable gifts, but it made certain types of income less vulnerable to taxation, and thus less in need of tax shelter. The maximum tax rate on many types of income was cut from 70 percent to 50 percent. The law also made certain tax-shelter devices less advantageous. While demand for shelter remained strong, many people became more discriminating in their investments and some companies' sales fell. The new provisions were phased in gradually and began to affect sales visibly in 1971.

In any event, the 1971 Home-Stake investor list remained impressive. Obviously, many wealthy people still took delight in beating the IRS any way they could, even if it meant investing in something risky. Despite all that was known or could have been learned by a diligent investor about Home-Stake by late 1971, the company still was alluring. Prominent investors attracted each other, and together they attracted a number of unknowns. Many of these people, of course, were ignorant of what was happening at Home-Stake, not because they lacked diligence but because they depended on others—lawyers, accountants, or financial advisers—to monitor their investments and the income from them.

As an extra inducement to invest in 1971, Home-Stake offered to finance 15 percent of an investor's purchase with a so-called nonrecourse loan, repayable only to the extent that the investment generated oil income. That is, if the investor received no income, he wasn't liable for repaying such a loan. To buy a $20,000 investment, for example, a client would put up $17,000 in cash, and Home-Stake would loan him the other $3,000. The first $3,000 of oil income would go toward repaying the loan. If there wasn't any income, the investor didn't have to repay.

The nonrecourse loan device has been used by many tax-shelter companies. Investors were given the impression that the entire investment, the loan as well as the cash outlay, was tax-deductible. The IRS subsequently challenged the loan portion of such deductions, stating that since the investor didn't have an absolute liability to repay, the loans weren't valid. The issue was before the courts and still unsettled in late 1976 when Congress finally prohibited tax deductions for much investment financed with nonrecourse loans.

It isn't known how many Home-Stake investors took advantage of the 15-percent loan offer in 1971. Fred Borch, who by then had retired as chairman of General Electric and hadn't invested in Home-Stake since 1966, put in $40,000, bringing his total to $640,787. Several of his former GE colleagues invested from $5,000 to $80,000 each.

Russell McFall, Western Union board chairman, contributed $140,000 in 1971, his highest investment yet, for a total stake of $374,000. Gerald Hoyt, Western Union's executive vice-president, and two other officers, John Evans and Charles Johnston, invested $20,000 each. Time Inc.'s James Shepley put in $20,000; Murray Gurfein, the judge who the previous June had written the original district court ruling on the Pentagon Papers case (upheld by the U.S. Supreme Court), $20,000; Gurfein's former law partner and former New York State attorney general

Nathaniel Goldstein, $20,000; and Wall Street lawyer George N. Lindsay, brother of John V. Lindsay, former mayor of New York City, $10,000.

Robert B. Fiske, Jr., a senior partner in the Wall Street law firm of Davis Polk & Wardwell, invested $10,000. "Another partner in the firm had invested in it. I read the stuff. Didn't see anything wrong. Other people in the firm said he [Trippet] was okay. They all liked him. The question never came up as to his honesty. It was just assumed he was honest. It didn't occur to anyone to question it."

(In 1975 President Gerald Ford appointed Robert Fiske to the post of U. S. Attorney for the Southern District of New York, which includes Manhattan. The position is one of the two or three most important and sensitive securities and tax law enforcement jobs in the federal government.)

Two prominent writers invested in Home-Stake in 1971: Calvin Tomkins II, of *The New Yorker*, put in $10,000; and George J. W. Goodman, who has written two best-selling financial books under the pseudonym Adam Smith, invested $110,000. Goodman was introduced to Home-Stake's Harry Fitzgerald, before he left the company, by one of Home-Stake's New York sales vice-presidents, Robert G. Killgore. Goodman also met Trippet in New York, where they chatted over drinks and lunch at The Brussels, an expensive restaurant around the corner from Home-Stake's Park Avenue offices, and at the Harvard Club.

Martin Bregman's agency, even as Bregman was arranging for his clients to donate their interests in previous programs to the Library of Congress, was steering still more of their money into the 1971 Home-Stake program. Liza Minnelli invested $105,000 for a total of $230,500; Alan Alda committed $25,000; Candice Bergen, $40,000; and Joseph Bologna and Renee Taylor, $40,000.

The events of 1971 were too much for the Rosenfeld, Meyer & Susman group, and they stayed out; however, other southern California investments at least partially compensated for their absence. Shirley Jones, the Oscar-winning actress and singer; Jack Cassidy, her husband at the time; and rock singer David Cassidy, Jack Cassidy's son by a previous marriage, invested a total of $150,000 in 1971. Their accountant, Leon T. Bush, was the link to Home-Stake. Bush put in $25,000 himself. Bush learned about Home-Stake through his brother-in-law, Joseph Gorelik, a wealthy businessman with palatial homes in Connecticut, Palm Springs, and Ecuador. Gorelik and his wife had been investing heavily in Home-Stake since 1965 after hearing about the company from William Murray. By the end of 1971 they had $1,075,520 at stake.

Comedian Jonathan Winters invested $20,000 in the 1971 venture.

As 1972 began, Trippet was still complaining about the size of Home-Stake's legal fees. William Blum wrote:

> I am very sure that after we [Home-Stake] were cited by the SEC and injunction filed, you made it clear that you wanted us to jump in and do everything that was necessary—and we sure did it—and I feel helped a great deal to keep them from putting you out of business as they threatened.

In another letter Blum told Trippet: "Things seem friendly and stable at the SEC, but Harry [Heller] has his usual pessimistic feeling that it's the lull before the storm. I think we're alright [sic] again and can stay that way by careful attention to detail."

Heller's assessment was the more nearly correct. A devastating storm was brewing. It had been building gradually for years. But more time would pass before the storm broke and destroyed Home-Stake. Throughout 1972 Trippet continued successfully to dodge squalls.

In January he hired an experienced oil man, Jackson M. Barton, to be president of Home-Stake. Trippet became chairman and remained in full control of the company. There are those who feel that Trippet, looking ahead to his own escape, was trying to set up Barton as a scapegoat. Although he was warned against taking the job by a friend who had known Trippet for years and was suspicious of his motives, Barton signed on anyway at an annual salary of $75,000. (Trippet was paying himself $96,000.) The company also hired a new treasurer, Marvin R. Barnett.

That same month saw a rash of resignations. Seven sales vice-presidents quit; and Thomas Landrith, J. D. Metcalfe, and Brooks

Gutelius, apparently upset over the revelations two months
earlier of Trippet's dealing with Kent Klineman, resigned from
the board of directors. In addition to Trippet the new directors
were Jackson Barton; Donald C. Larrabee, who had been hired
to replace Harry Fitzgerald as the company's top salesman;
Frank Sims, senior vice-president of operations; Herbert R.
Smith, a vice-president and petroleum engineer; and Marvin
Barnett, the new treasurer.

One of Trippet's most persistent problems in 1972 began on
January 21, when he received a letter from Robert Levine, a
New York lawyer representing Home-Stake investor Frank
Bendheim. A $100,000-plus investor in Home-Stake, Bendheim
had become suspicious of the company when he learned details
about the Klineman reversionary-interest transaction. Trippet
agreed to a March meeting with Levine in Tulsa.

Conrad Greer flew to Tulsa and had a long conference with
Trippet on Tuesday, February 8. According to Greer's diary,
Trippet said:

> Most of the participants in the 1964 through 1969 programs
> have become disenchanted and . . . have not reinvested in
> 1970 & 1971. . . . Therefore, Bob said, "Why should Home-
> Stake risk money to do work [in California] for those people
> who didn't like us anyway." I suggested that he should do it
> because he was under a contract to do the development work
> outlined in the prospectus. Bob said "I've done all I'm going
> to do; the hell with them."

Greer resigned as a Home-Stake vice-president effective immediately, but he was retained as a consultant at the same salary
he had been making.

By early 1972 Tulsa CPA Norman Cross had signed the accountant's letters in three Home-Stake annual reports and two
prospectuses, and was under considerable pressure from his
staff either to resolve Home-Stake's financial irregularities or
to resign as the company's outside auditor.

After Carl Clay left the Cross firm and joined Home-Stake
in mid-1971, Norman Cross had assigned four successive as-

sistants to handle Home-Stake. All four quickly spotted problems and either resigned from the firm or requested other assignments. One of the assistants, Ron Fiddner, told Cross that there appeared to be "massive fraud, misrepresentations, every indication that we should withdraw from the engagement." Fiddner said that Home-Stake effectively was bankrupt.

Marvin Stichka, who took over the Home-Stake audit from Fiddner in February 1972, drafted a letter for Cross to send to Trippet asking a number of embarrassing questions and demanding answers. Stichka needed the information to prepare Home-Stake's final financial report for 1971. Years later it remained unclear whether the letter was ever sent. In any event, Stichka never saw answers to his questions, and the problems continued to fester over the next two months. On Friday, April 14, Stichka and two other accountants at the Cross firm submitted their resignations. Two days later—on Sunday morning—Cross summoned his staff, including Stichka, to the office to discuss Home-Stake. At the end of the meeting, Cross dictated a memorandum that said in part: "I am not convinced that [Home-Stake] will develop fully [its] California properties. I feel the [SEC] would seriously question what happened to the funds that were raised for [previous drilling] programs."

Cross told Trippet the next day that his firm would have to write a "no-opinion" letter for the 1971 annual report—that is, a letter in which the accountant states that he is unable to certify the financial statement because of insufficient information. Trippet said that such a letter was totally unsatisfactory.

General Electric vice-president Milton ("Mink") Kent telephoned Conrad Greer to inquire about Home-Stake's problems. Greer wrote in his diary: "I told him I had resigned because Bob [Trippet] had elected not to continue with the development work, etc. Milton said he was going to 'get Bob where it hurt.'"

Blanche Dickinson and Dolly Yoshida asked Trippet to refund their investments—$77,770 to Dickinson and $10,000 to Yoshida. Trippet offered Dickinson $28,680 and Yoshida $3,585. "This is the very best we can do," he said. Angry but uncertain how to respond, they declined the offer.

David S. Greer, a Fall River, Massachusetts, physician, also was feeling confused and angry in the spring of 1972, but he was less doubtful about what to do. Greer (unrelated to Conrad Greer) was chairman of the board of trustees of Southeastern Massachusetts University. A recently completed inquiry into the SMU Educational Foundation, set up more than five years earlier to raise money for the school, showed that of the foundation's approximately $750,000 in claimed holdings, nearly $700,000 was in drilling units of the Home-Stake Production Company. The inquiry indicated that the Home-Stake units hadn't any apparent market value and weren't producing substantial income.

David Greer never had heard of Home-Stake. Nor was he familiar with any of William Murray's tax clients who had made the gifts. For the most part, none of them lived in Massachusetts or had any connection with the university. A source close to the inquiry said, "It appeared that, whether intentionally or not, the foundation constituted a vehicle for bailing out people who were stuck in Home-Stake and didn't want to give their shares to other established charities." The episode was particularly embarrassing because four years earlier—two years after Murray had helped to set up the foundation—the school had awarded him an honorary doctor of humane letters degree. The proclamation read: "Your commitment to, and service in, the cause of excellence in higher education has been graphically and measurably demonstrated in your unselfish devotion to this institution."

David Greer asked Murray to appear at a meeting of the university trustees. When questioned closely about the handling of the foundation's finances, Murray attempted to defend the foundation by citing a few small gifts it had made to the university. The discussion grew heated. Murray was asked about a long-pending request from the university that the foundation give it $10,000 to fund the school radio station. Murray offered to provide the money from another foundation, which was unrelated to the university. The trustees declined the offer.

Murray left the meeting, and the trustees voted to prohibit the foundation from further use of the school's name and seal. At subsequent meetings they voted to sever all relations between the university and the foundation. The directors of the foundation dismissed Murray as president. (He would later assert that he resigned because of a dispute unrelated to the Home-Stake gifts.)

Eventually, the foundation was dissolved and its remaining cash assets, about $30,000, were given to the university library. "Losing all that time set our whole fund-raising effort back," one trustee said.

By the end of April, Marvin Barnett, who had been Home-Stake's treasurer for only four months, had seen enough. "As we have discussed so many times during the last three months," Barnett wrote to Jackson Barton, the new company president:

> the company in the past has engaged in one practice which, in my opinion, we dare not continue in 1972. I am referring to disproportionate payments to investors who have made identical [investments]. It seems to me that sooner or later the SEC will discover that investors aren't being treated equitably and will shut the company down.
>
> This week distributions for the first quarter of 1972 are being made and I am convinced that they are again on a disproportionate basis. Also, we are sending out oil revenue to 1968 and 1969 program investors. Since there has been no production in these programs for many months, it is difficult to see where this revenue would come from. The treasurer of a company is responsible for the accuracy of the accounting records as well as the propriety of distributions. He cannot avoid that responsibility by saying "I didn't know what was happening" or "I was told to do it." Since I cannot agree with the practices and have no control over them, the only alternative is to resign.

Trippet convinced Barnett not to leave immediately.

On May 2 Trippet heard from Rosenfeld, Meyer & Susman partner Gary Schlessinger:

> We were shocked and dismayed at the reduction in payments for the last quarter in the various Home-Stake programs. Our clients and partners would like to know whether these reductions were caused by some occurrence which will apply only to

this last quarter or whether such reductions will be permanent? If the reductions will be permanent, our clients would like to know the exact amount spent on each program for drilling and other costs and the amount of oil which is now being produced from the various programs together with an explanation of why this drastic reduction in payments has taken place.

A few days later Home-Stake published its annual report to stockholders on 1971 activities. Like the 1970 report it was filled with color photographs. A drilling rig rose skyward amidst a cluster of bar graphs, all indicating a rising earnings trend. There was a color photo of Trippet shaking hands with Jackson Barton, and black-and-white pictures of the salesmen under the blue heading: "PEOPLE . . . Our Principal Asset."

The financial statement was followed by several footnotes, one of which gave a few, cryptic details of the Trippet-Klineman reversionary-interest transaction. Trippet had agreed to at least some of Norman Cross's demands for disclosure. The auditor's letter contained the qualification that the financial statement's accuracy depended on Home-Stake's ability to generate certain income from future oil production. A footnote said completion of drilling was "subject to conversion of assets to cash."

The report didn't mention the 1971 SEC action, the resignation of Harry Fitzgerald, or the departures of other officers.

New York CPA Louis Goldburt, whose firm had accepted more than $100,000 for referring clients to Home-Stake, had begun having serious second thoughts almost immediately after declining, in 1971, the opportunity for a refund of 1970 investments. He complained to Trippet by telephone, and even scrawled a long list of questions on lined, legal-sized sheets of paper and handed them to Trippet at a meeting in New York in late 1971. Now, in May 1972, he was gearing for more formal action. Referring to the list of questions, Goldburt wrote: "I now make formal demand for this data . . . I think it will save you and your company costs, expenses and goodwill if these items are amicably settled rather than require litigation."

On June 1 Trippet refused to buy back the 1968 and 1969 investments of former New York State attorney general Nathaniel Goldstein.

I have been reviewing every possible avenue for purchase of part of the 1968 and 1969 programs from you. The problem is that we operate strictly on a budget and our funds are earmarked. Just at this time we don't have any miscellaneous funds available for purchases. I cannot divert earmarked funds, as it would be illegal.

The following Monday, at the New York City headquarters of the IRS, agent Frank Caponegro, in a memorandum, complained again to his superiors that Home-Stake wasn't answering his requests for further information about its California operations. Caponegro recommended that a $47,930 charitable gift deduction taken by U.S. Trust Company chairman Hoyt Ammidon be cut to $4,314.

Robert Levine, the lawyer for New York investor Frank Bendheim, was pressuring Trippet, through Home-Stake lawyer Tom Landrith, to buy back Bendheim's interests. (Landrith still was serving as counsel for Home-Stake, even though he had resigned from the board of directors.) Levine threatened to go to the SEC with the full details of the Klineman-Trippet reversionary-interest deal, which he had gleaned from various sources. In April Trippet paid Bendheim $50,000 and dangled the possibility of more money later. Robert Levine said in May and June that Bendheim wanted more money immediately and renewed his threats to go to the SEC. An angered Trippet consulted William Blum about the possibility of "beating Levine to the punch" by having Blum complain to the SEC that Levine was harrassing Home-Stake about a matter (the reversionary-interest deal) that had been properly disclosed. Blum warned against such a move.

"I went to see Harry Heller and he went over everything and generally concurs with me . . . [that it wouldn't] be wise to go to the SEC's counsel. . . . It might encourage a reopening of the [earlier] extensive investigation." Blum suggested that Trippet simply let Bendheim know that continued pressure by his lawyer, Levine, only would lessen his chances of receiving additional payments from Home-Stake.

Robert Levine said that he was going to the SEC's New York office to report the matter on Tuesday, August 1. He didn't show up.

In mid-July Louis Goldburt, of Siegel & Goldburt, retained the Tulsa office of Lybrand, Ross Bros. & Montgomery, one of the nation's largest CPA firms, to audit Home-Stake's 1970 and 1971 programs. Goldburt had the impression from Trippet that he would cooperate with the audit.

On Friday, July 14, Trippet and Conrad Greer had breakfast with Christy Bell, of General Electric, in New York at the Union League Club. "Before Christy arrived," Greer said later in his diary, "Bob told me he wanted to get rid of Christy and all of his old participants. Christy asked Bob about the production, status of the development, etc. Bob misrepresented the facts in every case and Christy knew it."

All through the summer, investors continued to threaten Trippet, and depending on how influential they were and how much they had already been paid, Trippet refunded varying amounts of money. Michael Sovern, who would soon be dean of the Columbia University law school, received $6,000. He had invested $9,500 in Home-Stake's 1967 program. Robert McDonald, of Sullivan & Cromwell, was paid another $16,000 to cover interests for which he had paid $38,000. Los Angeles lawyer Barry Tarlow got back $40,375 from a $45,000 investment in 1969.

Tarlow's negotiations with Trippet, like those of many investors, were protracted and frustrating. Although Tarlow had recovered his 1970 investment at the time of the 1971 rescission offer, the SEC's charges against Home-Stake had aroused his suspicions about its other programs, too. A friend in the oil business, who had heard unfavorable rumors about Home-Stake, advised Tarlow to "get out." Moreover, Tarlow credited his experience as a criminal lawyer with giving him more insight into potentially fraudulent situations than the average person might have. "I had heard all the stories. I had heard all the answers." He demanded a full refund for 1969.

First Trippet offered him ten cents on the dollar; then, half the difference between the original investment and payments to date. Then he offered to let Tarlow exchange his 1969 interests at no extra charge for units in later programs that were "better." (A number of investors took this option, known as a rollover.) Trippet sent a Los Angeles-based Home-Stake salesman on repeated visits to Tarlow's Sunset Boulevard office to try to persuade him to accept one of the alternatives. Tarlow wouldn't budge. Finally he sent Trippet a formal letter accusing him of mismanagement and misrepresentations and threatening to sue if Trippet didn't pay. He paid.

Bruce Stiglitz, Walter Matthau's lawyer, queried Trippet again in August and got no satisfaction. Stiglitz then called Philip Goodkin, the New York CPA who had put Home-Stake in touch with Matthau's former lawyer, the late Arnold Krakower. Stiglitz said it appeared that "Home-Stake is trying to avoid giving me current information and it leaves me no choice but to take legal action to find out the status of Walter's investment and to protect his rights." Goodkin said that he would be meeting with Trippet soon and would report anything of interest to Stiglitz.

Louis Goldburt received a call in late July from H. O. Reyburn, a CPA at the Lybrand, Ross Bros. & Montgomery office in Tulsa. Apparently, Trippet was refusing to furnish part of the information needed for the audit that Goldburt had hired Lybrand to make. Goldburt told Reyburn to do the best he could, and on September 22 Lybrand sent a "report on limited examination" to Siegel & Goldburt.

> We have accepted as valid the documents furnished to us by Home-Stake . . . in support of expenses, income and well-completions without outside verification. . . . Because of the . . . limitation of our examination it didn't include all of the procedures to be performed in accordance with generally accepted auditing standards.

With those qualifications, the report said that Home-Stake appeared to have drilled only 29 new wells in the 1970

Venezuelan program out of a proposed 228. The report also contained a lot of other information, some of it confusing and therefore of limited use to Siegel & Goldburt. The report presented no conclusions or recommendations.

Tulsa attorney R. Dobie Langenkamp, who had forced refunds from Trippet for two clients in late 1970 and early 1971, was summoned to New York in October by attorneys for the Chase Manhattan Bank. They asked Langenkamp to represent the bank in its role as executor of the estates of two deceased Home-Stake investors. Langenkamp filed a lawsuit on October 25 in Tulsa federal court accusing Home-Stake of operating a "pyramid," or "Ponzi-type" fraud. It was the first suit formally to allege that Home-Stake was a Ponzi scheme. A headline in the Tulsa *World* read: "NY Bank Alleges Fraud in 'Pyramid' Suit Here." The lawsuit received no publicity elsewhere, however, and there weren't any Home-Stake investors in Tulsa. The suit was settled quietly a month later, when Home-Stake agreed to pay $303,690.

Despite its mounting problems, Home-Stake offered another drilling program in 1972; it proposed to drill gas wells in Ohio. The prospectus, passed upon by the SEC on October 11, contained more warnings than any previous version. In the "risk factors" section, participants were told to remember that the SEC had accused Home-Stake the previous year of violating the securities laws. The "tax aspects" section, explaining the various tax advantages of oil drilling, was written by William Murray's New York law firm, Murray, Patterson & Sharpe. Murray's name hadn't previously appeared in a Home-Stake prospectus, even though he had put Home-Stake in touch with many clients. For the first time, Harry Heller's name didn't appear. William Blum signed alone as the legal expert; Norman Cross's firm signed the auditor's letter.

Although it wasn't stated explicitly, tables in the "prior activities" section revealed again that Home-Stake had never come close to paying back an investor's outlay, much less making him a profit.

Home-Stake took in $5.4 million in 1972. Rumors, facts, speculation, and generally unfavorable talk were circulating widely, but a surprising number of people either didn't get the word, ignored it, or didn't believe it. William S. Lasdon, former executive committee chairman of Warner-Lambert, invested $160,000, bringing his total to $480,000. Former General Electric vice-president Virgil B. Day, by then a member of the Federal Pay Board under the Nixon wage-price control program, invested $30,000. Western Union's Russell McFall and Gerald Hoyt each put in $20,000: Time Inc.'s James Shepley, $10,000; Paul Miller of the Gannett newspaper chain, $10,000; Ross Millhiser, a Philip Morris Inc. vice-president, $35,000; Dennis G. Lyons, a partner in the Washington law firm of Arnold & Porter, $10,000; and Earl Kintner, of the Washington law firm Arent, Fox, Kintner, Plotkin & Kahn, $10,000; Kintner's totals: $127,000.

Martin Bregman's client Alan Alda invested $20,000. Shirley Jones, Jack Cassidy, and David Cassidy contributed another $150,000; their agent, Ruth Aarons, $10,000; and their accountant, Leon Bush, $60,000. Bush's brother-in-law, Joseph Gorelik, invested an additional $115,000.

The 1972 program, Home-Stake's seventeenth annual venture, brought the company's total collections since its founding to slightly more than $140 million from about three thousand investors.

Louis Goldburt and his principal client, Nicholas Marsh, had been pressuring Trippet to buy them out of past Home-Stake programs. In December 1972 an agreement was reached: Trippet would pay Marsh $1,915,000 for his units in the 1967 through 1971 programs and his stock, and Marsh simultaneously would invest $2 million in the 1972 program. Goldburt agreed to accept $77,125 from Trippet for 1970 and 1971 interests and, in turn, invest $75,000 in the 1972 venture. Marsh and Goldburt also agreed in writing, at Trippet's insistence, not to sue Home-Stake or make any claims against it.

Marsh was asked later why he hadn't sued after the unfavorable Lybrand, Ross Bros. & Montgomery report in September, or at least insisted on a better deal than he agreed to in December. "I was still foolish. I was gullible. He had excuses, and I fell for the continued excuses. When I heard the '72 program would be in Ohio I thought here we could watch it closer without sending the accountants in. Then again it was gas. We received a lot of clippings from *The Wall Street Journal* that gas is the thing for the future. So I was enamoured with this whole deal, gas; and I thought now I am going to really hit a bonanza." He added that the continued tax benefits of a reinvestment were another factor in the decision.

Gifts to charity increased in late 1972. Martin Bregman and his clients again donated Home-Stake interests to the Library of Congress. The clients included Alan Alda and actor Tony Roberts, who starred in the movies *Serpico, The Taking of Pelham—One Two Three,* and *Annie Hall,* and on Broadway in *Absurd Person Singular.* Bregman told the library that the 1972 gift was worth $250,000, raising his group's claimed total for 1971 and 1972 to $485,750. He said that the 1972 gift would pay the institution between $12,500 and $25,000 a year. If the forecast had proved accurate, the library by the end of 1974 would have received between $59,500 and $119,000 in income from the Home-Stake gifts. In fact, it got $1,660.87.

L. Quincy Mumford, librarian of Congress and secretary of its trust-fund board, which receives gifts to the library, made no effort to verify the claimed value of the Bregman group's gifts. Neither he nor anyone on the library staff knew of the SEC action against Home-Stake. Had the library examined the SEC's public file on Home-Stake, it would have been apparent that the estimates of value and yearly income were suspect.

Thomas Gates, the former defense secretary and chairman of the Morgan Guaranty Trust Company, is an alumnus of, and until being named U.S. envoy to Mainland China, was chairman of the executive board of the University of Pennsylvania's board of trustees. Gates donated more than half of his Home-Stake interests to the school. Trippet suggested that Gates make the charitable donations in order to get "the most [tax] mileage," Gates said later.

Other gifts were made by Tony Curtis, to the American Cancer Society, and by Jack Benny, to the Jewish Federation Council of Greater Los Angeles.

A number of investors asked Trippet to recommend a charity to whom they might give their Home-Stake units. In many instances he suggested the University of Oklahoma, his alma mater. As a result, the Oklahoma school has the dubious distinction of having received the largest concentration of Home-Stake gifts of all the nation's charities—units for which investors originally paid about $3.1 million.

The donors included Bill Blass; Bernard Broeker, executive vice-president of Bethlehem Steel; Heublein's Ralph Hart; General Electric's Milton Kent and William Dennler; and Corcoran Thom, Jr., of Riggs National Bank in Washington.

R. Boyd Gunning, the University of Oklahoma Foundation's executive director, had never seen so many people unconnected with the school give it shares of a particular security. But he didn't attempt to have the Home-Stake interests evaluated. Under repeated questioning, neither he nor the chairman of the foundation's board of trustees, H. O. Harder, was able to say why the large number of gifts didn't attract more scrutiny at the university.

Charities know that they sometimes are given junk by wealthy donors. "Everybody sort of smiled when we got our Home-Stake gift," recalled an official of a Boston hospital. For fear of offending donors, however, most charities don't often turn down gifts. "You take what you can get," said an officer of a Long Island charity. "You don't bargain and say to a donor, 'We'd rather have your General Motors.'"

This fear also has caused many charities to play down the extent to which the Home-Stake gifts hurt them. One prominent fund-raising figure took a different view. John J. Schwartz, president of the American Association of Fund-Raising Counsel, said, "This definitely does damage in at least one sense. If a charity is accustomed to getting a gift of value from a particular individual and then one year he gives it something that can't be sold and doesn't produce much income, it definitely leaves a gap."

Home-Stake's mystique was crumbling rapidly as 1973 began. The forces that eventually would destroy it, although not yet coordinated, had begun to form. But the mechanics of the swindle still functioned smoothly.

From the California properties included in its 1967 drilling venture, for example, Home-Stake produced 12,738 barrels of oil in December 1972 and in January and February 1973. The oil earned $32,940.38, or $65.23 for each of the 505 units of investment sold at $19,000 each in 1967.

Although each unit legally was entitled to the same payment, Trippet had established a hierarchy of sixteen pay categories, ranging from "full-pay" for people he wanted to appease to zero for charities and others he didn't fear. In the full-pay category, Trippet supplemented the $65.23 per unit in oil revenue with $277.99 in other funds—money from later investors and general funds that hadn't been spent for drilling. Trippet designated these additional funds as "pro. rev."—an abbreviation with no clear meaning.[1] It was simply intended to arouse the least possible curiosity and to camouflage the true character of the supplementary funds. The amount of pro. rev. was selected arbitrarily.

[1] Trippet told an IRS investigator that "pro. rev." meant program revenue; however, other Home-Stake people had the impression that it stood for program revision. Apparently, it raised fewer questions than "other," the previous designation for the supplementary funds.

The $277.99 plus $65.23 totaled $343.22. From that, Trippet subtracted $11.88 in expenses, for a net payment of $331.34 in the full-pay category.

The $65.23 oil figure remained constant in each category. But pro. rev. was reduced, and the expense charge increased in the lower categories. The "zero-pay" group were allotted $65.23 in oil revenue, charged $65.23 in expenses, and paid no pro. rev.

Every three months, Trippet would receive the oil-production figures from staff members and select the pro. rev. amounts himself. He would derive a full-pay figure for each drilling program. Then he would stroll to the office of Ouida Mae Back, the senior clerk in charge of paying the investors, and give her —usually orally—the oil-revenue, pro. rev., expense, and full-pay figures for each program. She would derive the figures for the other categories—80 percent of full pay, 70 percent, 60 percent, and so forth. (Trippet previously had assigned each investor to a pay category.)

The information would be put into a computer, which produced statements and checks for the investors. The statements, of course, didn't indicate that an investor was in a particular pay category and was being paid a different amount from other investors; only by comparing notes did investors learn that fact. (Trippet generally tried to keep investors who knew each other well in the same pay category, so that if they compared notes, no discrepancy would be evident. But it was impossible for him to know in every instance who was friendly with whom.)

Even those in the full-pay group, of course, were getting far less by 1973 than Home-Stake had projected. The $331.34 figure for the 1967 program over four quarters would have totaled $1,325.36 annually per unit in the 1972 to 1973 period. When Home-Stake sold the program in 1967, it projected that each unit would receive $10,125 in 1972 and $10,495 in 1973.

Ouida Mae Back, who was paid $16,800 a year, didn't question why investors were paid varying amounts. She just did as she was told.

The calm within Home-Stake's Tulsa headquarters belied the building momentum of events outside.

On the first business day of 1973—Tuesday, January 2—the Chase Manhattan Bank filed another lawsuit against Home-Stake. The bank was once again acting as trustee for a deceased investor and again alleged that Trippet was running a Ponzi scheme. On January 24 Trippet paid the Judson Streicher group in New York $60,000, only a little more than 1 percent of their $4,822,250 investment. On February 12 eight of Home-Stake's eighteen remaining sales vice-presidents resigned, including John Pogue of Chicago.

That same day, Trippet employed still another tactic for dealing with complainers. He filed a suit against a group of Los Angeles doctors and dentists who had been demanding a refund and threatening to sue Home-Stake. Trippet charged that the Los Angeles group hadn't fulfilled their contracts with Home-Stake. Some investors were frightened off by such tactics, but a few days later, the Los Angeles group brought suit against Home-Stake and Trippet for fraud.

The various excuses Home-Stake had concocted continued to assuage other investors. On February 26 financial vice-president John Lenoir wrote a letter to William D. Robertson, a Culver City, California, physician, blaming his low payments on a computer error.

In January and February Robert Trippet deposited $2.2 million in a personal checking account at the First National Bank of Tulsa and withdrew $2,388,284. It isn't known what his balance was at the beginning and end of the period or how much he had in other accounts.

More and more lawyers—including members of leading East and West Coast firms—were being consulted. In early February, Peter Van N. Lockwood, a young Harvard-educated partner in the Washington, D.C., law firm of Caplin & Drysdale, received a call from James Keeler, a Virginia CPA who handled the finances of Leland, James, and Lester Leachman. They were the cattlemen who had sold their company to Equity Funding Corporation in 1969, and had invested $1,245,000 in the 1970 Home-Stake drilling program on the advice of Kent Klineman.

Klineman had telephoned Jim Keeler saying that he had

become aware of certain problems at Home-Stake, and that he wanted to meet with the lawyers and accountants for people to whom he had sold 1970 Home-Stake investments. Keeler had called Peter Lockwood because Lockwood had been representing the Leachmans in an IRS audit of their 1970 income-tax returns. Caplin & Drysdale specializes in tax law; its senior partner, Mortimer Caplin, was commissioner of the IRS under John F. Kennedy. The agency was questioning the Leachmans' deduction of the 1970 Home-Stake investments, but the audit hadn't been completed.

A few days later, Peter Lockwood attended a meeting convened by Kent Klineman in the office of Joseph S. Hellman, a partner in the New York City firm of Kronish, Lieb, Shainswit, Weiner & Hellman, which had done legal work for Klineman. Lockwood had met Klineman two or three times in recent years when Klineman had tried to sell non-Home-Stake tax shelters to various of Lockwood's clients.

At the meeting in Hellman's office, Klineman said that the 1970 Home-Stake program had shown poor results, and that Trippet had been evasive when prodded for answers. Klineman suggested that Trippet be invited to New York for further discussion.

Trippet agreed to come, and met the group in Joseph Hellman's office on Wednesday, February 28. He acknowledged that Home-Stake had some problems but attributed them to production delays that he said were unavoidable. He tended to disclaim detailed knowledge of Home-Stake's affairs, blaming accounting confusion on accountants, engineering discrepancies on engineers, and so forth. After Trippet left, the worried group of lawyers and accountants decided that Joseph Hellman, on their behalf, should demand that Home-Stake refund their clients' money. Trippet refused.

It was obvious that negotiations were going to be difficult and protracted. Peter Lockwood was reluctant to have the Leachmans' interests represented by Hellman since he was Klineman's lawyer. Klineman himself eventually might be open to suit, having sold the Leachmans their investment. At that time, Lockwood still knew nothing of Klineman's extensive financial dealings with Trippet and Home-Stake. But after mid-March, Lockwood dealt directly with Trippet.

It wasn't Trippet's nature to fly to Brazil. The plan he devised for escaping from Home-Stake before it collapsed was characteristically more subtle and complicated than that. It appeared to offer the possibility of obscuring the Home-Stake fraud while allowing Trippet to ease himself out of the company, shifting at least part of if not all the responsibility and legal liability to others.

Citing failing health, Trippet quietly let it be known to certain business friends outside Home-Stake that he might want to transfer control of the company to new management. A new chief executive or management group, of course, would learn quickly of Home-Stake's precarious situation—lawsuits, complaints from investors, millions of dollars unaccounted for, and the strong possibility that the company had been defrauding its clients for years and thus was liable to them for many millions of dollars. New management would have to be willing to live with those problems in order to get its hands on Home-Stake's assets—$5.4 million in cash collected from 1972 investors and not yet spent, plus its various properties and whatever other funds might be stashed away.

One friend aware of Trippet's desire to leave Home-Stake was William Goudy, a Denver geologist who had known him since college. Around March 1, Goudy began exploring the possibility of putting Trippet in touch with an Albuquerque, New Mexico, business promoter named Elbert Myron ("Mike") Riebold. Trippet and Riebold were similar in one crucial respect: both were skilled swindlers. Neither man knew that when they first met, nor did William Goudy, it would seem. All Trippet knew for sure was that he was offering an oil company with at least $5.4 million in cash in the treasury; all Riebold knew was that he had a pressing need for a large amount of cash. Still, Trippet and Riebold were astute enough to realize that their needs could be fully satisfied only by a crook or a fool.

Mike Riebold, then forty-six years old, was as flamboyant as Trippet was conservative. Born in Oklahoma and raised in

the Missouri Ozarks, Riebold had been a carhop, a shoe salesman, a munitions worker, and a drama student. From his New
Mexico base, he flew around the Southwest in private planes
and helicopters, wheeling and dealing in the oil and mining
businesses.

When Riebold moved from Silver City, New Mexico, to
Albuquerque in 1971 he left behind thousands of dollars in
debts, lawsuits, and judgments against him; he had become
known as the "one-armed bandit." (He was born without a
right hand.) But his reputation didn't stop him from acquiring
a $200,000 home, with a swimming pool and riding horses, on
several secluded acres north of Albuquerque.

By early 1973, however, Riebold was in deep financial and
legal difficulty. He controlled three small New Mexico companies—Garfield Mines Ltd., Aqua Pura Inc., and American
Fuels Corporation—that purported to be in the oil, gas, and
mining businesses. Riebold and several associates raised more
than $5.5 million in 1972 and 1973 by touting and selling stock
in the three companies. They told investors that American Fuels
and Riebold owned or controlled oil, gas, coal, and other
mineral properties worth millions, and that American Fuels
anticipated drilling 350 gas wells with a total production of
70 billion cubic feet of natural gas per day.

Riebold flew potential investors to Albuquerque, where they
visited a suite of offices staffed with secretaries and technicians.
They were lavishly entertained and were flown by helicopter
about the picturesque countryside. They were impressed further
that the First National Bank in Albuquerque thought highly
enough of Riebold's operations to have loaned him well over a
million dollars between mid-1972 and the spring of 1973.

What the investors weren't told was that Riebold's claims were
vastly inflated. Some of his businesses actually were on the
verge of bankruptcy. The main reason that the First National
Bank had loaned him the money was that he had given $27,000
in cash and 722,242 shares of American Fuels stock to the bank
officer who had granted the loans—senior vice-president Donald
Travis Morgan. In all, Morgan made fifty-seven loans totalling
$6,239,339, partly unsecured, to Riebold and his associates.

No one could account for all the money that Mike Riebold

had obtained from investors and the bank. Undoubtedly he squandered much of it creating an appearance of prosperity and respectability about his headquarters and properties; buying and leasing several expensive airplanes; entertaining potential clients; and investing for his own benefit. He also paid off some of his loans. But Mike Riebold had a continuing and growing need for cash. He and Don Morgan knew that the loans from the First National Bank were illegal, and that eventually they would be discovered if they weren't all paid off or somehow covered before the next audit by national bank examiners. Since Riebold's mineral properties were of questionable value, they weren't producing much income.

Then one day in early March, Riebold got a call from Max Curry, an acquaintance and petroleum geologist in Midland, Texas. "I have just come back from Denver, Mike, and I ran across a situation that I think is interesting," Curry said. He told Riebold of Bill Goudy's effort to help Bob Trippet find someone to take over Home-Stake.

Just before noon a day or two later, Riebold walked into Don Morgan's office at the First National Bank. "I have had a call from Max Curry [whom Morgan also knew] and there is a gentleman who wants to talk to me and it may be an opportunity to associate with a company that has around five million dollars in cash which possibly can be moved to the First National Bank in Albuquerque," Riebold said.

Morgan cancelled his afternoon appointments and left immediately with Riebold for Midland, Texas, aboard Riebold's plane. A Riebold associate, Carlos Robinson, accompanied them; Robinson had worked for Riebold in various capacities for several years and could be counted on to follow orders. They met Bill Goudy in Max Curry's office that afternoon. Goudy's message, according to Don Morgan, was that "Trippet had had his problems in past years, namely with the SEC and I gathered with the IRS, and he was tired of fighting the battle and he was looking to find management that he would turn the company over to, who could carry forward with Home-Stake Production and wouldn't go out of its way, go back into past history and dig up things."

Riebold said that he would like very much to meet Trippet.

Three weeks later, on Monday, March 26, Home-Stake issued its annual report for 1972. According to the report, the Home-Stake Production Comapny had earned profits of $1,646,000, up from $1,593,000 in 1971. Assets at the end of 1972 were said to total $40,841,431. The report stressed that the National Association of Securities Dealers' automated quotation system had begun quoting the price of Home-Stake common stock, and that it was being traded by an increasing number of brokerage firms.

Several months after Blanche Dickinson and Dolly Yoshida rejected Trippet's settlement offer, Redvers Opie recommended that they consult a lawyer and consider suing Home-Stake. Opie put them in touch with a law-school professor he knew. In February 1973 the professor referred them to the San Francisco law firm of Broad, Khourie & Schulz, which has a national reputation for handling major securities and antitrust cases. A partner in the firm, William A. Wineberg, Jr., a graduate of the University of Chicago law school, examined Dickinson's and Yoshida's files on Home-Stake—letters, Black Books, prospectuses, profit projections, and payment vouchers. Wineberg also obtained Home-Stake material filed with the Office of the Corporations Commissioner for the State of California, including SEC documents. In addition, he looked up Home-Stake in a national digest of federal court cases and found the 1968 lawsuit filed by George McFadden of Memphis. By March, Wineberg was attempting to get Trippet to refund his clients' money.

That same month an IRS agent informed San Francisco businessman Ivan Anixter that his 1970 deduction of a $10,000 investment in Home-Stake was being challenged because the IRS had determined that Home-Stake hadn't spent investors' money for oil-drilling as promised. Anixter was incensed. He had had great difficulty deciding whether to take a refund of his 1970 investment at the time of the SEC-forced rescission offer in 1971. Having first asked for the money, he had then wired Home-Stake that he might change his mind, and finally had left the money in the program. The CPA handling the Anixter's IRS audit, Samuel Mendelson, was in the offices of Broad, Khourie & Schulz one day in March on another matter. He complained in passing about Home-Stake and what the IRS had found. Someone told Mendelson that the firm happened to be considering a lawsuit against Home-Stake for other clients. When Mendelson returned to his office, he telephoned Ivan Anixter and suggested that he contact William Wineberg.

Trippet refused Wineberg's demands for a refund, and tried the same countertactic that he had employed two months earlier against a group of complaining investors in southern California. He sued Ivan Anixter, Blanche Dickinson, and Dolly Yoshida, alleging that they had breached their agreements with Home-Stake.

On Friday, March 30, Wineberg filed suit against Home-Stake in the San Francisco federal court on behalf of Anixter, Dickinson, and Yoshida. The suit alleged fraud in Home-Stake's 1965 through 1971 drilling programs. It said that Trippet, Landrith, Fitzgerald, Kunkel, Cross, Metcalfe, and Gutelius had engaged in a continuing conspiracy to defraud investors over at least a seven-year period. Wineberg drafted the complaint as a "class action"—that is, it was filed not only on behalf of his three clients but all investors in the 1965–1971 ventures. If a lawsuit is accepted by a court as a class action and the plaintiffs win, damages usually are higher, because of the number of investors they represent, than if the defendant is sued by only one person or a few people.[2]

As William Wineberg was preparing his suit in San Francisco, Trippet's go-between, Bill Goudy, was arranging for Mike Riebold and Carlos Robinson to go to Tulsa to meet Trippet. Goudy attended the meeting, too. The men chatted in Trippet's Philtower office; it was a general discussion. When Trippet mentioned that he was looking for someone to take his place

[2] Apart from the possibility of winning damages for an entire class of victims, a class-action lawsuit affords the incentive of a possibly higher fee for their lawyer, whose original clients may have too little at stake or not be sufficiently wealthy to bear alone the financial burden of a sizeable legal proceeding. In contrast to many of Home-Stake's high-rolling investors, Blanche Dickinson and Dolly Yoshida had invested only $81,000 and $10,000, respectively, and neither was rich. Although Ivan Anixter was wealthier than Dickinson and Yoshida, he had only $20,000 at stake. The only feasible approach for Broad, Khourie & Schulz, therefore, was to bring a class action.

at Home-Stake, Goudy and Riebold recommended Carlos Robinson. It was understood, however, that Robinson worked for Mike Riebold and that Riebold would control Home-Stake if Robinson took Trippet's job.

In the meantime Trippet was being briefed on Riebold's background by Home-Stake senior vice-president Frank Sims and executive vice-president Donald Larrabee. After consulting a friend in Albuquerque, Sims wrote Trippet a memorandum.

> At the mere mention of [Riebold's] name, he was described as a rascal, unscrupulous, cheat, liar and confidence man. He had fleeced everybody that had had any association with him and my friend knew of no one . . . competent who would have anything to do with him. . . .

Sims also relayed to Trippet the comments of a prominent New Mexico lawyer, who had told Sims that Riebold "is very personable and actually 'hypnotizes' people into believing that what he contends is true. [The lawyer] knows of no instance where an association with the man has been anything but distress and in many, many instances has resulted in a lawsuit. The man is referred to locally as 'the one-armed bandit.' [Riebold] is still a topic of conversations at . . . lawyers' meetings where his escapades are laughingly discussed." The lawyer, describing Riebold as a "first-class swindler" and a "good money raiser," had told Sims that "if Home-Stake becomes associated with this man, . . . [Sims should] look for another job and tell me so I can sell your stock short."

Trippet wasn't deterred. He had at least a dozen meetings with Riebold and his henchmen over the next several weeks.

Rather than deal with lawyer William Wineberg on the Anixter-Dickinson-Yoshida suit, Trippet wanted to talk to Blanche Dickinson directly. He had difficulty locating her but finally learned that she temporarily was at the United States Embassy in Morocco. "What I have in mind can't be discussed satisfactorily with anyone else," he wrote on May 31. "I would appreciate it if you would call me. Please make the call collect." Trippet wrote Dickinson another note the next day sweetening his offer to refund part of her money. She sent the letters to her lawyer with a two-word reply scrawled across the bottom of the second: "Running scared?"

Mike Riebold and Carlos Robinson conferred with Trippet at the Home-Stake offices in Tulsa the last week in May, and Robinson and Trippet met again on Monday, June 11. They agreed that Robinson would start work at Home-Stake on June 18 and probably would become chief executive officer of the company shortly thereafter. They also discussed the possibility of moving Home-Stake to Denver, Colorado.

As Trippet and Robinson were meeting in the Philtower Building on June 11, Dobie Langenkamp, who had been sparring with Trippet on behalf of wealthy New York investors for two and a half years, was four blocks away in the Tulsa federal court filing a lawsuit for the Judson Streicher group. A four-column headline in the Tulsa *Tribune* said: "Investors Seek $10 Million in Suit Against Home-Stake." The suit recounted how the Streicher group had invested $4,822,250 from 1966 through 1971, and how it had been induced by larger-than-expected early payments to increase its stakes. Trippet was charged with running a pyramid scheme and paying disproportionate amounts to investors, the larger payments going to those expected to continue investing. Trippet "practiced deceptions with callous persistence," the suit said. Referring to the Santa Maria properties, particularly the painted irrigation pipes, Langenkamp asserted that Home-Stake tried to make it appear to visitors that "certain wells were producing oil when, in fact, such wells were mere shams and weren't producing or capable of producing" and that "certain equipment was being utilized for production of petroleum when, in fact, said equipment hadn't any relation to petroleum production."

The next day, Tuesday, Dobie Langenkamp flew to Los Angeles and rented a car. He spent Wednesday gathering statistics on Home-Stake's oil production from a Los Angeles consulting firm. On Thursday, he drove to Santa Maria, conferred with Conrad Greer, looked around the Home-Stake properties, and took color photographs of the pink irrigation pipes.

Meanwhile, most investors still knew nothing of the precariousness of Home-Stake's plight. They were unaware of the lawsuits and of Trippet's negotiations with a New Mexico swindler to take over the company. They knew only that payments to them were much lower than Home-Stake had projected, and that Trippet was fielding their complaints as calmly and routinely as ever.

"The distributions have been considerably less than the original projections," he wrote to Scott Taylor, a Beverly Hills investor, on Wednesday, June 13.

> There are several reasons for this. One is that we have experienced extremely difficult mechanical and production problems in California. We are working on techniques all the time to try to improve results. . . . I do want you to know that our people are working hard and to the very limits of their ability and will continue to do so.

Mike Riebold's first tactic for raiding the Home-Stake treasury was to try to arrange a $2.8-million loan from Home-Stake to one of his companies, American Fuels. Trippet agreed to the loan in principle, partly because repayment supposedly was to be guaranteed by the First National Bank in Albuquerque.

On Sunday, June 17, Riebold and Carlos Robinson flew by helicopter to banker Donald Morgan's weekend cabin northwest of Jemez, New Mexico, and asked Morgan to write and sign a guarantee of the proposed loan on behalf of the bank. What Morgan wrote wasn't an absolute guarantee. Rather, the letter stated, with some qualifications, that if the loan wasn't repaid by a certain future date, the First National Bank in Albuquerque would assume responsibility for it.

The letter was sent to Trippet early in the week. On Friday Carlos Robinson was named to Home-Stake's board of directors. A bland letter from Trippet to stockholders announcing the appointment said that Robinson "had extensive experience in all management phases of the oil and gas industry as an independent operator." Also named to the board was David E. Melendy, a forty-three-year-old CPA whom the announcement described as having been a chief financial officer in the oil and gas industry. The announcement didn't say that Robinson and Melendy represented the beginning of a takeover of Home-Stake by Riebold. The letter did add, however, that Home-Stake was considering moving its headquarters to Denver or Houston.

(David Melendy had been working at Home-Stake since April. By Riebold's later account, he got Trippet's permission to hire Melendy, a friend of Bill Goudy, Trippet's Denver crony, and have him examine Home-Stake's books. Soon, "Melendy was feeding me information I didn't like about Mr. Trippet," Riebold said. "I knew I had a bucket of worms on my hands, but I thought I could straighten them out.")

The next morning—Saturday, June 23—the telephone rang at the Tulsa home of Donald Larrabee, Home-Stake's executive vice-president. It was Trippet, asking if Larrabee could drop over to his home to discuss a business matter. Larrabee drove the short distance and found that Trippet wasn't alone. William Goudy was there with him. They showed Larrabee the papers covering the proposed $2.8-million Home-Stake loan to American Fuels and the Albuquerque bank's "guarantee." Trippet said that he had to leave for New York later that weekend and wanted Larrabee to take responsibility for actually transacting the loan—signing the loan note and so forth. It was urgent, Trippet said, because American Fuels needed the money by Monday.

Larrabee, who had been busy full-time planning the sale of a 1973 drilling program, knew little of Home-Stake's relationship with the Albuquerque group. Trippet had told him that Home-Stake might help American Fuels develop and sell a drilling program and that the two companies might enter other ventures together. Larrabee didn't know that the Albuquerque people intended to take control of Home-Stake. He had learned, however, about Riebold's bad reputation and had informed Trippet more than a month earlier.

When he was presented with the loan agreement, Larrabee was hesitant. Having had a lot of experience with banking and securities matters he knew that it can be illegal for a national bank to guarantee a "third-party loan"—a loan to which the bank itself isn't a party. But Larrabee was too diplomatic to flatly refuse Trippet's request. He recommended that Trippet consult James R. Ryan, legal counsel for the First National Bank of Tulsa.

When Larrabee left, Trippet telephoned Ryan and asked if he could come to the lawyer's home. Ryan examined the Albuquerque bank's letter and told Trippet that it wasn't a valid guarantee. Trippet relayed the opinion to Larrabee, saying that lawyers would research it further on Monday and that Larrabee should handle whatever developed.

Carlos Robinson and David Melendy arrived with the loan note at Don Larrabee's office on Monday morning and asked that he sign it. He told them that he wouldn't sign until he had a lawyer's approval.

"You know we don't have time for that, Don," Melendy said.

"Well, you're not going to get the money because I am not going to release it until I am absolutely certain that we will have it back under any conditions. That's the only way Trippet told me that he was going to make the loan."

"We can't wait for that," Melendy pleaded. But Larrabee was firm and Melendy and Robinson left in anger.

Meanwhile, James Ryan, the bank lawyer Trippet had consulted on Saturday, placed a call to the president of the First National Bank in Albuquerque, Cale W. Carson, Jr., to inquire about the letter signed by Donald Morgan. Ryan received a return call from Morgan himself. He claimed that the letter had been a "mistake" and that the loan was no longer being considered.

Trippet phoned Larrabee from New York that evening and accepted the news with equanimity. Mike Riebold would have to try some other means of raiding Home-Stake.

Three days later, on Thursday, June 28, Trippet sent Don Larrabee to Albuquerque to get acquainted with Mike Riebold. Trippet had portrayed Larrabee in conversations with Riebold as a "super salesman" who could be very effective in raising money for an American Fuels–Home-Stake venture. Riebold met Larrabee at the airport and drove him twenty miles north of the city to his home, which sat on a bluff overlooking the Rio Grande and facing the stark Sandia Mountains. They had drinks by the pool, and Riebold's wife served dinner. Larrabee stayed at the Riebold house overnight. The next day Riebold flew him out to the Four Corners region, where American Fuels purportedly had some oil properties. They landed at a small airstrip and surveyed the area by helicopter.

Larrabee was disturbed by something Riebold told him that day. Riebold claimed Trippet had promised to "deliver" the Home-Stake board of directors to Riebold but hadn't yet fulfilled the promise. Riebold was angry and said that he was going to "get Trippet's ass out of the company." The news bothered Larrabee because he knew it probably was illegal to change drastically the composition of a board of directors without the consent of the shareholders. The subject hadn't been raised at the annual Home-Stake shareholders meeting, held in Tulsa only three weeks earlier.

Larrabee, who flew back to Tulsa that evening, went to see Trippet at his home the next morning. Trippet acknowledged that he had agreed to turn over the company to Riebold. He said that his health was failing and that he couldn't run Home-Stake any longer.

Troubled by all he had learned, and concerned for his own potential liability, Donald Larrabee resigned on Sunday as executive vice-president and a director of Home-Stake.

On Monday, July 9, Mike Riebold's need for Home-Stake's cash suddenly became very urgent. Rodney Smith, a national bank examiner for the U.S. Treasury Department, strode unannounced into the Albuquerque First National Bank and identified himself. He was to begin a two-and-a-half-week examination of the bank's records. (All national bank examinations are unannounced.)

Riebold secured his takeover of Home-Stake the next day. At a 2:00 P.M. meeting of the Home-Stake board, three more Riebold associates were appointed directors: Richard M. Cottrill, Dean E. McKellep and David D. Thomasson. Frank Sims, Home-Stake's senior vice-president of operations, and Herbert Smith, another vice-president, resigned from the board. Cottrill, McKellep, and Thomasson had nothing in common except loyalty to Riebold or Donald Morgan. Cottrill was in the insurance business; Thomasson was a physician; and McKellep managed a company that manufactured a cleaning compound. "I was told Mr. Trippet was seeking new management, friendly to him, so as not to uncover his misdeeds," Dean McKellep explained later.

The changes gave Riebold four out of six board positions, with Trippet and Jackson Barton still holding the other two. It was decided to move Home-Stake's headquarters to Denver on August 31, less than eight weeks away. In an obvious attempt to increase the amount of cash in the company, the board also voted to sell a number of Home-Stake's assets, including many of its Kansas, Oklahoma, and Venezuelan holdings; its two California apartment complexes; and its Arizona limestone operations. The directors also budgeted $200,000 to try to settle the lawsuits pending against the company, and agreed to repurchase the interests of three complaining investors.

At four o'clock that afternoon, the board convened again and named Carlos Robinson chief executive officer of the company and a cosigner, with Trippet, of all banking transactions. Robinson's salary was set at $50,000 a year. He had been paid $18,000 in his previous job with Riebold.

The next day Robert Trippet deposited and then withdrew $1.2 million from one of his checking accounts at the First National Bank of Tulsa, which brought total activity in the account since January 1, 1973, to $7,820,000 in deposits and $8,061,519 in withdrawals. The balances at the beginning and end of the period aren't known.

Trippet telephoned William Bender, his long-time friend and the senior vice-president of the First National Bank of Tulsa, to say that he was leaving Home-Stake. Trippet sent Mike Riebold and Carlos Robinson to see Bender. They told Bender that they planned to transfer some Home-Stake funds to Albuquerque. When he asked them for an Albuquerque banking reference, they mentioned Donald Morgan. Bender phoned Morgan, who told him that Riebold and Robinson were "reputable individuals."

Bank examiner Rodney Smith soon discovered Morgan's loans to Riebold and asked about them. Morgan said that he expected them to be paid off within a few days. Smith didn't press the matter; he was to be in the bank for another two weeks and could take it up again later.

On Friday, July 13, Mike Riebold and Carlos Robinson went to Morgan's office in Albuquerque and told him there would be a transfer of Home-Stake funds to the bank.

"The whole five million?" Morgan asked.

"No, likely it will be something short of that, three point seventy-five million," he was told.

Morgan immediately opened a checking account for Home-Stake at the bank. Robinson signed a blank check drawn on the new account and payable to Riebold's company American Fuels. He left the check with Morgan and said: "Don, whatever Mike needs is what you do with the check."

The Riebold group wasn't announcing its strategy publicly, of course, but lawyer Dobie Langenkamp, who was getting fragmentary reports from sources within Home-Stake, was becoming very concerned. He knew that if the Albuquerque people sold a lot of Home-Stake's assets and moved the company to Denver, it would be much more difficult to trace and prove its frauds. Records could be destroyed; funds could be moved.

On Monday, July 16, at eight o'clock in the morning, Langenkamp began taking a series of depositions from persons familiar with the rapidly changing situation at Home-Stake. The overall purpose of the depositions, a prescribed procedure in prosecuting a lawsuit, was to gather information for his suit filed a month earlier on behalf of the Judson Streicher group. But the urgent need was to learn the plans of Mike Riebold.

Langenkamp first interrogated Jackson Barton, still nominally president and a director of Home-Stake. Barton confirmed the Riebold takeover and the plans for selling the company's assets, but he had to interrupt the deposition to attend a two o'clock Home-Stake directors meeting.

The board voted to fire Trippet as chairman and revoked his expense accounts, extensions of credit, and credit cards, effective immediately. Jackson Barton resigned, and Carlos Robinson was named president and chairman of the board, in addition to retaining the title of chief executive officer.

Trippet's dismissal was a formality arranged in advance by

him and Riebold. Although he registered opposition to the firing, Trippet wasn't really opposed. He wanted not only to transfer formal legal responsibility for Home-Stake's affairs to the new group as soon as possible, but also wanted to be able to claim later that he had been fired instead of resigning voluntarily. That would make it easier for him to blame the new management for any problems discovered at the company.

Actually, Trippet wasn't leaving Home-Stake—not just yet. He continued to occupy his old chairman's office and to exercise a degree of informal control over the company's operation. Dean McKellep, one of the directors Riebold had placed on the Home-Stake board, said he had the impression that Trippet himself the previous week had prepared the list of assets that could be sold quickly for cash and "was giving explicit direction to the directors for the future operation of the company." Trippet and Riebold both knew that Riebold's men weren't yet competent to run Home-Stake, and might never be. And Trippet and Riebold had a common interest in maintaining stability and avoiding chaos as long as possible.

After the board meeting, Jackson Barton returned to continue Langenkamp's deposition, which wasn't completed until the next day, Tuesday, July 17. At eleven o'clock that morning, Carlos Robinson called another meeting of Home-Stake directors. It was time for Mike Riebold's second run at the company's cash. The board approved a Robinson resolution to transfer $3,750,000 from Home-Stake's Tulsa bank account to the new Albuquerque account ($1 million more than Riebold had tried to get by means of a loan less than three weeks earlier).

Although Dobie Langenkamp didn't know specifically of the decision to transfer funds, he feared that such a maneuver was about to occur. So he drove to Oklahoma City the next morning and formally asked Luther Bohanon,[3] U.S. district judge, to enter a temporary restraining order barring the removal of Home-Stake funds or records from Tulsa. The judge complied but it was too late. The funds were transferred from Tulsa to

[3] Judge Bohanon, who divided his time between Tulsa and Oklahoma City, had been assigned the Judson Streicher lawsuit but happened to be in Oklahoma City on July 18, thus requiring Dobie Langenkamp to drive there to request the order.

Albuquerque and deposited in the new Home-Stake account before the court order could be served on the New Mexico group. The transaction was handled by teletype through the Federal Reserve System.

Using the blank check that Robinson had signed the previous week, Don Morgan immediately moved $2,880,000 of the Home-Stake money to the American Fuels account at the Albuquerque bank and paid off the illegal loans he had made to Riebold. On Thursday, Morgan showed examiner Rodney Smith that the debts had been paid.

Thus, for the time being at least, the bulk of the $5.4 million that Alan Alda, Shirley Jones, Jack Cassidy, Time Inc.'s James Shepley, Western Union's Russell McFall, and others had invested in the 1972 Home-Stake drilling program—and that they thought was being used to drill gas wells in Ohio—had, without their knowledge, been moved out of Tulsa to Albuquerque. And $2,880,000 of it had been used to conceal Mike Riebold's and Donald Morgan's loan-fraud conspiracy.

The Securities and Exchange Commission's investigation of Home-Stake in late 1970 and early 1971 was what the agency calls a home-office inquiry. The investigators didn't leave the the SEC's Washington headquarters, a plain seven-story box-like structure at 500 North Capitol Street near the Capitol. They called in Home-Stake's treasurer and its Washington lawyers for questioning, subpoenaed and analyzed several documents, and drafted and filed a lawsuit. The suit was directed only at Home-Stake's 1970 drilling venture in Venezuela. Its most serious allegation was that Home-Stake couldn't substantiate the amount of oil it said it could produce. The SEC hoped that enough investors would demand refunds to put Home-Stake out of business, or at least to drastically reduce its activities.

The investigation resulted from a complaint by a competing drilling company about Home-Stake's Black Books. Of course, it wasn't the first time Home-Stake had been brought to the SEC's attention. Tulsa accountant Keith Schuerman had warned the SEC in 1958 not to permit Home-Stake to sell common stock. In 1963 a prospective investor had suggested to the SEC that Home-Stake's drilling programs should be registered with the agency. The SEC had agreed and had instructed the company to file prospectuses beginning the next year. Also the SEC in 1963 had asked the IRS to analyze the viability of the tax deductions Home-Stake was promising. (There is no record of a reply from the IRS.) In 1967 Tulsa lawyer Richard Sonberg briefed the SEC's regional office in Fort Worth on the Rosen-blatt-Lyons lawsuit. In 1969 a lawyer representing Alan Pope, who had resigned as Home-Stake's chief New York salesman, told the SEC in Washington that Home-Stake was issuing Black Books rather than prospectuses to investors. That information was forwarded to the Fort Worth office.

A number of people, therefore, considered the 1970–1971 inquiry long overdue. But by 1972 and 1973 it became clear that the SEC hadn't looked closely enough; that its hopes about the effect of the 1971 rescission offer had been in vain; and that a complete field investigation was required. But Washington headquarters typically was swamped with more cases than it could handle, and the Fort Worth office, too, didn't have the manpower to give Home-Stake sufficiently high priority.

Throughout 1972 and early 1973 the Fort Worth investigative staff was fully occupied with two other major cases—the Four Seasons Nursing Centers fraud in Oklahoma and the Sharpstown Bank scandal in Texas. Four Seasons was a big commercial nursing-home operator whose stock soared on the American Stock Exchange in the late 1960s before collapsing amid allega-tions of fraud. Four officers and associates of Four Seasons were convicted of stock manipulation that was said to have cost in-vestors roughly $200 million in market value. The case dragged on through early 1973. Cecil S. Mathis, the chief SEC enforce-ment attorney in Fort Worth, spent eleven months in New York City on the case, flying home to see his wife every third week-end.

Meanwhile, other SEC lawyers in Fort Worth were investi-gating the Sharpstown bank case in Houston and related events. Several Texas politicians were implicated in that widely pub-licized affair.

The SEC therefore did very little about Home-Stake. A junior member of the Fort Worth staff was sent to Tulsa in 1972 to interview Dobie Langenkamp and Richard Sonberg. And during the summer of 1972 a law-school student interning with the SEC in Fort Worth prepared a report comparing the statements in Home-Stake's prospectuses with those in its Black Books. Not until the summer of 1973 did Cecil Mathis, then thirty-one years old, give Home-Stake his full attention. A burly six-footer with curly blond hair, Mathis had begun working for the SEC after graduating from Southern Methodist University law school in 1968.

Dobie Langenkamp had been keeping Mathis's boss, Richard Hewitt, assistant SEC regional administrator, informed of the fast-moving events of the spring and early summer of 1973—the filing of new lawsuits, the takeover of the company by the Albuquerque group, the planned move to Denver, and the danger of funds being transferred and of books and records disappearing or being altered.

The Fort Worth office discussed the situation by phone with SEC Washington headquarters, and on Wednesday, July 18— the day that the Riebold group transferred $3,750,000 from Tulsa to Albuquerque—the Fort Worth staff was formally authorized to proceed with a full investigation.

Cecil Mathis and another SEC investigator, Ben Simms, flew to Tulsa the next evening and checked into the Downtowner Motor Inn, a low-priced, three-story hotel in downtown Tulsa across a parking lot from the U.S. courthouse. Neither their air-conditioning nor the nearby ice machine worked.

At nine o'clock Friday morning, after a fitful night's sleep, Mathis and Simms arrived unannounced at the Home-Stake offices on the tenth floor of the Philtower Building. They served subpoenas on all company officers present; advised them of their constitutional right to say nothing; and informed them that any attempt to conceal or remove evidence was a violation of federal law. It turned out that Carlos Robinson, ill with a bad cold, was in his room at a Holiday Inn five blocks away. Mathis and Simms served him with a subpoena there and returned to the Home-Stake offices. Robert Trippet had appeared. He was smooth and cordial, and accepted his subpoena with a smile. Mathis and Simms then began the laborious task of examining the company's records.

Having obtained the court order too late to stop movement of the $3,750,000 from Tulsa to Albuquerque, Dobie Langenkamp asked lawyers for the Albuquerque group to have the money returned to Tulsa. Carlos Robinson said that, as far as he knew, the purpose of transferring the funds to Albuquerque was simply to establish a banking relationship for Home-Stake in a city where it would be doing business with American Fuels. When Robinson was served with the court order, he promptly telephoned Riebold in Albuquerque and told him of the order.

"So what?" Riebold said.

"We're in deep trouble."

"I don't think you're in deep trouble at all."

"They're going to sue everybody."

"Let them sue; I've been sued by experts. We made a fair and square deal, and let's go. Maybe you ought to put bone in your back instead of wet lettuce."

Robinson then called Don Morgan. "Don, we have to send it back. We have to undo the deal and send it back."

Morgan said, "I don't know whether we can do it or not. Let me get ahold of Mike and see what's up."

By the time Morgan reached him, Riebold had calmed down and grasped the ramifications of trying to keep the money. He told Morgan: "We are going to have to return the funds or else there will be lawsuits and the [Albuquerque] First National Bank will be named."

It was tentatively agreed that the money would be returned. Judge Bohanon in Oklahoma scheduled a court hearing on the matter.

Cecil Mathis and Ben Simms had barely begun to familiarize themselves with Home-Stake's voluminous records by Friday afternoon, July 20, when they had to fly back to Fort Worth to attend to other business. Mathis stayed in touch with Dobie Langenkamp by telephone but wasn't able to return to Tulsa until two weeks later.

What was to stop Home-Stake people from removing incriminating evidence from the company files in the SEC's absence? Some naturally were deterred by Cecil Mathis's warning that removing evidence is a serious federal offense. Also, Carlos Robinson, though he wasn't yet fully aware of the nature and condition of the company, was becoming more and more suspicious of Trippet and the other former officers. He ordered all Home-Stake employees to cooperate fully with the investigation and not to remove documents from the offices.

Still, Dobie Langenkamp was worried. He didn't trust the Albuquerque group any more than he trusted Trippet. (Trippet, still being permitted to occupy his old office at Home-Stake, had been seen in the Philtower Building on the evening of the day the SEC arrived to serve its subpoenas.) Attempting to gain greater insight into the new management's plans, Langenkamp took depositions from Carlos Robinson, Dean McKellep, and Trippet on Monday, July 23. Robinson gave further details on the intended sale of assets and the move to Denver. Information obtained from McKellep and Trippet was less useful. The Albuquerque group offered Dobie Langenkamp a position on the board of directors of Riebold's company, American Fuels. He declined.

Bank examiner Rodney Smith, satisfied that the Riebold loans had been repaid, had moved on to other departments of the Albuquerque bank. So Don Morgan made $2,880,000 in new unauthorized loans to the Riebold account and transferred the money back to the Home-Stake account. On Thursday, July 26, the $3,750,000 was returned to Home-Stake in Tulsa. Rodney Smith completed his work at the bank the next day and left, none the wiser.

The Albuquerque group agreed to a permanent court injunction requiring them to maintain an office in Tulsa and not sell assets or remove corporate records or funds unless fifteen days notice was given to Langenkamp so that he could oppose the actions in court. (The order didn't prohibit opening another office in Denver.)

William Wineberg, the San Francisco attorney representing Ivan Anixter, Blanche Dickinson, and Dolly Yoshida, obtained court permission to inspect Home-Stake documents. On Monday, July 30, Wineberg flew to Tulsa, accompanied by another lawyer, a paralegal assistant, and a portable microfilm machine. They hired two clerical workers from a local temporary agency and began examining Home-Stake's files. The Wineberg group didn't receive full cooperation from the Home-Stake staff, which Wineberg quickly concluded was because Trippet still not only was occupying his old office but also exercising a degree of control over the company.

The problem was solved two days later when Carlos Robinson, fearing the consequences of failure to cooperate with all investigations, evicted Trippet from the chairman's office and had the locks changed on the main tenth-floor office suite. Trippet was permitted to use a spare office on the ninth floor.

Over the next ten days the Wineberg group microfilmed roughly thirty thousand documents at Home-Stake and at the office of CPA Norman Cross. Some of the most revealing documents Wineberg discovered were the memoranda and questions that Cross's staff had prepared in the spring of 1972 concerning selling more than the registered number of units in a particular drilling program; supplementing paltry oil revenues with other money; and making unequal payments to investors.

Dobie Langenkamp wanted to interrogate Mike Riebold but couldn't locate him. Riebold's representatives in Tulsa claimed that they didn't know where he was. Langenkamp hired a private detective who searched for Riebold for a month unsuccessfully.

Robert Trippet also was consulting private detectives, but for a different purpose. At 11:40 on Wednesday morning, August 8, Trippet telephoned Gary Glanz, who is considered one of the most skilled private detectives in the nation. A former member of the Tulsa police vice squad, he wasn't widely known outside Oklahoma until June 1973, when *The Wall Street Journal* published a page-one profile of him. Since then he has had an international clientele and earned upwards of $100,000 a year.

Trippet told Glanz that he had just resigned as head of a local company because of a disagreement with other officers. It seemed that they had changed the lock on the front door of the company headquarters and Trippet needed to get in to recover some personal materials. Another detective Trippet had called said that he didn't do "lock jobs" but recommended Gary Glanz.

Glanz told Trippet to come see him at five that afternoon at his office in a residential area of Tulsa. Uncharacteristically,

Trippet was nervous when he arrived. Glanz asked why he didn't just ask the people at the company to give him his personal things; it seemed a legitimate request. Or why didn't he ask the night security-and-maintenance man at the building to unlock the door; it shouldn't take longer than a few minutes to gather what he wanted. Trippet said that it would take more than a few minutes. Actually, he wanted to stay in the office all night to make sure he got everything.

Glanz offered to drive to the Philtower Building and inspect the lock to see how difficult it might be to pick. It was past 5:30, and much of the rush-hour traffic had cleared out of the downtown area. When Glanz stopped his car at the entrance of the building, Trippet dropped down in the seat as if he had been shot. "Don't park here," he gasped. "I don't want to be seen." Glanz obediently pulled away and parked a block down the street in front of the Enterprise Building at the corner of Sixth Street and Boston Avenue.

Trippet waited in the car while Glanz returned to the Philtower Building. Inside it was quiet. Most of the office workers had left, but the elevators hadn't yet been put on reduced night service.

On the tenth floor Glanz found the Home-Stake office closed and locked for the day. Opening the door wouldn't have been difficult for Glanz. He could have picked the lock. The door was mainly glass, and he could have cut out a section large enough to reach through and open the door from the inside. He could have disguised himself as a telephone or typewriter repairman and talked the night maintenance man into opening the door.

Glanz returned to the car and questioned Trippet further. Trippet had decided he wanted to enter the building stairwell with a key he still had and walk up to the tenth floor so that he wouldn't chance being seen by the security man. He would move the material he needed from the Home-Stake offices down to a ninth-floor office he was being permitted to use temporarily. He would enter the building late in the evening and stay through the night until the next business day had begun. Then it would be simple to come and go, transporting his material in briefcase-loads to his car, without attracting undue attention.

Glanz told Trippet that he could handle the job easily but

that his fee would be at least $1,000. Trippet, who seemed relieved, agreed without hesitation. While driving back to his office, however, the detective decided against taking the job. He didn't believe Trippet's story that he wanted to take only "personal" items from the office. He suspected that Trippet might be engaged in some sort of illegal activity, and Glanz didn't want to become involved. Since he had more than enough business, he could well afford to turn away clients he didn't trust. Trippet was angry but Glanz was firm.

SEC investigator Cecil Mathis returned to Tulsa in early August. He was accompanied by Sammy L. Hughes, a certified public accountant on the agency's investigative staff. The SEC men moved into an office near the one that lawyer William Wineberg's group was using on the ninth floor of the Philtower Building. Mathis conferred with Bill Wineberg on his findings. Essentially, Wineberg's and the SEC's objectives were the same: to fathom how the company had been operated; to find the roots of the apparent fraud; and to document their findings with evidence usable in court.

Mathis and Hughes concentrated on Home-Stake's accounting records in an attempt to determine whether the officers had stolen any money, and if so, how and how much. It became apparent that the company was insolvent, but finding missing money proved difficult.

Although Wineberg had been asking the Home-Stake staff for days to show him the company's master records of payments to investors, he had received little cooperation. Then, early Wednesday evening, August 8—the same day Trippet consulted Gary Glanz—Wineberg was given a computer printout of investors' names with various numbers next to them. He and Cecil Mathis examined it but couldn't make much sense of it. They asked a company accountant what it was. He chuckled.

"That's how we paid the participants," the accountant said. He showed them how the code had allotted higher payments to important investors, lower payments to less important people, and nothing to charities. Worksheets attached to the lists bore the name of Ouida Mae Back, the clerk who had handled the payments.

The investigators were elated. The list was the most comprehensive documentation yet uncovered showing that Home-Stake's unequal payments stemmed from a calculated, highly refined, and in their view, clearly fraudulent Ponzi-type plan carried on within the company. The list essentially completed the broad outlines of the picture they had begun to assemble with examples of unequal payments to investors, for which Trippet had always had excuses (for example, "computer error"), and the detailed allegations contained in the files of accountant Norman Cross.

The SEC men served Ouida Mae Back with a subpoena when she arrived at the offices the next morning, summoned a court stenographer, and immediately began interrogating Back under oath. It quickly became apparent that she would need a lawyer. Patrick Waddell, a Tulsa attorney who had been in Cecil Mathis's class at the Southern Methodist University law school, was retained. Mathis told Back to appear for further questioning the following Tuesday at the federal courthouse.

Cecil Mathis, Sammy Hughes, and Wayne Whitaker, another SEC lawyer who was summoned from Fort Worth, spent the remainder of August in Tulsa examining Home-Stake records and taking sworn testimony from present and former officers, employees, and others familiar with the company.

William Wineberg stayed for a few days, then returned to San Francisco to begin analyzing the thirty thousand pages of material he and his assistants had microfilmed.

Cecil Mathis and Sammy Hughes interrogated Ouida Mae Back for more than two hours on Tuesday morning, August 14. She led them patiently and laboriously through the intricacies of Home-Stake's "full" to "zero" payout categories.

Dobie Langenkamp took formal testimony from Back the following week, and she explained the payout system to him. Langenkamp's questioning also revealed that Back had a bachelor's degree in accounting from Oklahoma State University.

"Did you ever develop any curiosity," Langenkamp asked, "as to why some people would permit themselves to be paid at two percent while others got eighty and ninety percent?"

"Curiosity, but it didn't go beyond curiosity."

"In other words, it never manifested itself in a question to Mr. Trippet?"

"No, I didn't ask him."

"Were you ever asked by any of the other girls that worked on this?"

"Probably, but I didn't feel that it was my position to pass judgment on any of it. It was my job to do the mathematical figurations on it."

That same day, the SEC conducted a rambling and inconclusive interrogation of Norman Cross. The interview was made difficult because all Cross's files on Home-Stake—hundreds of documents—were at that very moment being examined by IRS agents at Cross's office six blocks away. Since it was difficult for Cross to answer questions without the files, the SEC had to wait for the IRS to finish. (After years of sporadic auditing of a few Home-Stake investors by local IRS offices, the IRS finally had begun a full investigation of Home-Stake itself. The agency's challenges of charitable-gift deductions taken by Procter & Gamble officers and several New York investors a few years earlier had failed to penetrate the fraud. For the most part, the IRS compromised on those audits, leaving intact major portions of the investors' deductions. By the late summer of 1973, however, the IRS was challenging hundreds of drilling and gift write-offs and had told Home-Stake itself that it owed $9,740,349 in extra taxes for 1969 alone.)

The SEC and IRS investigations weren't the only inquiries in progress. The new Home-Stake directors from Albuquerque, surprised and frightened by the sudden crisis in the company they had taken control of, had begun their own effort to assess the situation. Carlos Robinson asked CPA David Melendy, who had joined Home-Stake with Robinson in the spring, to help sort out its tangled affairs. The records were a shambles; some appeared to be missing or to have been tampered with.

At 8:30 Monday evening, August 27, Melendy reported to the Home-Stake board—which still comprised only the four Riebold representatives, Robinson, McKellep, Cottrill, and Thomasson—that there was evidence of fraud, diversion of corporate funds, self-dealing, and mismanagement by Robert Trippet and other former officers. The board decided that it had no choice but to retain legal counsel and sue Trippet and the others.

The next morning at the federal courthouse, the SEC staff

interrogated Thomas Landrith, Home-Stake's Tulsa legal counsel and a director from 1967 to 1972. It was a short session. When the questioning became substantive, Landrith took the Fifth Amendment.

On Thursday, August 30, Washington attorney Peter Lockwood, who had begun monitoring the Tulsa investigations closely after months of fruitless negotiation, filed a fraud suit against Trippet and Home-Stake in the federal court of the District of Columbia on behalf of James, Leland, and Lester Leachman.

By the end of August, the SEC had all it needed to prepare a lawsuit. Mathis, Hughes, and Whitaker returned to the Fort Worth office, called in a stenographer, and worked through the Labor Day weekend drafting the suit and accompanying papers. The material was mailed to SEC headquarters on September 5.

Meanwhile, William Wineberg had prepared a long legal brief on the Home-Stake fraud in support of his suit. He filed the brief in court on Thursday, September 6, along with numerous documents selected from those he had collected in Tulsa.

SEC headquarters the following Monday authorized the Fort Worth investigators to proceed, and their suit was filed in Tulsa federal court the next day. The SEC suit and accompanying documents alleged, among many other things, that Trippet had been operating a massive Ponzi scheme at least since 1964, when the company first registered a program with the SEC. (The SEC chose to ignore prior years.) Trippet was charged with "orchestrating" the swindle himself by promising huge oil profits and big tax-write-offs; making higher-than-promised early payments to induce larger investments; paying investors from other investors' funds under the guise of oil revenues; and employing various devices to deal with disgruntled investors, including encouraging charitable gifts and preparing false evaluations to support them. The 1971 rescission offer, which was supposed to have complied with the SEC lawsuit against the company that year, was itself fraudulent, because it perpetuated a blatantly misleading portrayal of the company's true character.

In an accompanying affidavit, the agency's CPA, Sammy Hughes, showed that Home-Stake's drilling ventures had made a profit—a small one—in only one year, 1964; otherwise, they had operated at a loss. The company's main source of income wasn't oil and gas; it was the increasing annual flow of investments from the public. Hughes concluded that since Home-Stake's liabilities far exceeded its assets, the company was insolvent. The SEC asked the court to enjoin Home-Stake and Trippet from further violations of federal securities law; to declare Home-Stake insolvent and appoint a trustee to preside over it; and to assess the feasibility of reorganizing the company under the bankruptcy laws.

That same day, across the street at the Tulsa County courthouse, lawyers hired by the new Home-Stake management filed a suit making many of the same allegations that the SEC had made. But the SEC named only Home-Stake and Trippet as defendants. The management suit also named the other principal officers and directors of the company in recent years—Harry Fitzgerald, Thomas Landrith, Donald Larrabee, Frank Sims, Jackson Barton, J. D. Metcalfe, and Brooks Gutelius.

Despite the gravity of the allegations, neither lawsuit on the surface clearly revealed the full dimensions or importance of the fraud, or the names of any of the investors. Court reporters for the local newspapers and the wire services read the suits only cursorily, and didn't write long or analytical stories. *The Wall Street Journal* ran only a brief article.

The new Home-Stake officers also filed an insurance claim with Aetna Casualty and Surety Company on September 12, attempting to collect on a policy insuring the company against employee dishonesty. The claim said that Trippet had, in effect, stolen $4,054,103.28 from the company. The figure later would be increased. Documents accompanying the claim showed records of the allegedly dummy companies that Trippet had created over the years as devices for funneling money out of Home-Stake.

On Thursday, September 20, Home-Stake was declared officially insolvent. The federal court appointed a trustee—a former U. S. district court judge, Royce H. Savage—to run the company as prescribed by federal bankruptcy laws, and to determine whether it could be salvaged. Savage had resigned his judgeship in Tulsa in 1962 to become general counsel of the Gulf

Oil Corporation in Pittsburgh. He retired in 1970 at the age of sixty-five and had been conducting a small law practice in Tulsa before being named Home-Stake bankruptcy trustee.

The appointment of the trustee brought the Home-Stake Production Company swindle formally to a close. The investors were protected against further fraud by either Trippet or Riebold. But nobody cheered. In eighteen years Home-Stake had taken in slightly more than $140 million, much of it under false pretenses. The company had returned only about $45 million to $50 million to investors. Its common stock had deteriorated in value from more than $12 million to zero. The total loss, therefore, was at least $102 million. In all probability, a substantial portion of the loss would be borne by the U.S. Treasury—the American taxpayer—because of the investors' mostly improper tax deductions.

The time had come to assess damage, determine what had happened to all the money, and fix blame and liability. That would prove to be a massive and extraordinarily difficult task.

His elaborate escape plan having failed, Trippet chose what often proves to be the most effective alternative course for a man in his position: a direct and vigorous confrontation with his accusers. Such a confrontation can itself be a form of escape for a skilled white-collar criminal. If a swindle is as complex as Trippet's, and the swindler is as smart and as well-financed as he, proving him guilty of a crime or liable for damages usually is far from simple, no matter how blatant the fraud may appear to be. White-collar criminals frequently emerge from litigation and the criminal-justice process with light punishment and much of their fortune intact.

After a brief stay in his temporary quarters on the ninth floor of the Philtower Building, Robert Trippet rented an office in the First National Bank building across the street; retained his long-time secretary, Helen Loop; and began marshalling his defenses.

Trippet wasn't naive about the seriousness of the allegations he faced, but he wasn't intimidated either. The charges were just that—charges. To him, they had no inherent moral legitimacy; they were merely tactical thrusts in a contest over money—a strictly amoral dispute over who had bested whom in a series of business deals.

Trippet knew that he might have to relinquish a part of his modest fortune in order to settle the lawsuits pending against him, but he would still be very well off financially. The investors would go after the company's remaining assets as well as his.

And the IRS was sure to lower its tax claims eventually; the IRS always backs down in the end. The investors then could divide what was left of the company, relieving some of the financial pressure on Trippet.

The SEC, of course, might try to develop a criminal case against him. But the agency had shown itself to be incompetent in the past, and Trippet was willing to take the chance that it would be no more skillful in stalking him this time.

His accusers almost certainly underestimated the fight they were in for. The tumult that he and Home-Stake had been through hadn't shaken his aggressive self-confidence. He was tougher and smarter than most of if not all his victims and pursuers. As an adversary in a business or legal dispute, he had few equals. "There isn't a government attorney in this country that's half as smart as you, Bob," one Tulsa friend had said. Trippet would modify his tactics to fit particular cases, but basically he saw three lines of counterattack.

First, he would argue that much of whatever money his rich clients had lost would have gone to the government in taxes anyway. Who gets excited about the U.S. Treasury losing tax revenue? It wastes billions of dollars every year.

Second, even if fraud were proven, Trippet could blame others. He had relied on lawyers for advice on tax and securities law. He had relied on engineers for advice on how much oil was in the ground and how to extract it. He had relied on accountants for advice on how to present the company's finances. If anyone had done anything wrong, it was they, not he.

Third, he would stall. He would delay. He would wear down his opponents with tactical maneuvering. He would be more patient and tenacious than any of them. He knew that tactics have a crucial effect on the outcome of many cases, both civil and criminal, and he planned to use them to the fullest.

The battle would be long and difficult but he didn't fear it. In a sense, he rather looked forward to it.

The decision to proceed with a criminal investigation of the Home-Stake swindle wasn't a difficult choice for the SEC Fort Worth staff. Its September 11 lawsuit was intended primarily to put the company out of business and under the control of a court-appointed trustee. Theoretically, that would secure Home-Stake's remaining assets and make it impossible for anyone to use the company for further fraud. The next question was how severely to attempt to punish those responsible for what had happened. The SEC faces that question in every fraud case it brings. Usually it is forced by manpower limitations to be content with civil injunctions and hand-slapping penalties. But when a fraud is as huge and as willful as the Home-Stake swindle appeared to be, the SEC is obligated to develop a criminal case and present it to the Department of Justice for prosecution.

Cecil Mathis knew that the investigation could turn out to be particularly sensitive and difficult. He had finally found time to study a master list of the investors. The show-business names caught his eye immediately. He also recognized a few of the corporate executives' names, and knew that all those people with addresses at General Electric, Western Union, and Sullivan & Cromwell weren't clerks and janitors. Many of them might be reluctant to undergo the public embarrassment of admitting their losses, and thus be unwilling to give more than grudging aid to the investigation.

Mathis spent most of the week of Monday, September 17, in New York City questioning people familiar with Home-Stake's activities. He talked with a few of the company's salesmen, some of whom were still using their company expense accounts to entertain people. One sales vice-president, Roy A. Foulke, Jr., listed September expenses of $650.31 including more than $200 for entertainment extending through September 18. He submitted a separate claim for reimbursement of $636.23 in fees that he paid a lawyer to represent him at the SEC. Mathis interrogated Foulke the morning of September 19.

Wayne Whitaker and Sammy Hughes returned to Tulsa to question present and former Home-Stake officers in more detail.

In Albuquerque, meanwhile, Don Morgan's days as senior vice-president of the First National Bank were numbered. Other bank officers had discovered his illegal loans to Mike Riebold and called in the Federal Bureau of Investigation. "I can't believe you have done this—I just—I can't believe it," an incredulous Cale

Carson, the bank's president, said to Morgan. "You have either lost your mind or you are in cahoots with them."

Trippet followed the course of the SEC probe in Tulsa closely. Donald Larrabee, who had resigned on June 30 as Home-Stake's executive vice-president, was scheduled to be interrogated Monday, October 15. The previous Tuesday, a friend invited Larrabee to have lunch at the Summit Club, a private retreat atop a new downtown office building. Trippet joined them. After lunch Trippet asked Larrabee to come to a vacant office next to his own in the First National Bank building. (Trippet suspected that his office was being bugged.) He brought up the investigation.

"When are you going to the SEC?"

"Next Monday afternoon."

"Don, you've never given testimony," Trippet said. "I'm a lawyer and I believe I can be of help. The first thing to remember is to just answer the questions. Don't volunteer information. Don't anticipate questions."

"I'm going to tell the truth," Larrabee said. "I'm not a good enough liar to lie."

Larrabee took out a small pad and began taking notes.

"It's not necessary to take any notes," Trippet said.

"Well, I just want to think about these things later."

"'You don't know,'" Larrabee wrote, quoting Trippet. Then, using the abbreviation *IDK* for "I don't know," Larrabee listed the questions that Trippet anticipated the SEC would ask.

> Were participant payments disproportionate? IDK.
> False reports to participants on oil production. IDK.
> Lewis & Ganong reports false. IDK.
> Pyramiding. IDK.
> Induce gifts [to charity]. IDK.
> Repurchases. IDK.
> False prospecti. IDK.

Later that week Trippet telephoned Nathan Graham, the U.S. attorney in Tulsa. In years past Nate Graham had practiced law in Bartlesville, Oklahoma, Trippet's home town. He had

advised Trippet's mother, and his law firm was counsel for
Trippet's father's savings and loan association. But Nate Graham
hardly knew Bob Trippet himself. Trippet, however, made small
talk on the telephone that morning as if they had been close
friends for years. Finally he said that he had called to offer
$30,000 to endow a chair at the University of Oklahoma law
school in the name of Graham's late law partner, Richard K.
Harris. Could he come over and discuss it with Nate? Somewhat
taken aback, Graham at first agreed to see Trippet. Later he cancelled the appointment; it mightn't look right in view of the
Home-Stake investigation. (Whether Nate Graham would become involved in the Home-Stake inquiry hadn't yet become
clear, but the odds favored it, since Graham's office was responsible for prosecuting federal crimes committed in Tulsa and the
the rest of northern Oklahoma. Eventually Graham reported
Trippet's call to the FBI and the SEC.)

Early the next Monday morning, Trippet phoned Don Larrabee and again asked when he was to testify before the SEC.

"This afternoon."

"Oh, I thought it was this morning."

"No."

"Well, good luck."

The SEC asked Larrabee that afternoon whether anyone had
tried to influence his testimony. After huddling with his lawyer,
he gave the investigators his notes from his conference with
Trippet.

Former judge Royce Savage, the bankruptcy trustee, took full
control of Home-Stake by early October. He dismissed all the
Albuquerque people and installed Herbert Smith, a former
company vice-president, as the titular president. Appointed as
legal counsel to the trustee were Anthony F. Ringold and Gene
L. Mortensen, of the Tulsa law firm of Rosenstein, Fist and
Ringold.

Savage retained the Tulsa office of Coopers & Lybrand, the
national CPA firm, to conduct a full audit of the company.
Coopers & Lybrand—formerly, Lybrand, Ross Bros. & Montgomery—had audited the 1970 and 1971 drilling programs in the

summer of 1972 for Siegel & Goldburt in New York. Its access to records and cooperation from Trippet were limited then. This time there would be no restraints.

By the end of 1973 eight lawsuits alleging fraud were on file against Home-Stake and Trippet in Tulsa federal court, not counting the ones that had been settled. Suits filed elsewhere —for example, the Anixter-Dickinson-Yoshida class action in San Francisco and the Leachman suit in the District of Columbia —had been transferred to Tulsa. Actor Walter Matthau had joined the Anixter group in prosecuting that case. The defendants denied all allegations of wrongdoing.

Meanwhile, another major group of investors was counting its losses and preparing to take legal action. Top officials of the General Electric Company, including at least three dozen incumbent and former executives, had invested more than $3.5 million in Home-Stake from 1960 through 1972. Naturally they had followed the company's collapse with great interest.

In late 1973 they formed a committee under the chairmanship of vice-president Milton Kent, who was nearing retirement and had sufficient time to devote to the Home-Stake problem. The committee was asked to evaluate the situation and decide whether to sue. It retained the New York law firm of Gilbert, Segall & Young, and a partner in the firm, Roland A. Paul, began an inquiry.

The General Electric group enlisted the support of a number of other disgruntled investors. Thomas Gates, of Morgan Guaranty, signed on, as did Ted Westfall, of IT&T; Russell McFall, of Western Union; and Ralph Hart, of Heublein. Home-Stake's payments to the group had varied, but their returns averaged roughly 20 percent of their investments after profit projections of 400 percent. Fred Borch, a favored client, received about 36 percent; Ralph Hart got only 12 percent.

The group met on Friday morning, January 4, 1974, in a basement auditorium of General Electric's New York City headquarters at 570 Lexington Avenue. Chairman Milton Kent turned the meeting over to Roland Paul, who reviewed the grounds for a lawsuit against Home-Stake and discussed the individuals who would be logical targets.

The first people Paul mentioned weren't Trippet and the other former Home-Stake officers. They were Harry Heller of Simpson Thacher & Bartlett, William Blum, and other lawyers, as well as the CPAs who had worked for Home-Stake. "One reason the attorneys and accountants were selected as likely defendants was that they were probably well insured," the minutes of the meeting quoted Roland Paul as saying. "Some haven't yet been sued in other lawsuits . . . growing out of the Home-Stake fraud."

In other words, Roland Paul logically was suggesting that the GE group concentrate its recovery efforts on potential defendants known to have sufficient financial resources to pay damages. He recommended pursuing Trippet, Fitzgerald, and the others also, of course. But since lawyers and CPAs generally carry substantial amounts of malpractice insurance, they present tempting targets in fraud situations where the assets of the fraudulent company itself and its principal officers may be depleted or subject to competing claims from tax authorities. (Robert Trippet, Harry Fitzgerald, and several other Home-Stake officers and associates were lawyers or accountants, too, but since they served the company as managers or salesmen, rather than as legal or accounting advisers, they didn't carry malpractice insurance. If found liable by the courts, however, they would be subject to disciplinary actions by bar or CPA authorities, as would those who functioned in purely professional capacities.)

To collect damages from a lawyer or accountant, an investor must prove that he participated in or aided the fraud. Frequently, that is difficult to prove, since the law is ambiguous and the courts have disagreed on how deep a lawyer's or accountant's involvement must be in order to make him liable for damages.

The SEC had set off a vigorous and bitter debate within the legal community in 1972, when it filed a civil lawsuit charging White & Case, a leading Wall Street law firm, and a White & Case partner, Marion Jay Epley III, with aiding the fraud of the National Student Marketing Corporation. The company's rise and fall in the stock market was a celebrated episode in the late 1960s and 1970. After more than five years of tussling in court, the SEC and White & Case settled the suit on the eve of trial. The U. S. District Court for the District of Columbia enjoined Marion Epley from certain violations of federal securities law and ordered him to comply with White & Case's procedures for handling securities transactions. Epley agreed not to practice before the SEC for six months. Epley and the firm neither admitted nor denied the SEC's allegations. The court said it would retain jurisdiction to enforce the terms of the settlement.

In criminal proceedings, two CPAs who audited National Student Marketing's books were convicted of criminal fraud by a federal jury in New York. The accountants were employed by the nation's biggest CPA firm, Peat Marwick Mitchell & Company. Three other CPAs were found guilty in Los Angeles of participating in the Equity Funding Corporation of America fraud. In a notable case that the government lost, however, three Arthur Andersen & Company accountants were exonerated of criminal wrongdoing in their audits of the Four Seasons Nursing Centers of America, another stockmarket highflier of the late 1960s. (Arthur Andersen had audited certain of Home-Stake's financial statements in 1967.)

Private investors and the government had brought charges against a number of other lawyers and accountants with mixed results. In each case, it was argued that a lawyer or accountant was aware of illegal or improper actions by his corporate client and should have reported them to authorities. By not doing so, it was said, he was in effect participating in or at least aiding the fraud. The lawyers and accountants generally denied wrongdoing; many members of both professions question whether under normal circumstances they necessarily should be expected to discern wrongdoing by a client, or if they do learn of it, whether the responsibility for reporting it necessarily is theirs. Some lawyers and accountants fear that if the government has its way, they could be forced to perform a policing function in the business world. They say that such a role could erode the confidentiality essential to the performance of their primary task: advising the client and representing his interest.

(The roles of attorney and accountant aren't identical, of course. A lawyer is expected generally to be a partisan advocate of his clients' interests. An outside accountant, by contrast, purports to be more independent and objective. Both, however, operate under professional canons requiring them to be honest and ethical.) [1]

On that January morning in 1974, Roland Paul told the GE investors he believed that there were solid grounds for suing Harry Heller and William Blum. Among other things, Paul discussed Heller's and Blum's work on Home-Stake's 1971 prospectus and their trip to Tulsa in November to discuss whether a supplement to the prospectus should be distributed. Paul said that Heller and Blum knew or should have known by then that Home-Stake was producing "hardly any" oil and gas revenue; that it was insolvent; and that it was a Ponzi scheme.

Paul cited the oblique and legalistic footnote buried near the end of the 1971 prospectus, which seemed to say, on close reading, that only a little oil was being produced, and that most of the money paid to investors was nothing more than a small portion of their own and others' money coming back to them. According to Paul, the footnote, which he said Harry Heller had written, "was totally inadequate as a notice to prospective investors of the magnitude of the fraud . . . but does demonstrate that [Heller and Blum] had knowledge of such fraud."

Milton Kent and Roland Paul flew to Los Angeles a few weeks later and delivered the same pitch to a group of south-

[1] In March 1976, the U.S. Supreme Court narrowed the circumstances in which a private-damage suit can be brought against an accountant for securities fraud. The Court said that an accountant cannot be sued under the basic federal securities fraud statute, Section 10(b) of the Securities Exchange Act of 1934, unless he is accused of "intent to deceive, manipulate or defraud." Negligence in auditing, even if it has the effect of aiding fraud by the auditor's client, isn't sufficient grounds for suing the accountant under the fraud statute, the Court said. It pointed out that accountants can be sued for negligence under other sections of the federal securities laws. Furthermore, the Court stated that in discussing negligence, it wasn't addressing the question of whether a lawsuit for "recklessness" by an accountant, presumably a worse sin than negligence, could properly be brought under the fraud law. The Court also stressed that it was ruling only on private-damage suits; it wasn't ruling on whether an accountant's negligence was sufficient grounds for an SEC suit seeking a civil injunction under the fraud statute.

ern California investors assembled by Donald McKee for breakfast in a private dining room of the California Club.

Bankruptcy trustee Royce Savage reported to the Tulsa federal
court in January that it was too early to determine whether
reorganization of Home-Stake would be feasible. On February
19 Coopers & Lybrand completed the audit that Savage had
requested. Coopers & Lybrand estimated the total remaining
assets of the company to be about $18.6 million, including
$4.7 million in cash or liquid securities. But it declined to issue
a firm opinion on Home-Stake's financial status: the company's
books and records weren't in satisfactory condition; federal and
state tax claims against it exceeded $20 million; and investor
lawsuits sought actual and punitive damages of over $17 million.

Trippet knew he would need a lawyer. He expected to mastermind his own defense, but he needed at least one lawyer, and
probably more, to advise him and handle the cumbersome
mechanics: filing formal responses to lawsuits; negotiating with
lawyers for the government and investors; and arguing motions
in court.

Thomas Landrith had handled Trippet's and the company's
responses to the initial lawsuits. Landrith, however, was a
defendant himself now, and like Trippet, faced possible criminal
charges. So Trippet quietly approached Tulsa's foremost law
firm, Connor Winters Ballaine Barry & McGowen, and asked it
to take his case. But the firm already had been retained by
Donald Larrabee and thus wasn't available to Trippet.

Trippet hired James C. Lang, a thirty-three-year-old Tulsa
lawyer. Lang formerly was an FBI agent and an assistant Tulsa
County district attorney. Later, Trippet contacted Jay H. Topkis,
a partner in the New York law firm of Paul Weiss, Rifkind,
Wharton & Garrison. Topkis became moderately well known in
the fall of 1973 as the man who masterminded the defense of
Spiro Agnew. (The U.S. Justice Department had a strong case
against Agnew for bribery, extortion, and income-tax evasion.
In the end, however, he was allowed to plead no-contest to a
single tax charge and was placed on probation without a jail
term.)

Topkis took Trippet's case for a while. He conferred with Trippet in Tulsa and with the SEC in Fort Worth. Topkis discussed hypothetically with federal investigators the possibility that Trippet might testify against others, thus assuring himself light punishment. But the talks proved fruitless and Topkis left the case.

Trippet also retained Lester A. Klaus, an Oklahoma City attorney with wide experience representing people accused of white-collar crimes; his clients included one of the defendants in the Four Seasons Nursing Centers case. Klaus eventually became Trippet's chief counsel.

The SEC's criminal investigation continued through the early months of 1974. Dozens of former officers, employees, and investors were questioned. Wayne Whitaker flew to California and questioned former Home-Stake engineer Conrad Greer in Santa Maria on Friday, April 26. Accompanying Whitaker was another SEC lawyer, Jess Elliott, who has a degree in geology. (It had become evident that analyzing some of Home-Stake's activities would require geology expertise.) Greer went to Los Angeles for further interrogation the following Tuesday. According to an SEC digest of Greer's testimony, he portrayed himself as a "conscientious employee caught up in a bad situation in which he tried to make a go of a very frustrating work atmosphere." (Greer had been questioned the previous week in Santa Maria by Trippet's lawyers, Lester Klaus and James Lang.)

On May 22 the group organized by the General Electric investors filed nine lawsuits in Tulsa federal court, one for each Home-Stake drilling program from 1964 through 1972. The suits charged that Trippet had "looted" Home-Stake of millions of dollars; that the company had been insolvent from 1964 onward; and that it had operated pre-1964 drilling ventures at substantial losses.

In addition to Trippet, Fitzgerald, Landrith, and the other former Home-Stake officers and directors, one or more of the lawsuits named as defendants Harry Heller and his firm, Simpson Thacher & Bartlett, William Blum, William Murray, and most other lawyers and accountants, and their firms, who had worked on Home-Stake prospectuses, financial statements, or legal opinions. Also sued were Richard Ganong and William Lewis, the California engineer and geologist who had prepared the evaluation reports for Home-Stake. (In a partnership such as a law or accounting firm, the partnership itself may be liable and can be sued for the actions of an individual partner.) The suits charged that Heller, Blum, and the others knew or should have known that Home-Stake was a fraud.

The General Electric suits were prepared by Harold F. McGuire, Jr., a young partner at the New York firm of Gilbert, Segall & Young. McGuire, who had taken over the Home-Stake matter from Roland Paul, had recently completed several years as an assistant U.S. attorney in Manhattan. He conducted the government's investigation of the National Student Marketing case, among others.

William Wineberg, Dobie Langenkamp, and Peter Lockwood also filed amended versions of their clients' lawsuits and included most of the lawyers and accountants as defendants. Wineberg accused William Blum and William Murray of taking money to sell Home-Stake interests. Wineberg and Lockwood alleged that the reversionary-interest transaction in which Klineman participated with Trippet should have been disclosed to Klineman's clients. The lawyer-accountant defendants in all the suits denied that they had done anything wrong, and the principal defendants repeated previous denials.

Despite the abundance of activity the Home-Stake affair had generated by mid-1974—an intense criminal investigation, several multi-million-dollar lawsuits, and a major bankruptcy proceeding—the public in general still knew nothing of the case. The few small articles that had appeared in the Tulsa papers and *The Wall Street Journal* didn't even hint at its size and significance. In the early spring, however, *The Wall Street Journal* became aware of the dimensions of the case, and on Wednesday, June 26, after a three-month inquiry, it published a major front-page story under the headline: "The Big Write-off: Rich Investors' Losses in New 'Ponzi Scheme' Could Hit $100

Million." The article described the swindle and its history and listed 126 show-business figures, lawyers, businessmen, and politicians, together with the amounts of their investments.

The Associated Press and United Press International had the story on their national news wires by noon that day. CBS News dispatched a camera crew by helicopter from Los Angeles to Santa Maria to photograph the pink irrigation pipes. The New York *Post* was on the streets of Manhattan by midafternoon with a front-page headline: "Bare $100 Million Show Biz Swindle." David Brinkley devoted his NBC commentary that evening to the Home-Stake story. The *New York Times*, the Washington *Post*, the Chicago *Tribune*, the San Francisco *Chronicle*, the *Financial Times* of London, the *International Herald-Tribune* in Paris, and many other papers featured *The Wall Street Journal* story the next day. The *New York Times* sent a reporter to Tulsa for a follow-up story. *Time* magazine ("Gulling the Beautiful People") and *Newsweek* ("A Star-Spangled Swindle") devoted major articles to the subject the following week. *Fortune* magazine assigned two writers to prepare an article for its September issue.

Investors who had dodged inquiries earlier were more accessible after the story broke.

"It's the best group of people I've ever been listed with," said Senator Ernest Hollings of South Carolina.

Andy Williams: "I don't know anyone in show business who has enough know-how to make wise investments. We simply have to take other people's advice. And this time we all were duped."

Barbra Streisand: "None of my investments have ever made money."

Alan Alda: "I went into the investment not because it was a speculative thing but because it was described to me as being extremely safe. I'm really sore. It's going to take me a lot of time to salvage what I've lost. I'll have to work harder now. I'm told this was a classical swindle. That doesn't make it any easier. I'm not used to being conned—except by people I vote for."

Bob Hope said that he believed one reason so many entertainers invested in Home-Stake was that he and Bing Crosby many years ago *made* a lot of money in an oil deal. After that "every star in town wanted to get into oil."

Johnny Carson joked about Home-Stake on "The Tonight Show." He hadn't invested in Home-Stake himself, he said, but his business manager, "Bombastic Bushkin," had induced him to put money into several other questionable ventures—a tall men's shop in Tokyo, a McDonald's in Calcutta, and a limousine service that drives live lobsters from Maine to the West Coast.

The day that *The Wall Street Journal* article was published, Stanley Sporkin, chief of the SEC's Division of Enforcement in Washington, telephoned Robert Watson, the SEC regional administrator in Fort Worth, and asked the status of the criminal investigation. Watson said that his staff planned to have the case ready by Labor Day for presentation to the Justice Department. Sporkin instructed Watson to make arrangements to refer the case sooner if possible.

The choice of where and how to prosecute the Home-Stake case involved tactical as well as substantive considerations. The prosecution was to demonstrate, in fact, the extraordinary extent to which tactics, pure chance, and other factors not directly related to guilt or innocence can affect the course of a case. The prosecution could have been mounted in New York or Los Angeles, two cities where many investors lived, or in Tulsa, home of most of the alleged swindlers. The SEC preferred Los Angeles or New York to Tulsa. Generally, the government likes to prosecute major fraud cases in big cities. A trial will attract more national press coverage in New York or Los Angeles—deterrent publicity, as the government sees it—and will have a greater impact on the nation's financial community, which is headquartered in New York, with sizeable contingents in other major cities. A second factor also favored New York or Los Angeles: They are the principal cities where the Justice Department maintains large staffs of lawyers specializing in complex financial prosecutions. So Tulsa was eliminated.

In choosing between New York and Los Angeles, the SEC —especially its Fort Worth office—was influenced by its experience with an earlier case, the Four Seasons Nursing Centers fraud. Although the company was based in Oklahoma City, many Four Seasons investors were New Yorkers, and the stock was traded on the American Stock Exchange in New York. So the prosecution was centered in Manhattan.

Five of eight defendants moved to shift their trial to Oklahoma City. New York federal judge Thomas Griesa granted their motion. The ruling was considered unusual; the government historically has been given wide discretion in choosing where to prosecute a nationwide fraud. The ruling was a major psychological blow to the Four Seasons prosecution. The Justice Department's Manhattan fraud unit, which had devoted thousands of manhours to the case, decided that it didn't want to handle the Oklahoma trial; the department therefore named a relatively inexperienced lawyer from its Washington headquarters to take over the prosecution. Of four defendants who went on trial in Oklahoma City, three were acquitted. The jury deadlocked on the fourth, and charges were dismissed. The other defendant in Oklahoma City and the three in New York pleaded guilty, and generally were given light sentences.

The SEC and the Justice Department considered the Four Seasons prosecution a tactical failure and wanted to avoid a similar experience with Home-Stake. Several of the then-potential defendants in the Home-Stake case were expected to seek a Tulsa trial. It was assumed that a New York judge, ruling after Judge Griesa's precedent, was more likely to grant such a motion than a Los Angeles judge would be. So the SEC's Fort Worth office recommended that the Home-Stake case be prosecuted in Los Angeles.

There was a brief delay. The New York fraud unit decided that it wanted the case, despite the Four Seasons experience. The Home-Stake prosecution was bound to generate a lot of publicity and bring prestige to the office handling it, assuming the defendants were convicted. The Manhattan U.S. attorney's office sent a letter to Washington asking that it be given the case instead of its Los Angeles counterpart.

Justice Department headquarters chose Los Angeles. It believed the Four Seasons rationale was valid. Furthermore, the reputation of the Manhattan fraud unit had been tarnished slightly because it had recently lost the John Mitchell-Maurice Stans case; a jury had acquitted the two men of bribery and conspiracy in connection with campaign contributions by financier Robert Vesco. The Los Angeles fraud unit, although smaller than the one in New York, had a solid record of convictions.

Thus, in July 1974, the Home-Stake case was placed under the supervision of William D. Keller, the U.S. attorney in Los Angeles, and Stephen V. Wilson, chief of Keller's fraud and special prosecutions unit. Stephen Wilson, then thirty-three years old, has an impressive string of convictions to his credit and is a specialist in tax-fraud prosecutions. It had been decided that the tax aspects of the Home-Stake case would be featured. The case would be the first of its size in which federal authorities would bring criminal charges to combat abuses in the murky, multi-billion-dollar world of tax shelters.

Cecil Mathis flew to Los Angeles and discussed the case with Wilson. Mathis described Home-Stake as an "octopus . . . there is one singular 'head' who controlled the entire operation, but who couldn't have survived without the aid of various conspirators who prostituted themselves and their professions."

Mathis also briefed top IRS officials in Los Angeles, and they enthusiastically assigned two lawyers and two special agents to the investigation. (An earlier attempt by the SEC to interest Oklahoma IRS officials in the criminal inquiry had proved futile, although the IRS in Oklahoma was conducting a civil audit of Home-Stake's tax liability and the agency nationally was auditing the investors.)

Mathis, Wayne Whitaker, Sammy Hughes, and Jess Elliott —along with some two hundred thousand Home-Stake documents in cardboard cartons and metal filing cabinets—were installed in two vacant adjoining offices on the twelfth floor of the Los Angeles federal courthouse down the hall from Stephen Wilson's office. The SEC men spent the month of August preparing evidence for presentation to a grand jury. They had to work fast. Wilson wanted to indict the defendants by late November or early December, when the statute of limitations on some crucial aspects of the case would run out.

In early September a grand jury was impaneled, and Wilson and the SEC and IRS investigators began the laborious, exacting task of organizing documentary evidence, subpoenaing witnesses, and presenting both to the grand jury, ideally in logical sequence. Witnesses with busy schedules—for example, some of the New York business executives who had invested in Home-Stake—had to be flown to Los Angeles, put before the grand jury, and released as efficiently as possible. There were a number of snafus. Some witnesses arrived unexpectedly; others didn't arrive when needed. There was further confusion because the government's investigation wasn't complete yet. Wilson, who had been busy with other matters through August, was still familiarizing himself with the details of the case—even as he was presenting witnesses to the grand jury—and the SEC and IRS men still were finding and assimilating new evidence.

Witnesses in such investigations typically are questioned several times. The SEC had taken informal and subsequent formal statements from a number of people in Tulsa, New York, and California over the months since the investigation began in July 1973. As more evidence was assembled, these people were called back for more questioning. Once the investigation was moved to Los Angeles and placed under Justice Department supervision, Wilson and the others interviewed many people again in order to refine or amplify testimony before a witness was taken before the grand jury.

The treatment of certain witnesses by Wilson and the SEC investigators later would become the focus of bitter dispute. Elmer Kunkel, the lawyer-CPA who had been Home-Stake's treasurer, was summoned to Los Angeles and questioned at the courthouse by Wilson, Mathis, Whitaker, and Hughes throughout the afternoon and evening of Sunday, September 8, and most of Monday. Wilson berated Kunkel for being a "whore." The prosecutor likened Home-Stake to a "whorehouse," and said the lawyers, accountants, and engineers who knew of its frauds were whores because they allegedly prostituted their professional reputations for money. Kunkel acknowledged that he had been involved in various audits of Home-Stake as far back as 1961. He told of the procedure used to derive the 1968 profit figure ("backing into income"); of warning Trippet repeatedly that some of the company's activities were fraudulent; and of eventually going to work for the company as a full-time officer. Kunkel testified before the grand jury at noon, Wednesday, September 11. He later accused Stephen Wilson of tricking him into incriminating himself by assuring him prior to his grand-jury testimony that he wouldn't be indicted. Wilson, Whitaker, and Hughes denied the allegation, stressing that Kunkel was reminded repeatedly of his right to say nothing.

Harry Fitzgerald was interrogated in Los Angeles for three days beginning on Tuesday, October 1, and at several later times. Wilson told Fitzgerald that he didn't want any "bull shit" because the case against him was overwhelming. Fitzgerald said that he would cooperate, and according to the government men, agreed to plead guilty to one or more counts but later changed his mind. After he refused to plead guilty, Fitzgerald claimed that Wilson "angrily pointed his finger and shook it in my face indicating he was very disappointed in me, that I was a fool, that I was going to be convicted, that he was going to work me over like no one else, that he was going to make the trial so long it was going to ruin every defendant." Fitzgerald denied that he ever agreed to plead guilty. He said that Wilson's tactics upset and depressed him so much that he had to hospitalize himself to keep away from liquor. Wilson acknowledged becoming angry at Fitzgerald but disputed the particulars of Fitzgerald's version. Fitzgerald wasn't put before the grand jury.

Kent Klineman gave grand-jury testimony on Tuesday morning, October 15. His lawyer later asserted that Klineman was duped into testifying by being assured that he wasn't a "target" of the investigation.

William Murray was subjected to several hours of biting interrogation by Wilson on November 26. Wilson was particularly interested in how Murray characterized the money Home-Stake paid him.

"Would it have been commissions for selling units of Home-Stake?"

"No, I don't—I don't recall it as commissions, no."

"Tell me how you regard it. Use your own words."

"Just fees for business advice."

"You know what a bird dog is?"

"Sure, I grew up on a farm."

"I figured you did. And you know a bird dog is a dog that goes out and is pretty good at finding things; isn't that right?"

"A bird dog is good at finding birds, yes, uh-huh."

"Right. Were you pretty good at finding people who would invest in Home-Stake units?"

"I don't know that I was good. I found a number of people who were interested, yes."

"Was Trippet rewarding you for finding these people by giving you consulting fees?"

"Undoubtedly that was one of the factors in his mind."

"It was not a factor in your mind?"

"Not particularly."

The early December deadline forced Wilson and the others to work extremely long hours. There were loud, protracted arguments over how many people to indict and how to word the indictment. Although everyone agreed that Trippet was the principal defendant, there was disagreement on how many additional people to charge. The SEC wanted only six defendants—Trippet, Fitzgerald, Landrith, Cross, Sims, and Ganong. Others wanted as many as fifteen.

The indictment was difficult to draft. It had to reflect the complexity of the case, yet be simple enough to be understood by a lay jury.

The government men were in a state of exhaustion as the deadline for returning the indictment neared. A tentative date of Tuesday, December 3, was postponed until Thursday, the fifth; then Tuesday, the tenth; and finally, Thursday, December 12.

Wilson settled on thirteen defendants and a thirty-nine-count indictment of eighty-seven pages. Three stenographers were kept at the U.S. attorney's offices through the evening of December 11. Pages of the indictment were spread across desks amid half-eaten sandwiches and refilled coffee cups. Edited pages were retyped, reread by the weary lawyers, and edited and typed again. A stenographer's radio softly played Top Forty music. At 9:30 P.M. Wilson yelled to no one in particular, "How do you spell 'commingled?'" (as in "Home-Stake commingled the investors' funds")."

Wilson thought that the indictment was in final form at midnight. He was wrong. Quibbling over wording continued through the next morning. Several pages again were retyped. The grand jurors voted to approve the indictment, and at two o'clock Wilson led them into Courtroom 9 and handed the document to the judge Irving Hill.

The indictment said that the Home-Stake conspiracy began the day the company was founded in April 1955 and lasted until January 1, 1974. Generally, it accused Robert Trippet and twelve others of conspiring to conceive and carry out a vast array of schemes designed to mislead Home-Stake investors into believing that they would reap huge profits and could take large tax deductions; to placate investors disgruntled about low payouts; to foster investors' filing of false income-tax returns; and to divert millions of dollars to the defendants' personal use.

All the defendants were named in a single, broad count of conspiracy to perpetrate the swindle. In addition, Trippet was accused of thirty-seven specific violations in three categories of federal criminal law: twenty-two counts of securities fraud and making false statements in SEC prospectuses; twelve counts of fostering the preparation of false income-tax returns; and three counts of using the U.S. mails to defraud.

The other defendants and allegations, in addition to conspiracy:

Harry Fitzgerald: twenty-two securities fraud, five tax fraud, three mail fraud.

Frank Sims: twenty-two securities fraud, three mail fraud.

Norman Cross, Jr.: twenty-two securities fraud, three mail fraud.

Conrad Greer: twenty-two securities fraud, seven tax fraud, three mail fraud.

Richard Ganong: twenty-two securities fraud, seven tax fraud, three mail fraud.

Elmer Kunkel: twenty-two securities fraud, five tax fraud, three mail fraud.

John Lenoir: twenty-two securities fraud, five tax fraud, three mail fraud.

Herbert Smith: twenty-two securities fraud, one mail fraud.

David Davies: twenty-two securities fraud, three mail fraud.

Larry Martin: twenty-two securities fraud, three mail fraud.

Kent Klineman: one count of perjury before the grand jury.[1]

Most of the defendants had been warned that the indictments would be returned that Thursday. At his Tulsa home Trippet had prepared a statement for the press.

I haven't seen a copy of the indictment. However, I am confident it wouldn't contain a recital of the evidence in the case. At the trial, all of the facts and evidence will come out and I sincerely believe that I will then be vindicated and my innocence will be established.

The others issued general denials or said nothing. Stephen Wilson said that the defendants would be arraigned in early January.

As the Los Angeles indictment was being rushed to completion in early December, the FBI, the Denver office of the SEC, and the U.S. attorney in Albuquerque were concluding a relatively leisurely inquiry into the frauds of Mike Riebold, banker Donald Morgan, and their friends. On Friday, December 20, a federal grand jury returned an eighty-four-count indictment against Riebold, Morgan (who by then had been dismissed from the First National Bank in Albuquerque), and three other Riebold associates. They were accused of misapplication of bank funds and a variety of other frauds. The indictment said that Riebold and Morgan had plotted the takeover of Home-Stake essentially to gain control of Home-Stake's funds so that they could cover the illegal loans the bank had made to Riebold.

The indictment didn't name as defendants Carlos Robinson or the other Riebold associates who became Home-Stake officers

---

[1] Klineman was accused of having denied using the Black Book to sell Home-Stake interests when in fact he had used it.

and directors. Investigators concluded they were unwitting tools of Riebold rather than conscious participants in the conspiracy.

The Home-Stake defendants all pleaded innocent on January 13 in Los Angeles, and the case was assigned to Albert Lee Stephens, Jr., the chief U.S. district judge. (Cases are assigned to judges generally by lot. The position of chief judge is awarded on the basis of seniority.) Stephens's competence as a judge is considered to be no higher than average, and observers weren't pleased when he drew the highly complex Home-Stake case. A pre-trial hearing was set for February 24.

In late January, Tulsa accountant and former Home-Stake financial vice-president John Lenoir decided to plead guilty to the conspiracy count and to one of the tax-fraud counts. He was motivated partly by a lack of funds to hire an adequate lawyer for his defense.

Lawyers for Trippet and several other defendants, however, had found a loophole in the government's strategy for trying the case in Los Angeles. It seemed that Stephen Wilson and his staff had overlooked an obscure provision of federal law that permits people accused of certain tax crimes to be tried in the jurisdiction where they live if they so choose. The provision meant that ten of the twelve remaining defendants—all except Californians Greer and Ganong—could elect to have their trials on the tax charges held in their home cities—New York for Klineman and Tulsa for Trippet and the others. (Even though Kent Klineman wasn't accused of a specific count of tax fraud, he was named in the conspiracy count, which alleged that tax fraud was one of the means of the conspiracy. Thus Klineman felt as entitled as the others to have his case transferred.)

In an effort to thwart such a move and keep the trial in Los Angeles, Wilson decided to draft a new indictment, dropping tax-fraud charges against the defendants not from California. He also decided to broaden the case against Kent Klineman to include securities fraud and mail fraud as well as conspiracy and perjury.

In the days preceding the February 24 hearing, Wilson and the investigators sifted through their files, made a number of telephone calls, and paid at least one visit to potential witnesses around Los Angeles in an effort to piece together additional evidence against Klineman. An amended indictment was drafted. The grand jury approved it, and the government announced it at the hearing.

Assistant prosecutor A. Howard Matz, a member of Wilson's fraud and special prosecutions unit, said that the changes were intended to "clarify" the first indictment and to correct errors made due to time pressure and fatigue in December. Matz said that the case had always been essentially a securities and mail fraud prosecution. (That was a change from the government's earlier characterization of it as a major assault on tax-shelter abuses.)

Defense lawyers called the new indictment a "shabby, improper maneuver" and a "preemptive strike," and accused the prosecutors of deleting the tax charges in order to deny their clients' right to have the trial of the tax counts moved. "It is a tax shelter and tax case from beginning to end," said Trippet's lawyer, Lester Klaus.

Kent Klineman's attorney, Seymour Glanzer,[2] of Washington, D.C., charged that the additional allegations against his client also were part of a government effort to camouflage the real motive of the amended indictment—keeping the trial in Los Angeles.

The ten defendants from outside California all filed general motions to transfer the trial, contending that holding it in Los Angeles would be unduly expensive and inconvenient for them. They also filed separate motions to have the trial of the tax counts moved. They claimed that the government hadn't really dropped the tax charges; it had merely recouched them

[2] Glanzer had become moderately well known in late 1972 and early 1973 as the second-ranking assistant U.S. attorney on the team of three prosecutors who conducted the original Watergate investigation, resulting in the indictment of the five burglars plus E. Howard Hunt and Gordon Liddy. Special prosecutor Archibald Cox took over the investigation in May 1973. The head of the original prosecution team, Earl Silbert, eventually became U.S. attorney for the District of Columbia, after protracted Senate hearings that featured much opposition to his appointment. Seymour Glanzer entered private practice with the Washington firm of Dickstein, Shapiro & Morin, where Charles Colson once was a partner.

in mail-fraud terms without changing the substance of the allegations.[3]

The defendants' lawyers cited the Four Seasons Nursing Centers case as precedent for moving the trial to Oklahoma. But assistant prosecutor Matz argued that the "case would be decimated" if moved from Los Angeles, because neither he nor Stephen Wilson would be able to handle it in Oklahoma and new government attorneys would have to be appointed. "The complexity of this case, the monumental array of issues and defendants which far exceed the Four Seasons case, is something that even a very brilliant attorney couldn't get a handle on in . . . less than several months," Matz said.

Judge Stephens didn't rule on the transfer motions until August 25, more than eight months after the original indictment. He ordered the trial on all counts moved to Tulsa for the non-California defendants, including Klineman, posing the necessity of a separate Los Angeles trial for the two California residents. The judge accepted the government's amended indictment, but agreed with the defense that dropping the tax allegations had been a tactical maneuver by the prosecution to keep the trial in Los Angeles.

Judge Stephens's failure to rule until August 25 disturbed many observers of the case but didn't surprise them. When Stephens was appointed a judge in 1961, the American Bar Association rated him "well qualified" on a scale of "exceptionally well qualified," "well qualified," "qualified," and "not qualified." However, he is widely regarded as a procrastinator. (Stephens denies procrastinating, but says his administrative tasks as chief judge sometimes keep him from performing his judicial duties as promptly as other judges.)

The transfer of the case to Tulsa placed it in the hands of Allen E. Barrow, the sixty-one-year-old chief federal judge there. Barrow had been named to the bench in 1962, largely because of his close association with the late U.S. senator from Oklahoma,

[3] In the first indictment, the defendants were charged with fostering the filing of false income-tax returns by sending false tax information to investors for use in completing their returns. In the amended indictment, the defendants were accused of the same acts—sending the false information by mail—but the alleged crime was changed to mail fraud.

Robert S. Kerr. The American Bar Association rated Barrow "qualified," third position down on its rating scale of four. He is somewhat inarticulate and tends occasionally to misstate facts in extemporaneous remarks from the bench.

Barrow is known for being lenient toward both white- and blue-collar criminals. A controversial figure in Tulsa, he is extremely sensitive to press criticism—particularly by the Tulsa *Tribune,* whose editor and publisher, Jenkin Lloyd Jones, is the father-in-law of one of Tulsa's assistant federal prosecutors, Kenneth Snoke. Barrow's reputation for unorthodox judicial moves was bolstered by his actions in the Home-Stake case.

In October the judge asked the U.S. attorney in Tulsa, Nathan Graham, to file a motion to transfer the case back to Los Angeles. Graham complied, but withdrew the motion when the Justice Department instructed him to do so because there was little if any precedent for it. Judge Barrow ordered the case retransferred anyway. He cited statistics purporting to show that the caseload in the Tulsa federal court was heavier than in the Los Angeles court. He said that he had tried unsuccessfully to recruit an additional federal judge from outside Tulsa.

Judge Barrow noted that the government planned to present 150 witnesses, which would require an estimated four months, and that the defendants anticipated taking even longer to present rebuttal. Allowing time for other parts of the trial, he said, "It appears we are confronted with a trial period of up to a full year. It is obvious that this district isn't in any position to hear a protracted trial without outside help."

Judge Barrow assailed Los Angeles Judge Stephens and the Justice Department for delaying the criminal case. "It is most unfortunate," he said, "that the transfer should be held up by the [Los Angeles] court . . . then to receive this stale and untouched case in this district in the same month that the federal judiciary is implementing plans for speedier trials." (That statement was a reference to a recently enacted federal law intended to expedite trials.) As for the prosecutors, Judge Barrow said that the case was a "showplace of U.S. Government indecision in the area of prosecutory discretion." He called the government a "nervous chameleon—constantly changing its color and position." (That statement in part referred to the Justice

Department's decision not to support retransfer of the case to Los Angeles after it had tried so hard to keep it there in the first place.)

The defendants immediately asked the federal appeals court in Denver to overturn Judge Barrow's order and keep the case in Tulsa. The case files were returned to Los Angeles, however, and Judge Stephens assigned the case to another Los Angeles judge, A. Andrew Hauk. Judge Hauk's ABA rating was "qualified." Like Judge Stephens, he isn't considered a judicial giant by southern California lawyers who've tried cases before him.[4]

On November 10, 1975, Tulsa CPA Norman Cross filed a motion to dismiss the pending indictment on grounds that his Sixth Amendment guarantee of a speedy trial had been violated. He accused the government of subjecting him to "prosecution by investigation" for more than twenty-seven months.

Cross said that the investigation had severely damaged his accounting practice.

> Several bankers, with whom I have had a close relationship since I started in public accounting, have no longer indicated a desire to refer clients to me. . . . Because of the nature of my business and the ethics of the profession, it is nearly impossible to survive without referrals from bankers, attorneys and clients. . . .
> The effect on my wife has been very upsetting to me. She has had to take tranquilizers regularly to overcome her anxiety over our well-being.

The same day that Cross filed his dismissal motion in Los Angeles, a federal court jury in Albuquerque convicted Mike Riebold and Donald Morgan of conspiracy, securities fraud, misapplication of bank funds, wire fraud, mail-fraud, interstate transportation of stolen property, and making false statements to the

---

[4] In 1973 the San Francisco U.S. appeals court, in reversing a ruling by Judge Hauk in a criminal case, not only accused him of a "glaring error" but also found that he had permitted his court reporter to overcharge for transcripts and had "humiliated" a lawyer who had challenged the overcharging. "What he did is inconsistent with what is expected of a federal judge," the appeals court said.

SEC. The trial had taken nine weeks. The three men charged along with Riebold and Morgan had pleaded guilty to lesser charges prior to trial. Riebold was sentenced to five years in prison, Morgan to two years. Each was fined $10,000. They announced they would appeal.

On December 2, the IRS subpoenaed Robert Trippet's checking account records for 1972, 1973, and 1974 from the First National Bank of Tulsa. The summons served on the bank indicated that Trippet had deposited a total of $8,550,272 in two accounts and had withdrawn $8,824,019 between January 10, 1973 and December 17, 1974. The summons didn't say how much was in the accounts before and after the deposits and withdrawals.

Justice Department lawyers were convinced that Judge Barrow's retransfer of the Home-Stake case to Los Angeles would be overruled and the trial ultimately held in Tulsa. Prosecutor Stephen Wilson's duties as head of the Los Angeles fraud and special prosecutions unit prevented him from handling a major trial outside Los Angeles. Howard Matz, the lawyer who had aided Wilson in the early months of 1975, was by autumn otherwise occupied. So Wilson named a new prosecutor, thirty-one-year-old William R. ("Will") Hawes. Although he was on Wilson's staff in Los Angeles, Hawes was placed under the direct supervision of the Justice Department's criminal division in Washington for the duration of the Home-Stake criminal case.

An intense, impulsive man of medium build with curly light-brown hair, Hawes grew up on a ranch in northern California. His normal daily attire is a conservative business suit and cowboy boots. He speaks rapidly in a resonant baritone voice with just a slight country twang, and his courtroom manner and phrasing tend to be formalistic.

Although considered a competent prosecutor, Hawes wasn't as experienced as Wilson, particularly in complex tax prosecutions. After reviewing the Home-Stake case, he told lawyers for the defendants in late 1975 that he intended to seek still another indictment in order to "streamline" the prosecution. Hawes let it be known that the new indictment would be brought in Tulsa in early 1976; it would contain only about ten counts and would highlight the relatively simple mail-fraud aspects of the case. That meant disregarding some substantive elements of the swindle as perceived by the original investigators, prosecutors, and grand jury.

Among other things, Hawes wanted to drop the conspiracy and fraud charges against Kent Klineman and proceed against him only on the single charge of perjury before the grand jury in Los Angeles. "Wilson and Matz are hot to try Klineman but the evidence can't put him in bed with Trippet—no way," Hawes told Klineman's lawyer, Seymour Glanzer. Will Hawes also noted that neither the SEC nor the IRS had recommended that Klineman be indicted.

Hawes's suggestion that Klineman be excluded from the new Tulsa indictment was rejected by both the Justice Department in Washington—in the person of Edward Barnes, head of the criminal securities fraud unit—and by the Los Angeles U.S. attorney's office, which was still playing a strong advisory role. When Hawes told Steve Wilson he wanted to drop Klineman from the Tulsa case, Wilson cursed him and hung up. The Justice Department asked Hawes if he could "live with Klineman in the conspiracy count." He said that he could, and told Seymour Glanzer that Klineman would be named in the new indictment after all. Glanzer angrily accused Hawes of misrepresenting Klineman's status and "cow-towing" to his superiors. Hawes retorted that Stephen Wilson's judgment had prevailed because Wilson had the "nose of a bloodhound."

On January 30, 1976, *The Wall Street Journal* published an article describing the lagging prosecution and reporting the government's intention to seek a new indictment in Tulsa. Judge Barrow considered the government's move an insult and an attempt to skirt his retransfer of the case to California. He telephoned Deputy Attorney General Harold Tyler, in Washington, to complain. He also threatened to have a U.S. marshal arrest William Hawes or other prosecutors if they appeared in the grand jury room at the Tulsa federal courthouse to prepare for a new Home-Stake indictment. The Justice Department men assured Judge Barrow that they didn't intend to insult him or circumvent his authority; they simply believed that bringing a new indictment in Tulsa appeared to be the quickest and most direct route to an early trial. The judge relented and permitted Hawes to proceed.

Judge Barrow's attitude wasn't the only reason that Hawes felt unwelcome in Tulsa. At about 2:00 one morning in early February, just as Hawes was preparing for bed in his room at the Downtowner Motor Inn, he heard a noise outside his door. It was a man with a gun, who fled after Hawes brandished his own fourteen-shot, fully loaded and cocked 9-mm automatic. Hawes, a gun buff, kept the weapon in his room at all times. He reported the incident to the FBI as a possible threat against his life stemming from the Home-Stake case, but the FBI did nothing; it apparently felt that the episode more likely was a random robbery attempt.

Hawes began presenting evidence to a Tulsa grand jury on Tuesday, February 17, and on Friday he obtained a new, simplified indictment charging Robert Trippet, Norman Cross, Frank Sims, Harry Fitzgerald, Elmer Kunkel, and David Davies each with one count of conspiracy and up to nine counts of mail fraud. Kent Klineman was charged with conspiracy only. Allegations of overt instances of tax and securities fraud were dropped, although tax, securities, and mail fraud, as well as false statements to the SEC, were cited in the conspiracy count as being means of the conspiracy. The indictment sketched the scope of the conspiracy more modestly than the first two indictments had. Instead of alleging that it began when the company was founded in 1955, the new indictment said that it started in 1967. Allegations against Thomas Landrith, Larry Martin, and Herbert Smith were dismissed. Their inclusion in the previous indictments was "deemed legally defective after a complete review of the law and facts," Hawes said in a press release.

In a tactical sense, the new indictment constituted an effort to expedite the prosecution and reduce chances for further delay. It also was an acknowledgment that William Hawes lacked experience in prosecuting highly complex tax-fraud cases. In a broader sense, the new indictment was indicative of the U. S. criminal-justice system's inability to grapple effectively with one of the largest and most complex fraud cases ever to confront it.

Judge Barrow scheduled trial for May 24. The seven defendants filed a total of twenty-eight motions to dismiss the indictment. They contended that their Fifth Amendment "due-process" and Sixth Amendment "speedy trial" guarantees had been abridged, and that the government in handling the case had "abused its prosecutorial discretion" to the detriment of the defendants' rights.

Conrad Greer, one of the two defendants still facing charges in Los Angeles, chose to have a nonjury trial before Judge Hauk beginning Tuesday, May 4. William Hawes interrupted trial preparation in Tulsa to return to Los Angeles for Greer's trial.

The case against Greer also had been reduced, to one count of conspiracy, two counts of mail fraud, and three counts of fostering the preparation of false income-tax returns. The trial took four days. After hearing testimony from four prosecution witnesses and Greer himself, as well as seeing 161 documents, many of which were highly technical and complex, Judge Hauk found Greer not guilty on all counts.

"He generally did the best he could in good faith to present the engineering facts . . . until he got to the point where he couldn't stand it anymore, what with his ulcers and all that," Hauk said.

> The defendant here, in my view, was a fish, not an octopus, and the fact that he may have been in the environment or presence of an octopus doesn't make him part of the octopus. I think . . . he was a fish, who, in my view, was duped almost as much as the investor participants apparently were duped— I'm not going to pass on that because that's not the case before me.

Richard Ganong, the other California defendant, had chosen to await a jury trial. But William Hawes acknowledged at the end of the Greer trial that the evidence against Ganong would be essentially the same as that presented against Greer. So Judge Hauk declared Ganong not guilty, too.

Hawes spent the weekend at his Pasadena home, then rushed back to Tulsa to continue preparing for the May 24 start of the main Home-Stake trial. On Wednesday, May 19, however, Judge Barrow, saying that he needed more time to consider the defendants' twenty-eight motions to dismiss the indictment, postponed the trial to July 6. On June 29 the judge denied all the motions. He ruled that the various investigations of the Home-Stake affair by the government had been "correct, proper and thorough" and weren't "for the purpose of delay." On the contrary, Barrow said, the defendants' pretrial motions were the "root of most of the delay." Still, the judge expressed chagrin that he couldn't justify dismissing the case because of his crowded docket. Separately, Barrow granted a motion by Kent Klineman to transfer his trial to New York.

On Friday, July 2, as preparations for the Tulsa trial were being completed, Irvine E. Ungerman, the lawyer for defendant Frank Sims, suffered a heart attack. On Tuesday Judge Barrow rescheduled the trial for early September, saying that if Ungerman wasn't well enough by then to represent Sims, he would have to get another lawyer.

Meanwhile, the government announced that former Home-Stake treasurer Elmer Kunkel had decided to plead guilty to a misdemeanor securities-law violation, and that the felony conspiracy and mail fraud charges against him would be dismissed. At a public court session before Judge Barrow, Kunkel admitted that he was guilty of the misdemeanor. A week later, however, when Kunkel was to enter his plea formally, he pleaded no-contest [5] instead of guilty. For most purposes the pleas are identical; a no-contest plea stands as a conviction of the alleged crime. But there are two important practical differences. First, a no-contest plea sometimes is considered slightly weaker grounds than a guilty plea for disbarring a lawyer or revoking an accountant's license to practice. Kunkel is both a lawyer and an accountant, and Judge Barrow said that since he didn't consider Kunkel guilty of "moral turpitude," he didn't want to jeopardize his professional licenses.

The second difference between a no-contest plea and a guilty plea is that while a no-contest plea can't be used against the defendant by plaintiffs in a civil lawsuit, a guilty plea can.

[5] The formal plea is expressed in the Latin phrase *nolo contendere,* "I do not wish to contend."

Thus, Kunkel's plea didn't weaken his position as a defendant in lawsuits pending against Home-Stake and its former officers and directors.

Judge Barrow fined Elmer Kunkel $5,000 but withdrew the fine a few days later at the request of the government, which expected Kunkel to be an important witness against Trippet.

Will Hawes also announced in July that the government was dropping all charges against David Davies. No explanation was given. With John Lenoir having pleaded guilty in Los Angeles, that left Trippet, Sims, Fitzgerald, and Cross awaiting trial in September in Tulsa, and Kent Klineman facing a single conspiracy count in New York.

Lawyers for the government and the defendants continued to maneuver throughout the summer. Hawes flew to Albuquerque and questioned Mike Riebold on the details of his negotiations with Trippet in 1973. Riebold was free on bail while appealing his conviction. After a five-hour interrogation in a room at the Albuquerque Hilton Inn, Hawes tentatively decided to use Riebold as a witness against Trippet. Riebold told Hawes that CPA Dave Melendy had given him unfavorable reports about Home-Stake's finances. As a result, Riebold said, he had asked Trippet about how Home-Stake drilling funds had been used and Trippet had said: " 'Sometimes you have to borrow from Peter to pay Paul.' " Trippet also had said that raising money with a new drilling offering was necessary to "cover some mistakes and keep the wheels greased," according to Riebold.

Trippet heard about the government's renewed interest in the Albuquerque connection and it concerned him. In late August, he made a move that, at least to kibitzers in the bars and locker rooms of the Tulsa Club, signaled a major break in the case. He hired Patrick Malloy, a Tulsa lawyer known for being particularly adept at plea-bargaining and for being a close friend of Judge Barrow. Malloy, once a contender for mayor of Tulsa and a former candidate for Congress, has been active in Democratic party politics for many years, as was Allen Barrow before being named to the federal bench.

Word circulated that Malloy was negotiating a deal whereby

Trippet would agree to change his plea from not guilty to no-contest and Judge Barrow would agree to refrain from sending Trippet to jail, limiting his penalty to a fine and probation. It was expected that if Trippet changed his plea, other Tulsa defendants would, too, thus eliminating or substantially reducing the dimensions of the trial that Judge Barrow wanted so much to avoid.

Trippet portrayed the purported plan as a great victory. To him, a fine and probation were meaningless. It was jail that had concerned him all along. Moreover, a no-contest plea couldn't be used against him in the civil suits.

"I'm better than Muhammad Ali," he bragged to a friend over lunch at the Tulsa Club one day near the end of August. "I've gone fifteen rounds each with three of the government's best [Stephen Wilson, Will Hawes, and Edward Barnes, the Justice Department supervisor from Washington] and won every time."

On Thursday afternoon, September 2, five days before the scheduled start of the trial, Trippet and his lawyers appeared in court before Judge Barrow to announce the change of plea. Barrow first made everyone swear that there had been no pressure from him to plea-bargain; an Oklahoma newspaper story had contended that the judge did apply pressure. Then Barrow read the entire indictment aloud, and began to extemporize in his typically imprecise fashion.

"It's one of the most complex, complicated cases I have ever seen and it was a mastermind that put it together as it worked out. I am amazed at what might have happened if Mr. Trippet had used his mind for talents and efforts toward a legitimate end, what might have ended up. He might have owned General Motors and Exxon, I don't know."

"That is correct, Your Honor," Hawes said. "One individual who would testify in this case wrote a letter to Home-Stake after finding out what was actually going on and said in essence what I have uncovered, once it is completely unraveled will disclose to the American investing public the greatest Ponzi scheme since this gentleman, Ponzi, went to jail over a half a century ago for mail fraud.[6] And this is what the government expected to prove against the defendant Trippet."

Barrow continued, "I note two or three things casually, that the Moneymaker Man who wrote the book [he meant Adam Smith, author of *The Money Game*] was one of the investors in this and some of the biggest businessmen in the country, as you know as well as prominent people, but the thing that still never fails to amaze me is how any investor or anyone with common business sense would expect a 358% return on their investment after two years. Someone is looking for something that isn't there."

Hawes gently corrected the judge. The 358 percent return on the 1970 drilling program was to be paid over 15 years, not two.

"I understand," Barrow said. "All over 300%, though."

"Yes."

"I say, to have that idea, let's say there is not a dry eye in the house for those type men who knew better. The small investor I would agree, but anyone who would go in with the idea of getting a return of 358 percent in two years I don't exactly cry for or weep for, particularly those knowledgeable people."

Hawes didn't bother to correct "two years" again. He pointed out, however, that not all Home-Stake investors were wealthy or knowledgeable. And he added that Trippet, "in carrying out this very long and very involved Ponzi scheme, hurt a lot of people who worked with him, some of whom were named as defendants and have their reputations destroyed, so there are other victims in this case."

After a few more largely irrelevant remarks, Judge Barrow asked Trippet to step forward. "Now, do you tell the Court . . . that you have no defense to offer and that you in no way contest these charges against you?"

"That is correct."

". . . Now, Mr. Trippet, based on your statements and your demeanor and your clear and responsive answers to my questions, the Court finds that the evidence against you would be strong and conclusive, that you have no defense or contest to offer to the prosecution's charges, and that your plea of nolo contendere

[6] A reference to the letter from Grant Anderson of Portland, Oregon, cited on p. 117.

should be accepted. . . . The court further finds that your plea is voluntary with your understanding of the charges against you and with your knowledge of the consequences of your plea. Do you understand that?"

"I do."

"It would be the same as a guilty plea."

"Yes, sir."

"The court therefore accepts your plea of nolo contendere and finds that you are convicted as charged by a plea of nolo contendere."

The next day Frank Sims changed his plea to no-contest to the entire indictment, and Harry Fitzgerald pleaded guilty to two felony securities violations in exchange for dismissal of the conspiracy and mail-fraud charges. Under the law, Trippet and Sims each could have been sentenced to fifty years in prison and fined $19,000. Fitzgerald could have gotten ten years and a $10,000 fine. Sentencing was postponed.

The trial of CPA Norman Cross, who stuck to his not-guilty plea, was set for September 21. Kent Klineman's trial in New York was put off indefinitely.

Norman Cross was acquitted of criminal wrongdoing. It was the only possible verdict under the circumstances, which were that in a forty-four-day trial, the government attorneys failed, in the opinion of Judge Barrow, to meet the legal requirement for a guilty verdict—proof of guilt beyond a reasonable doubt. Barrow didn't let the case go to the jury. He directed acquittal at the end of the prosecution and defense presentations. "The government's evidence is equally strong to infer innocence of the crimes charged as it is to infer guilt, and there has been no finger of guilt pointed at this defendant," Barrow said.

For the most part, the Cross trial was an anticlimax for everyone except Cross and his family. Out of thirteen original defendants, he was the twelfth to be disposed of. He wasn't as important a figure as Home-Stake's principal officers—Trippet, Sims, Lenoir, and Fitzgerald. With their convictions, the prosecution could claim a measure of success.

Still, the trial must be examined briefly. As in so many other facets of the Home-Stake affair, what actually happened was more complicated and elusive than what might be inferred from the result.

The merits of both the prosecution and defense cases unfortunately were somewhat obscured by two factors. First, the prosecution was startlingly inept. From the opening statement to the verdict, the Justice Department representatives' conduct of the trial appeared to be a law-school demonstration of how *not* to present a complex fraud case to a jury of laymen and a less-than-astute judge. That analysis is only partly hindsight; it was the opinion of a number of lawyers observing the trial in progress.

In addition, facing an ineffectual prosecution, Norman Cross didn't need much help from Judge Barrow. But he got some anyway. Allen Barrow lost few opportunities to display his long-standing antagonism toward the Home-Stake prosecution; his warmth toward Cross's very able attorney, B. Hayden Crawford; and his disdain for the rich, out-of-state city slickers who claimed to have been cheated by Bob Trippet.

It should not be inferred, however, that Cross would have been convicted if the prosecution had been skillful and the judge wholly impartial. Rather, these points are made to stress an obvious but often ignored fact: Criminal trials aren't conducted in isolation chambers by identically skilled robots. They are conducted by human beings of varying competence and psychological bent who are subject to all manner of stimuli from outside the courtroom. These factors, as well as guilt or innocence, inevitably affect the course and results of trials.

Prosecutor William Hawes was assisted by Jay C. Johnson, a young attorney from the fraud section of the Justice Department's criminal division in Washington, and Kenneth Snoke, an assistant U.S. attorney in Tulsa and the son-in-law of Tulsa *Tribune* editor and publisher Jenkin Lloyd Jones, whose editorials often attacked Judge Barrow. To convict Cross, the government lawyers were required to prove that he aided the Home-Stake fraud by signing financial statements that he knew, or had strong reason to suspect, were false and misleading. In a technical sense they had to demonstrate three things: that there was a criminal conspiracy to swindle investors by means of securities fraud, mail fraud, and fostering the preparation of false income-tax returns; that Cross was part of the conspiracy; and that Cross was guilty of nine specific instances of mail fraud. (One need not mail anything to commit mail fraud. It's enough to participate knowingly in the production of a fraudulent document that is sent through the mail.)

Hawes, Johnson, and Snoke inexplicably ignored some elementary tactical logic in presenting their case. For example, they failed to keep the case sufficiently simple. Although the basic thrust of most frauds—misrepresentation and concealment—is simple, the substance frequently is very complex, and the role of an accountant can be the most complex element of all. The defense will try to mire the trial in complexity in an effort to confuse and bore the judge and jury. The prosecutors, therefore, must use every possible means to keep attention rooted on the main themes. They didn't.

The government attorneys also failed to focus attention from the outset on Home-Stake's character as a tax shelter. The defense obviously would contend that the Home-Stake investors deserved no sympathy: They were wealthy. They derived tax advantages from their investments. They were able to compensate for some of their losses through tax deductions. To blunt that line of reasoning, the prosecution should have openly acknowledged the tax angles at the beginning but stressed that because of improper tax deductions, the big loser was the U.S. Treasury —the nation's taxpayers. Moreover, the government should have made the obvious point that wealthy people are entitled to the same protection under the fraud laws that is afforded everyone else. Tax deductibility isn't a license to steal an investor's money, nor is it a legal defense to a charge of fraud. After all, a bank-robbery loss is tax-deductible to the bank, to the extent it isn't covered by insurance. But courts aren't permitted to use that as an excuse for treating the robber leniently.

Hawes and his helpers, furthermore, failed to prepare their early witnesses adequately to answer such basic questions as: How much money did you lose? Do you believe you were defrauded? Many investors were somewhat apathetic and hadn't focused on these questions. And since they were not properly prepared, their honest answer in the beginning of the trial was: "I don't know."

Will Hawes assigned Jay Johnson to make the opening statement to the jury. The statement was poorly organized and filled with technical terms—such as *units of participation, steamflood,* and *quit-claim*—that Johnson didn't adequately define. Incredibly, Johnson didn't mention the tax-shelter aspect of the case until half way through the statement, and then referred to it only briefly. The Trippet-Klineman reversionary-interest transaction—complex to be sure but not beyond comprehension —also was poorly explained.

Hawes assigned the crucial questioning of the investors during the trial to the least able member of the prosecution team, Kenneth Snoke, who had even less experience with major fraud cases than Hawes and Johnson. The first of these witnesses was George Vandenhoff, a rich Los Angeles stockbroker. Snoke was nervous, his questions imprecise and superficial. He neither explored the tax aspects of Vandenhoff's investment nor asked how much money Vandenhoff lost. Defense counsel Hayden Crawford thus had the opportunity, while cross-examining Vandenhoff, to stress his tax deductions, lack of specific knowledge of his losses, and unfamiliarity with Norman Cross's role in the affairs of Home-Stake.

The government handled some later witnesses more skillfully. Heublein's Ralph Hart, for instance, testified that he had lost between $50,000 and $75,000, after taking account of tax savings protected by the statute of limitations, and that his loss would be substantially greater if the IRS succeeded in barring his post-1969 deductions. But Hart's impact was diminished because of the inept questioning of early witnesses, from whom judge and jury got their basic impression of the strength of the government's case.

No government attorney, moreover, was the match of Hayden Crawford, who once served as U.S. attorney in Tulsa and is an experienced trial lawyer. Crawford's chief success in defending Norman Cross was nurturing the idea that auditing the books of a corporation is an extremely complex activity involving judgments on which honest accountants can and frequently do differ. He convinced the judge that even if Norman Cross's accounting judgments were open to question, they didn't constitute participation in a criminal conspiracy. The government failed to sway the judge to its position: that despite room for disagreement on many accounting questions, Cross's work for Home-Stake was outside the bounds of legitimate accounting judgment and constituted fraudulent conduct.

Two of the most important trial witnesses were Elmer Kunkel, the former Home-Stake treasurer and outside auditor who pleaded no-contest to a misdemeanor securities violation in exchange for the dropping of felony charges, and John Lenoir, the company's former financial vice-president who had pleaded guilty to felony conspiracy and one felony tax-fraud count in the first indictment in Los Angeles.

Kunkel told how he had become concerned that investor tax deductions were improper because money wasn't being spent for its intended tax-favored purposes; that unequal payments were made to investors in identical drilling programs; and that the payments weren't derived from oil income. He also explained how he had worked backwards from an earnings-per-share figure given to him by Trippet to derive the earnings Trippet wanted (the government called this practice "backing into income"), and how he had warned Trippet that he would end up like Billy Sol Estes.

On cross-examination, however, Hayden Crawford used Kunkel's testimony to develop his theme that auditing is very complex and that differences of opinion are common. "If you get ten [accountants] you have ten disputes," Kunkel said.

Kunkel also agreed with Hayden Crawford that the remark about Billy Sol Estes and Trippet's reply that he was "smarter than Billy Sol Estes" were made in anger. "You aren't here to tell us, are you, that this conversation was evidence of a conspiracy?" Crawford asked.

"Certainly not, no sir."

"No, of course not," Crawford added.

"It had nothing to do with conspiracy," said Kunkel.

Under later questioning, Kunkel acknowledged that he didn't know the legal definition of a criminal conspiracy. Still later he testified that he understood the "essence" of a conspiracy but hadn't "willfully" become a part of a conspiracy. He was never asked whether in his opinion there had been a conspiracy involving others.

John Lenoir corroborated much of Kunkel's testimony about the operations of Home-Stake. Lenoir testified that Trippet said that the 1968 and 1969 drilling programs weren't worth "spending too much money on"; that the inflated payments to investors (termed "pro. rev.") were "dreamed up . . ." to show that the program was making some money; that Home-Stake routinely tried to conceal unequal payments by grouping investors who knew each other and paying members of a particular group equally; that the company frequently blamed fictitious "computer errors" when investors complained about payment discrepancies; and that there had been a betting pool among office employees on what earnings-per-share figure Trippet would select.

As with Kunkel, there was extended discussion during cross-examination of whether Lenoir had participated in a criminal conspiracy. "You have never been part of any conspiracy to defraud anybody, have you?" Hayden Crawford asked Lenoir.

"Not that I know of, sir."

Later Crawford asked, "You know of no fraud or conspiracy, isn't that true?"

"None that I could pinpoint, no."

Lenoir said that he had pleaded guilty to felony conspiracy and felony tax fraud because of poor health and lack of funds to hire a defense lawyer. When questioned by prosecutor Jay Johnson, however, Lenoir took precisely the opposite position. Johnson read lengthy excerpts from Lenoir's sworn guilty plea in Los Angeles in 1975. Lenoir said that he still would make the same admissions.

"Would you have entered the plea considering your health and economic conditions if you didn't feel in your heart that you had done some things wrong and had seen some things done wrong at Home-Stake?" Johnson asked.

"There were certain allegations in the indictment that I knew would be more or less true, and I had to take those into consideration . . . and I didn't feel like I wanted to fight those through the court."

"You didn't wish to fight the charges that you knew were true?"

"That's right."

Allen Barrow's prejudices and his limitations as a judge were on display throughout the trial. "When the so-called Okies left Oklahoma, it improved the IQ of Oklahoma and California also," he to'ld a Los Angeles witness who had invested heavily in Home-Stake. Of entertainment celebrities Barrow said, "I wouldn't go across the street to get a photograph of one upside down standing on their head."

Furthermore, as he had in pre-trial proceedings, Barrow showed a remarkable propensity for misstating certain facts of the Home-Stake case. In an effort to portray the wealthy investors as stupid, greedy, and undeserving of sympathy, he again castigated them for purportedly accepting a promise that they would get a 300 percent return in *two years*. In fact, Home-Stake's projection was a 300 percent return over a period of twelve to eighteen years. To George Vandenhoff, the first investor witness, the judge said, "As a stockbroker weren't you a little bit doubtful of the rate of return they promised you?"

"You are referring to the [drilling] units now?"

"Yes. Could you tell any customer you had of any stock you know that would pay over 300% return in two years?"

"Well, no, it worked out 300% by 1980—this was in 1966—a 12 to 16 year program," said the nonplussed Vandenhoff.

"Weren't you told you could get your money back within two years?"

"Oh, no, no, no, I didn't want it back within two years."

"You were not told that?"

"I was not told that."

Barrow also misunderstood and repeatedly misstated the essence of the Trippet-Klineman reversionary-interest deal. That is somewhat understandable since the prosecution never explained the deal properly and since the defense naturally did everything it could to foster confusion.

In addition, the judge misconstrued the government's characterization of Home-Stake as a Ponzi scheme. Barrow said, in effect, that a company's operations can't be called a Ponzi fraud unless the company has no legitimate core of business whatsoever. "Isn't a Ponzi scheme where you have no ownership of anything except money, . . . rob Peter to pay Paul?" Borrow asked.[1]

The government, of course, never contended that Home-Stake

[1] The expression "rob Peter to pay Paul," originally used by an IRS witness, was similar to the phrase "borrow from Peter to pay Paul" that Mike Riebold claimed Trippet had used to describe certain aspects of Home-Stake's handling of investor funds.

was a pure Ponzi scheme with no oil wells. Rather, it alleged that because Home-Stake produced far less oil than it projected, it used money from later investors to inflate the return paid to earlier investors under the guise of oil revenue. Even the original 1919 Ponzi scheme in Boston began with a tiny core of business activity.

Throughout the trial, Barrow also repeatedly stressed something that was irrelevant to the trial: the current financial condition of Home-Stake. Barrow had authority over the Home-Stake bankruptcy proceedings as well as the criminal case, and he displayed a proprietor's pride in the way the company's remaining assets had been managed. The government had never contended that the company was without assets, but Barrow insisted on inferring that the government was making such a contention and that it needed to be rebutted. He proudly trumpeted Home-Stake's $16 million in assets without placing the figure in context: It represented only a small fraction of the amount Home-Stake had raised, squandered, and stolen. In any event, the amount of current assets had no bearing whatsoever on the trial's central question: whether Home-Stake had committed fraud.

Norman Cross hardly needed character witnesses, but Hayden Crawford presented some anyway. Judge Barrow made it obvious to everyone in the courtroom that a few of them were old friends of his. "Bill, nice to have you. Say hello to your wife," the judge said to one witness. At the end of another's testimony he said, "Thank you, Maybelle. Nice to have seen you."

"Nice to have seen you," said Maybelle. "Merry Christmas."

Barrow acquitted Cross on Wednesday, December 15. Ironically, the celebrants included a number of people who had accused Cross of wrongdoing: the investors who had filed suit against Home-Stake and its officers, accountants, and lawyers. Had Cross been convicted of criminal violations, his acts probably wouldn't have been covered by his malpractice insurance. The typical policy carried by lawyers and accountants doesn't cover willful dishonesty. The investors' best hope, therefore, was proving that Cross and other CPAs and lawyers were liable for some lesser sin, which would be covered by insurance and might be expected to trigger damage payments. (Cross, of course, continued to deny any civil or criminal wrongdoing.)

To the extent that the Cross trial had been confusing, leaden, and long, what happened next was brief, simple, amusing to some, and utterly hypocritical. Judge Barrow scheduled sentencing of Trippet, Sims, and Fitzgerald for Tuesday morning, December 21. All three, of course, had been free on bail since December 1974. Barrow abruptly revoked their bail as of nine o'clock Monday morning, the day before sentencing, and ordered them to surrender to the U.S. marshal at the federal courthouse. The marshal took them in his car across the street to the federal section of the Tulsa County jail. They weren't handcuffed, but at the jail they were spreadeagled against a wall and frisked; their belongings were confiscated and inventoried; and they were made to change out of their suits and ties and into prison blue-denim trousers and shirts. They were fingerprinted, given numbers, and photographed. Then they were led into a cellblock and locked in a standard cell equipped with a double bunk bed, a single bed, an open toilet, a wash basin and mirror, and a table and two benches.

The unnatural presence of the three Home-Stake figures amused the other inmates, many of whom had read of the case in the Tulsa papers. "How in hell did you steal $40 million?" asked a man in the next cell. "I broke my ass to steal $200 and I'll probably be here for ever. You'll do a few months or a year if you're unlucky."

The Home-Stake Three chuckled. "Don't believe everything you read in the papers," Trippet said. (The third indictment focused on investments totaling about $40 million.)

"If you give back the $40 million they'll go easier on you," another prisoner said.

"Give it back, shit. They'll be a few months in jail, then they'll get out and start spending it," retorted the first inmate.

Trippet quietly cautioned his colleagues against idle talk of Home-Stake. He feared the cell might be bugged.

The day dragged, partly because the prisoners weren't allowed to wear their watches. There was no television or radio. The jail offered only a small selection of magazines and paperback books. Harry Fitzgerald had brought along a hardcover edition of James Joyce's *Ulysses*, his lifelong passion, which he had read dozens of times and from which he still derived pleasure. But hardcover books aren't permitted in the Tulsa County jail, Joyce was confiscated, and Fitzgerald had to settle for a mystery novel. Trippet leafed through an old issue of *U.S. News and World Report*. Sims, who wasn't feeling well, read nothing.

Fitzgerald won $3 from Trippet at gin rummy.

All three men slept poorly that night, unaccustomed to the bright overhead lights and the hourly clanking of the cell-block door as a guard made his rounds.

Early Tuesday morning they washed and shaved at the cell basin and were given breakfast. They weren't allowed to shower. At nine they changed back into their own clothes, reclaimed their belongings, and were escorted back across the street to the federal courthouse.

A number of Trippet's friends and members of his family were present in the courtroom, as were several local business-men and lawyers. There were smiles all around. Everyone knew the defendants wouldn't spend another night in jail. "The next time I commit a felony, it's going to be a white-collar one," an attorney whispered.

After a brief proceeding concerning a dungaree-clad truck-driver accused of interstate transportation of stolen securities, Judge Barrow took up the case of *the United States of America* v. *Robert S. Trippet et al.* The judge began by reading, haltingly, a vague and clumsily phrased formal statement.

Now, at the conclusion of long manipulations, pleas of guilty, nolo pleas and three acquittals, transfer and retransfer, three indictments, a costly trial, thirteen weeks of trial and 6,580 pages of transcript in daily copy, certain aspects of the so-called Home-Stake trial have become clear to me as the trial judge. Not the least of these is that the whole thing is not what was pictured by some Eastern newspapers and magazines in their colorful or sensational reporting, however you want to call it, as the century's greatest swindle. . . . I have seen evidence that there was a grandiose promotional scheme that went sour. . . . I know that men concerned in the matter confessed by their pleas a degree of wrongdoing in that pleas of guilty and nolo contendere have been entered to various charged offenses. . . . These men admit having done wrong, having violated the trust that the individuals reposed in them. One must accept these confessions of fault and abide by the judgments upon themselves thereby pronounced.

As an individual, I can but wonder if the price of oil had been then as it is now . . . would the outcome have been the same. I doubt it. . . .

Now each man comes before this bench having tasted, each of them, for the first time and each in his middle years having tasted what jail is like, each having served approximately 25 hours incarcerated, each man has sat in a cell, each man has had his fingerprints taken, his belongings inventoried and was assigned a number. Yes, for some who would delight in sensationalism and seem also to delight in the evil that happens to men and suffering, each one of these men has been treated as a common criminal. . . .

I am not influenced by the howlings of certain media and other people who make their livings dramatizing the misfortunes of others so as to appeal to popular imaginations. . . . I must decide what sentence, given to each man, will relate to his individual circumstances, will deter him from ever again violating the law, and will likewise encourage him to behave lawfully in the future. . . .

I have carefully considered the facts in each case, and among them the real sufferings of a man, once proud and respected, now held in disrepute by his own admissions.

Judge Barrow then asked, "Mr. Trippet, you have spent a night in jail, a day. I don't think you like what you saw, did you?"

"No, your honor, I think that the experience I have had would have a big impact on anybody. I am certainly no exception. The room was fully spotlighted all night long, very noisy, and I slept not a wink, and I remember it vividly."

"I imagine you will remember it forever."

"I am sure I will."

"But you can imagine what fifty years would be like, then."

"Yes, sir."

"I think this will give also a lot of people a view of some reform that needs to be done in jails, the over-crowded conditions of places of incarceration, as well; it's a serious problem," Barrow said.

Trippet was invited to be seated. He settled into a chair at the defense table, leaned back, and surveyed the scene like the chairman of the board he once was.

Barrow then called on his long-time friend and confidant, Pat Malloy, the lawyer who had negotiated the no-contest plea for Trippet. Malloy—a bluff Irishman with long silver hair, a flushed face, and a small potbelly—orated for fifteen minutes. He pleaded for mercy for his client. He said Trippet had entered his plea not because he was guilty but because of the "persistent and recurring tragic and serious health problems plaguing not only the defendant, but also members of his family." In addition, the Home-Stake criminal case had been based mainly on "falsehoods originally initiated by the press," he said.

A lack of serious investigation and a flare for sensationalism and the dramatic all led to the appearance in *The Wall Street Journal* of a feature article that catapulted the California prosecutors into the hurried and irresponsible indictments—"Ponzi scheme," "pink pipes," "fraud of poor investors," "Black books," "missing money stashed in Swiss bank accounts," catch phrases, movie stuff, Arthur Haley novel material but not evidence. Fortunately, your honor, still in this country newspapers do not convict when the judges involved are guided by the evidence, not headlines, and by facts, not pressure. . . .[2]

[2] Malloy's remarks, like much that was said on all sides on December 21, was courtroom bombast that few people if any took seriously. However, it would seem wise to state for the record that the press, of course, "initiated" nothing in the Home-Stake case, "falsehoods" or otherwise. As Malloy and Judge Barrow well knew or should have known, the original *Wall Street Journal* article and other stories reported the existence of some thirty lawsuits and voluminous other documents filed months earlier by the SEC and well over one hundred investors. The lawsuits asserted unanimously that Home-Stake had operated a giant Ponzi scheme and offered substantial evidence to support their allegations. It appeared as this book was written that most of those lawsuits would be settled out of court, as most are. No *Wall Street Journal* article nor any other article of which the author is aware nor any lawsuit said anything about "fraud on poor investors" or "missing money stashed in Swiss bank accounts." As for the

Finally, your honor, I shall submit to you, as you know better than I, that sentencing is a lonely task. It is my opinion predicated on years of observation that you approach the task of sentencing with great seriousness and with but one thought in mind, to see justice done.

Barrow recognized William Hawes, who had arrived only shortly before the court session after an all-night flight from Los Angeles. Hawes reiterated a memorandum the government had filed asking "very substantial sentences" for Trippet and Sims.

Any less imposition of penalty by the court in this case would sanction the flagrant thievery and the calculated, premeditated crimes of Trippet, Sims and others in similar situations. That the defendant is a so-called "white-collar criminal" with status and education provides no basis whatsoever for judicial treatment more lenient than criminals who have not obtained the "white-collar" label. Indeed, the defendant's advantaged background only serves to underscore the calculated, premeditated nature of his crime. Moreover, this court should not condone a double standard of justice which accords lighter sentences for those criminals from the middle and upper classes.

At stake is the integrity of the criminal justice system. If it is to have any real meaning . . . then individuals such as Trippet and Sims must be held responsible for their conduct and significant punishment must follow from their pervasive criminal activity.

Hawes's extemporaneous remarks were weaker.

The Holy Bible talks about our Father in Heaven being the ultimate judge of our fellow man. I subscribe to the Christian religion, your honor, and I think it would be very difficult for me to take your position and sentence any of these gentlemen, even though I know the facts, I think I appreciate the facts, I would still have a very difficult time, Your Honor, and I would be swayed by the eloquence presented by counsel for Mr. Trippet and I would also be swayed by Mr. Trippet's comments.

---

so-called pink pipes and Black Books, their existence was certified repeatedly under oath by numerous witnesses at the Cross trial and in other official proceedings and was never refuted.

Judge Barrow said that Trippet's health and the health of his family were the "main things influencing this court" in imposing sentence. (Trippet underwent open-heart surgery in May 1975 and recovered. Certain members of his family were under psychiatric care in 1976.) Barrow placed Trippet on three years supervised probation and fined him $19,000, the maximum fine for the ten felony crimes of which he stood convicted. The judge also ordered Trippet to pay $100,000 to the Home-Stake bankruptcy trustee.

> The money shall be held by the Trustee for the benefit of widows, orphans or children of participants or for destitute participants who file a claim with the trustee within one year showing proof of actual loss from their Home-Stake investment.[3]
> This group of claimants shall not include the sophisticated and knowledgeable investors, heads of corporations, investors who had the advice of investment counselors, CPAs or stockbrokers. Any loss shall be computed so as not to include any amount saved by the claimants as a result of income tax benefits received.

Barrow stipulated that if there weren't enough valid claims to exhaust the $100,000, the remaining money would be returned to Trippet.

"I wish you well, and I hope that was a good experience last night," the judge told Trippet.

"Thank you, your honor."

Barrow called Frank Sims to the bench.

"Is there anything you would like to say to the court now as to why the court should not impose sentence at this time or anything you would like to say in mitigation?"

---

[3] "Widows and orphans" is an expression used by sophisticated investors and investment salesmen to describe, usually condescendingly, investors of little sophistication and meager means. Judge Barrow's literal introduction of this category of investor into the formal Trippet sentencing order caused a great deal of confusion. Apparently Barrow was trying to affect droll wit and at the same time stress the obvious point that very few unsophisticated people invested in Home-Stake and emphasize his belief that the other investors deserved no sympathy. The prescribed disposition of the $100,000 was so vague that Barrow was forced to issue a formal order on December 30 clarifying it, and another on January 26 clarifying the December 30 order.

"No."

"I don't suppose you enjoyed your experience of 25 hours in jail, did you?"

"The worst day in my life."

"You will never forget it?"

"It wasn't one day, it was 1,440 minutes times 60 seconds. I suffered, we all suffered in our own way, but we all concluded that we can't go to jail. We aren't the type. We would die."

"This is a great gamble I wanted all of you to see you were taking. Here you are exposed to fifty years imprisonment if the court accepted this plea."

"I thought of that."

"And you see what one night is. Of course, this is something else in tailoring the sentence to suit the crime and the individual. People don't sometimes realize it. I have pros that are in here, 20 years is nothing, and to others, one day is a lifetime. So, I think this will probably accentuate, just from your own statement it is something you will never forget. The whole thing wasn't worth it, was it?"

"No sir."

". . . I hope you see the severity of the gamble you were taking when you were involved in this whole—it's the type situation if you rub shoulders, you can almost be involved in it by just mere appearance. That is the danger of a conspiracy."

Barrow didn't fine Sims, but he placed him on probation for a year and ordered him to pay $5,000 to the fund for civil claimants under the same terms prescribed for Trippet's $100,000.

That left Harry Fitzgerald, who had pleaded guilty to two felony securities violations, for which he could have been sentenced to ten years in prison and fined $10,000. "We do have a few comments to make," Fitzgerald's lawyer said, "especially in light of the fact that some of the press is still here that followed this case so closely for so long. Maybe they can communicate to their readers what criminal justice is about."

Judge Barrow said to Fitzgerald, "You have done well under your control of drinking, apparently, for 17 years, except for a couple of slips. Do you still have it under control?"

"I beg your pardon."

"Do you still have it under control, your drinking problem?"

"Yes, sir, your honor, day by day."

"Seventeen years except for two or three slips?"

"Yes, your honor, almost made 12 years completely."

"That is very commendable."

"Thank you."

"And as you say, it is a day by day thing with you, isn't it?"

"Indefinitely into the future, yes, your honor."

Fitzgerald had filed a financial statement with the court indicating that he was bankrupt. Barrow put him on unsupervised probation for a year and didn't fine him or order him to contribute to the civil claimants' fund. The judge also invited Fitzgerald to change his guilty plea to no-contest.

"Thank you, Mr. Hawes," Barrow said. "Nice seeing you, and I hope you come back again on a shorter case."

"Your honor, I think I will retire, it's over. I wouldn't miss this for anything in the world. . . . It's a culmination of a really difficult experience for me, but it has been very rewarding, too, and I would like to appreciate or express my appreciation to your honor, you have been very, very cordial to me. I remember the first time I walked into the building I wasn't too popular. I was, as your honor indicated, carrying the ball in a case that has experienced many difficulties, and I would like to express my appreciation to your honor and to your honor's staff for the diligence that they expressed and to everyone in this courthouse and this town."

"Thank you, Mr. Hawes."

"It's been a good experience, your honor."

"I appreciate it, and we appreciate having you."

"I enjoyed it."

"I hope it will be under more favorable circumstances next time."

"I hope so, too."

"Have a nice Christmas and trip home."

"I would like to extend that courtesy to you, have a nice Christmas and a Happy New Year."

"Thank you very much."

The Tulsa *Tribune*'s lead editorial on the day following sentencing was entitled "One Night in Jail."

On Tuesday, U.S. District Judge Allen E. Barrow of Tulsa seemed to have accomplished the difficult feat of topping himself in the matter of trivial sentences.

Although the [Home-Stake] principals did not put on a defense, having pleaded guilty or nolo contendere, it was the general theory of the defense that investors lost little since most were seeking shelters from high income taxes. Judge Barrow seems to have eagerly seized on this idea. It is true that by adroitly combining "charitable giving" and the statute of limitations, a clever operator could get robbed and still feel no pain. Nevertheless, for most Home-Stake investors there were obvious losses. . . .

Was the judge indicating that he takes a light view of any larceny that doesn't wipe out its victim? There is no doubt that the U.S. Treasury was a big loser in Home-Stake. For any write-offs for bad Home-Stake investments reduced income taxes.

Judge Barrow referred gently to the Home-Stake caper as a "grandiose promotional scheme that went sour." It was much more than that. It was a Ponzi game, featuring technicolored oil production claims and the old business of keeping older investors happy by paying "dividends" out of the proceeds of the sale of new shares.

Bob and Helen Grey Trippet sent separate notes and a Christmas card to Allen Barrow's home.

On Tuesday, you saved four lives—my wife's, my two daughters[1] and mine. This Christmas will indeed be a happy and joyous one for our little family, all thanks to you. . . . You have always acted courageously and fairly. You are a credit to your profession and to your high calling.

Most sincerely,
Bob

The Christmas card, with the engraved signature "Helen Grey and Bob," was the same one they sent to all their friends. It ended with a quotation: "This day shall change all griefs and quarrels into love."—William Shakespeare

The Home-Stake criminal case was concluded formally on Monday, February 7, 1977, when the office of the U.S. attorney in New York City, acting on behalf of the Justice Department, dismissed the criminal conspiracy charge against tax lawyer and shelter salesman Kent Klineman. It was the only practical course. Some people in the Los Angeles U.S. attorney's office still were willing to try Klineman. But fraud unit chief Stephen Wilson, who had conducted the original grand jury investigation, decided that the same reasons which prevented him from spending an extended period in Tulsa also would preclude his going to New York for a trial. The Justice Department didn't particularly want to entrust the case to William Hawes, who already had lost two Home-Stake trials. Washington-based Jay Johnson was tired of being on the road away from his family.

As far as the New York U.S. attorney's office was concerned, it couldn't work up any enthusiasm about prosecuting the peripheral thirteenth defendant in what was alleged to have been a thirteen-man conspiracy. No glory in that. Besides, the trial inevitably would be long. Since Klineman was accused of conspiracy, a certain amount of evidence against the other alleged conspirators, as well as the evidence against Klineman, would have to be presented. Most important, the government lawyers in New York felt that the Tulsa indictment was poorly drafted, and that the Klineman evidence wasn't as strong as Stephen Wilson believed it was when he sought the original indictment.

---

[1] It wasn't clear why Trippet didn't mention his third daughter.

Prosecuting Klineman had been Wilson's idea all along, of course. William Hawes hadn't been enthusiastic about it, nor had the SEC. Even if Klineman were convicted, his sentence, in view of the light penalties imposed on the major defendants, would be limited to probation and possibly a fine.

The New York fraud unit therefore recommended to the Justice Department that the indictment be dropped. The department's formal statement said: "It has been concluded that the evidence against Klineman isn't sufficient to justify the expenditure of the resources necessary to try the case since it appears unlikely that the prosecution would be successful."

Two years, two months, and countless thousands of manhours and dollars after the initial indictment, the Home-Stake criminal case showed the following results:

Robert S. Trippet: pleaded no-contest; convicted of one count of conspiracy and nine counts of mail fraud; one day in jail; three years supervised probation; $19,000 fine; $100,000 to fund for civil claimants.

Frank E. Sims: pleaded no-contest; convicted of one count of conspiracy and nine counts of mail fraud; one day in jail; one year probation; no fine; $5,000 to fund for civil claimants.

Harry L. Fitzgerald: pleaded guilty; convicted of two felony securities violations; changed plea to no-contest at the invitation of the judge; conviction stood; one day in jail; one year unsupervised probation; no fine; no payment to fund for civil claimants.

John T. Lenoir: pleaded guilty; convicted of one count of conspiracy and one count of aiding and abetting the preparation of false federal income-tax returns; no jail, no fine, two years probation. (The counts to which Lenoir pleaded guilty were in the first indictment, returned in December 1974, which alleged that the conspiracy began when Home-Stake was founded in 1955.)

Elmer M. Kunkel: pleaded no-contest after admitting to the judge that he was guilty of one misdemeanor securities violation; $5,000 fine revoked.

Norman C. Cross, Jr., F. Conrad Greer, Richard A. Ganong: acquitted of criminal wrongdoing after trial.

David C. Davies, Larry A. Martin, Thomas A. Landrith, Jr., Herbert A. Smith, Kent M. Klineman: charges of criminal wrongdoing dropped by the U.S. Justice Department.

Less glamorous but financially far more significant than the criminal prosecution were the civil lawsuits against Home-Stake, Trippet, and the others,[2] which languished through much of the protracted criminal proceeding. As long as the criminal defendants were under indictment, they could assert their Fifth Amendment privilege against self-incrimination in the civil suits as well as in the criminal case. But as the prosecution struggled through its final months, the civil litigation began to move faster.

Senior U.S. District Judge George H. Boldt, the circuit-riding judge from Tacoma, Washington, who had been assigned to preside over the Home-Stake civil suits, tentatively certified as a class action the suit filed in March 1973, and amended in May 1974, by San Francisco lawyer William A. Wineberg, Jr., on behalf of Walter Matthau, businessman Ivan Anixter, World Bank economist Blanche Dickinson, Pentagon civil servant Dolly Yoshida and others. The suit and accompanying documents alleged that a "continuing conspiracy" to defraud investors by means of a Ponzi scheme began at Home-Stake sometime prior to July 1960. The class-action ruling essentially gave Home-Stake's three thousand investors a roughly equal chance to recover damages in proportion to the relative size of their investments. In effect, the other suits filed against Home-Stake became part of the class-action suit. The other principal attorneys—R. Dobie Langenkamp repre-

[2] As of mid-1977, the persons named as defendants in one or more lawsuits included all the original defendants in the criminal case except Conrad Greer, Larry Martin, and David Davies. The civil defendants also included former Home-Stake directors Brooks Gutelius, Jr., and J. D. Metcalfe; former officers Carl E. Clay, Jackson M. Barton, Marvin R. Barnett, and Donald Larrabee; lawyers Harry Heller, William Blum, William E. Murray, and Kent Klineman; the law firms of Simpson Thacher & Bartlett, and Murray, Patterson & Sharpe of New York; McAfee, Taft, Mark, Bond, Rucks & Woodruff of Oklahoma City; and Kothe & Eagleton of Tulsa; the CPA firms of Arthur Andersen & Company of Chicago, McKee Atkins & Schuler of Tulsa, and Cross & Company of Tulsa; petroleum geologist William D. Lewis and the California consulting firm of Lewis & Ganong; and the First National Bank & Trust Company of Tulsa.

senting the Judson Streicher group, Harold F. McGuire, Jr., representing the General Electric group, and Peter Van N. Lockwood representing the Leachman group—became William Wineberg's co-counsel.

In the summer of 1976, Judge Boldt ordered the civil plaintiffs and defendants to begin gathering evidence for trial. That required months of depositions—formal transcribed interrogations conducted by the plaintiffs' and defendants' counsel of all the important figures in the case. One of the first people to be interrogated was Conrad Greer; his deposition alone took up several weeks. Early in the Greer deposition, it was discovered that he had kept a diary throughout much of the time he was a Home-Stake engineer and officer. The diary somehow had escaped the attention of the SEC and Justice Department lawyers during their unsuccessful prosecution of Greer. It became important evidence in the civil litigation. As chief engineer at Santa Maria, Conrad Greer had had extensive personal contact not only with Trippet and Sims but with consulting engineer Richard Ganong; IRS agents investigating the value of Home-Stake gifts to charity; a large number of investors; and other figures on both the plaintiffs' and defendants' sides of the case. His record of these contacts was very useful in reconstructing Home-Stake's history and the actions and states of mind of key figures.

Depositions also were taken from investors, Home-Stake officers, and others close to the company. Although the class-action lawsuit did not estimate damages in dollar terms, the plaintiffs clearly were seeking many millions of dollars.

Meanwhile, the IRS continued to press tax claims against Home-Stake totaling more than $30 million. The agency also challenged about $37 million in tax deductions that investors had taken for drilling investments and charitable gifts since 1969. An additional $100 million-plus in investor tax deductions was protected from IRS audit by the statute of limitations.

Separately, bankruptcy trustee Royce Savage proceeded with a series of lawsuits against Trippet, Sims, Fitzgerald, Landrith, several other former Home-Stake officers and directors, and New York lawyers William Murray and Kent Klineman. The suits were drafted by Savage's legal counsel, Anthony Ringold and Gene Mortensen of the Tulsa law firm Rosenstein, Fist &

Ringold. They accused Trippet, and to a considerably lesser degree the others, of fraud dating back to 1958. Damages of $108.4 million were sought—$55.4 million actual and $53 million punitive. The suits accused Trippet of having illegally removed a minimum of $6 million from Home-Stake for his personal use or for his family or close business associates. In addition, the lawsuits said, Trippet had bilked the company in other ways that couldn't be measured because he had altered, removed, and canceled entries in the company's books. The complaints charged that from 1958 through 1973 Trippet had "caused Home-Stake to make unauthorized, illegal and fraudulent payments and gifts without any or adequate consideration"; continually had "borrowed money from Home-Stake" without paying interest; and had used Home-Stake credit cards and funds to buy, use, or "otherwise receive the benefit of" cars, food, and other personal items for himself and his family.

Trippet and the other defendants continued to deny all allegations of wrongdoing in the lawsuits. In a deposition in the late winter of 1977, Trippet rebutted various charges. Among other things, he said that Home-Stake had had "many sources of income" and hadn't made payments to investors from their own funds. He said that he had sold his reversionary interests to provide funds for his retirement; his health was deteriorating and he wanted to leave Home-Stake. He sold the interests in 1969, he said, because capital gains taxes, which would be applied to the sale, were expected to rise in 1970. Trippet also asserted that he hadn't misled the Home-Stake directors in August, 1971, when he told them about the reversionary interest deal.

As for the allegedly dummy corporations, Trippet said they had, in fact, been real and had actually performed valuable services for Home-Stake. He said that the only things he took from the company were a couple of used cars, which he gave to his daughters instead of to "the junkie," presumably a reference to a junk dealer.

William E. Murray, as one of several lines of defense, said he had been "instrumental in adding safeguards" for investors to the 1972 Home-Stake program. Murray added that after Home-Stake filed for bankruptcy reorganization he advised investors to form a committee to protect their interests. A committee was formed and represented the 1972 investors' interests effectively, he said.

The bankruptcy trustee's suit against Kent Klineman was settled in April 1977, when Klineman agreed to pay the company $100,000.

The poor condition of Home-Stake's books made it impossible to account for every dollar, or even every hundred thousand dollars, of the approximately $140 million that had passed through the company. It appeared from rough calculations that Home-Stake had spent about $50 million over the years solely to operate and conceal the Ponzi scheme—buying back drilling units from disgruntled investors, making quarterly pro. rev. payments in the guise of oil revenues, and paying dividends on common stock to make it appear that the company was earning legitimate profits. The company likely had expended an additional $15 million or more since it was founded on its sales efforts: salaries, travel, entertainment, office overhead, and other costs.

It may never be known how much Home-Stake actually spent drilling for oil, but the figure probably is in the $30 million range, or only about 21 percent of what it was committed to spend.

The sum of those major components—$6 million allegedly diverted by Trippet; $50 million spent lulling investors; $15 million in selling expenses; and $30 million drilling for oil—is $101 million, leaving $39 million to be accounted for of the $140 million believed to have been collected. Much of that $39 million appears to have been used for a large number of other general expenses of running the company over eighteen years as well as for various miscellaneous activities in which Home-Stake was involved. It invested more than $5 million, for example, in limestone mining and processing in Arizona and more than $2.5 million in apartment complexes in California. In addition, there were many relatively small outlays, such as $20,000 for the plot of land in Mexico where *The Night of the Iguana* was filmed. And a sizeable amount of money was consumed by taxes; the company reported part of investor contributions as income each year and paid taxes on it.

Regardless of how the $140 million is accounted for, it was

clear that neither the IRS, the investors, nor the bankruptcy trustees on behalf of the creditors would collect more than a small fraction of the huge amounts they sought. The one indisputable fact was that out of $140 million, only about $16 million in cash and property was left. It was that amount that the contending parties were fighting over and ultimately were to divide.[3]

In addition to getting far less than it wanted out of the carcass of the company, the IRS apparently would have to settle for only a small portion of the amount it sought from the investors. Of the $37 million in tax deductions that was disputed, the IRS was reasonably sure of denying successfully only about $14 million—the amount deducted in 1970, 1971, and 1972 for gifts of Home-Stake units to charity. The other $23 million represented drilling deductions; and to the extent that the IRS succeeded in barring them, the investors could attempt to substitute theft-loss deductions.[4]

The difficulties of tracing every dollar Home-Stake collected also hampered efforts to compute losses. There was no question,

[3] The $16 million was the assets left in the company. The amount didn't include Trippet's or other defendants' personal funds or potential collections from lawyers' and accountants' malpractice insurance policies.

[4] In mid-1977 it was by no means certain that the IRS would allow theft-loss deductions. Taxpayers are required to meet very exacting criteria to sustain the deductions. And, even if granted, theft-loss deductions loomed as a mixed blessing. The investors still were liable for interest on whatever additional tax was assessed as a result of losing the drilling deductions. The interest accrued from the years of the barred deductions (1970-1972) until the year of settlement or court judgment (probably no earlier than 1978 and maybe later). Furthermore, the theft deductions weren't allowed for the year of the original drilling deductions. Because some investors' tax situations varied substantially from year to year, the need to switch years disrupted tax planning. Theft-loss deductions normally are granted only in the year a theft is discovered, or in the year when it becomes clear that the taxpayer hasn't any reasonable prospect of recovering the loss. It could be argued that the year of discovery in the Home-Stake case was 1973, when the SEC accused Home-Stake of fraud. It appeared, however, that the amount of damage recovery, if any, might not be known until 1978 or later, when the lawsuits were expected to be disposed of. Thus, it was anticipated that the theft-loss deductions wouldn't be granted until then, if at all.

however, that the biggest loser of all was the Treasury Department—and thus the U.S. taxpayer. Rough estimates indicated that the Treasury lost about $75 million in tax revenues denied it as a result of improper tax deductions fostered by Home-Stake. (See Estimate of Losses, page 301.) The value of Home-Stake's common stock declined from more than $12 million to zero. On investments in drilling units, Home-Stake's clients lost about $90 million, before tax considerations. After deductions, taxes, and interest, it looked as if the investors emerged from the swindle with about $25 million less than they would have had if they had not made the investment and had paid full taxes on their $140 million. Thus, instead of sheltering the investors from taxation, the swindle in effect lifted them into a higher tax bracket with no shelter.

The net loss to all concerned parties, then, was at least $112 million—the sum of $75 million, $12 million, and $25 million. That figure, however, doesn't measure the investors' loss in terms of profits they might have netted had they invested their money elsewhere during the time that Home-Stake had it. Nor does the figure include an estimate of the petroleum energy lost to society as a result of Home-Stake's failure to spend most of the money it collected on oil drilling. Although these calculations would be speculative, they would boost the total loss much higher. On the other hand, the loss estimate excludes any projection of damages the investors might collect from their lawsuits, and any return they might receive from drilling on properties that other oil companies have taken over from the Home-Stake bankruptcy trustee.

It is not necessary to discourse at length here on the lessons of Home-Stake. What the case says about the U.S. tax-shelter system; the government's ability to enforce the law; the white-collar criminal justice apparatus; and the financial perspicacity of some wealthy people is clear from the foregoing narrative. Moreover, although a number of valid generalizations can be drawn, it must be recognized that Home-Stake was not a typical case. It was extraordinary. Robert Trippet unquestionably was one of the most skilled swindlers of this or any century.

Although the Home-Stake affair made many investors wary,

it didn't make them wary enough to stay away from tax shelters, only to look for alternatives to Home-Stake. Some got lucky; others didn't.

From 1964 through 1971, Spottswood Wellford Corbin, then a high-level vice-president of the General Electric Company, invested $155,000 in Home-Stake drilling programs. He was one of the many who later sued to try to recover damages.

In 1972 Corbin switched tax shelters. He invested $20,000 in Prudential Funds Inc., another oil drilling concern. The SEC later alleged that Prudential had misrepresented its 1972 drilling programs. The company consented to a court order against securities law violations without admitting any wrongdoing.

In 1973 Spottswood Corbin found yet another shelter, Lafayette Funds of Shreveport, Louisiana. By the end of 1975 he had put $40,000 into Lafayette, an oil company run by J. C. Trahan, a flamboyant former oil-field worker. Trahan used to visit New York's 21 often enough to be assured of a good table and a hug from the hat-check girl. He sported a pair of cufflinks made from large gold discs bearing miniature oil wells spewing diamonds.

On December 14, 1976, after several months of investigation, the SEC charged Lafayette and Trahan with fraud and misuse of funds. They said that they had done nothing wrong, but agreed to an injunction against securities violations.

The Home-Stake affair and other instances of tax-shelter abuse helped spur Congress in late 1976 to enact additional curbs on the ability of the wealthy to defer taxation by investing in shelters. But the shelter laws remained extremely complex, and the IRS's ability to enforce them still was limited. The nation's tax lawyers and accountants pounced on the 1976 tax act like a new toy. Before long they were finding fresh opportunities to shelter their clients' income. Greed, it seemed, was still deductible.

Estimate of Losses *

* These figures represent a rough financial profile of the Home-Stake swindle as a whole. Based on the latest data available in mid-1977, the figures are general estimates and involve a degree of oversimplification for the sake of clarity. Some investors' cases, because of widely varying individual financial circumstances, may differ considerably from the proportions and percentages shown here. For example, by no means have all investors made gifts to charity.

Amount Home-Stake collected from investors, 1955–1972	$140,000,000
Projected return to investors (300 percent) [NOTE 1]	420,000,000
Actual return to investors	50,000,000
Difference between projected and actual return	370,000,000
Loss on drilling investments (outlay minus return, not counting tax considerations)	$ 90,000,000
Decline in market value of common stock	12,000,000
Total loss to investors (not counting tax considerations)	102,000,000
Tax deductions taken for drilling investments	$140,000,000
Tax deductions taken for charitable gifts	40,000,000
Total tax deductions	180,000,000
Drilling deductions validated by actual drilling	30,000,000
Gift deductions validated by actual income and value	1,000,000
Improper drilling deductions (total minus those validated by drilling)	110,000,000
Improper gift deductions (total minus those validated by value)	39,000,000

Total improper tax deductions	149,000,000
Improper deductions beyond IRS challenge because of statute of limitations (deductions taken in 1969 and earlier) [NOTE 2]	102,125,000
Improper drilling deductions under actual or potential challenge by the IRS (1970, 1971, 1972) [NOTE 3]	30,000,000
Improper gift deductions under actual or potential challenge by the IRS (1970–1972)	14,000,000
Total improper deductions potentially under IRS challenge	44,000,000
Deductions for which theft-loss deductions possibly may be substituted [NOTE 4]	30,000,000
Total unrecoverable improper deductions (assuming theft-loss deductions are allowed)	132,125,000
Loss of tax revenue to U.S. Treasury from unrecoverable improper deductions (assuming average taxpayer is in 60-percent bracket)	79,275,000
Energy loss to society from Home-Stake's failure to spend $110,000,000 drilling for oil	Incalculable
Tax savings to investors from drilling deductions (assuming they are in 60 percent bracket and theft-loss deductions are allowed)	$ 84,000,000
Tax savings from charitable gift deductions beyond IRS challenge	15,000,000
Net investment (after subtracting tax savings)	41,000,000
Tax on $50,000,000 return on investment [NOTE 5]	20,000,000
Net return on investment	30,000,000
Net loss (net investment minus net return)	11,000,000
Potential interest on back taxes [NOTE 6]	14,000,000
Total net loss, considering tax savings, taxes on return, and interest on back taxes (in addition to investors' expenditure on Home-Stake of an amount equal to what they would have paid in taxes had they not made the investments)	25,000,000
Difference between Home-Stake's actual return to investors (after taxes) and amount they would have received if Home-Stake had paid them a return equal to their investment, with no profit or loss [NOTE 7]	63,000,000

Minimum after-tax loss from Home-Stake swindle:

U.S. Treasury [NOTE 8]	$ 79,275,000
Drilling units [NOTE 9]	25,000,000
Common stock	12,000,000
Total	116,275,000

NOTE 1: Home-Stake normally projected at least a 300-percent return, and often higher.

NOTE 2: It is assumed that Home-Stake spent 21 percent (30/140) of its collections on drilling each year, and that the other 79 percent of the deductions is improper. The 21 percent is an estimated average. The percentage varied from year to year, and generally declined during the eighteen years of the Home-Stake affair.

Under the statute of limitations, the IRS generally must audit a tax return within three years after it is due, normally on April 15. The IRS did not begin blanket audits of Home-Stake investors until after April 15, 1973, the deadline for auditing 1969 returns. Thus, most deductions taken in 1969 and earlier are protected.

NOTE 3: This is a very conservative estimate.

NOTE 4: See the explanation of theft-loss deductions in footnote on page 298.

NOTE 5: The effective tax rate on the return that Home-Stake paid to investors is assumed to have been 40 percent. The returns were taxed at various rates, most of them lower than the 60-percent ordinary income-tax rate. The rate depended on the form of the payment from Home-Stake, for example, repurchase of a drilling unit, "pro. rev.," or the minimal actual oil revenues.

NOTE 6: It is assumed that most of the tax audits will be settled in 1979.

NOTE 7: Had Home-Stake been legitimate and the deductions withstood IRS scrutiny, the tax savings would have totaled $108 million—$84 million from the $140 million in drilling deductions, and $24 million from the $40 million in charitable deductions—leaving a net investment of $32 million. If Home-Stake had paid the investors a legitimate return equal to their $140 million investment—no profit, no loss—the effective tax rate on the return problably would have been around 40 percent, $56 million, leaving a net return of $84 million. Subtracting the $32 million net investment leaves a $52 million after-tax profit—an excess of $63 million over the $11 million net loss (excluding interest on back taxes) that the investors actually experienced.

NOTE 8: Some might feel that the $14 million in interest on back taxes that investors may have to pay amounts to partial compensation to the U.S. Treasury for the lost income-tax revenues. Under that concept, the Treasury's net loss would be $61,405,600.

NOTE 9: This amount constitutes the investors' loss in excess of the portion of their Home-Stake investment that would have been payable in taxes had they not made the investment. The figure does not include an estimate of energy loss resulting from Home-Stake's failure to spend $110 million on drilling. Nor does it attempt to measure loss in terms of profits that investors might have realized had their money been invested in legitimate, profitable tax shelters for the same amount of time rather than in Home-Stake. These factors considered, the total loss would be much higher, although it would be reduced to the extent that the investors collected damages from their lawsuits. And interest payments to the government on back taxes are deductible just like any other interest payment.

Investors

Listed here are some of the more prominent investors in the Home-Stake Production Company.

THE ARTS AND SPORTS

Alan Alda
Ed Ames
David Begelman: President, Columbia Pictures.
Jack Benny
Candice Bergen
Jacqueline Bisset
Bill Blass
Joseph Bologna and Renee Taylor: Husband and wife, screen writers and actors (*Lovers and Other Strangers, Made for Each Other*).
Martin Bregman: Film producer (*Serpico, Dog Day Afternoon*) and business and career manager for entertainers.
John Calley: Vice-chairman, Warner Bros.
Diahann Carroll
David Cassidy
Jack Cassidy
Oleg Cassini
Saul Chaplin: Film producer (*That's Entertainment, Part Two*).
Tony Curtis
Phil D'Antoni: Film producer (*The French Connection*).
Delmer Daves: Film director, producer, and writer (*A Summer Place, An Affair to Remember*).
Sandy Dennis

Phyllis Diller
William Dozier: Television producer.
Faye Dunaway
Bob Dylan
Mia Farrow
Freddie Fields: Prominent talent agent and film producer.
Bobbie Gentry
Leopold Godowsky: Violinist, chemist (coinventor of Kodachrome processing), and brother-in-law of George and Ira Gershwin.
George J. W. Goodman: Author (under the pseudonym "Adam Smith") of *The Money Game* and *Supermoney.*
John Guedel: Television and radio producer (Art Linkletter's "House Party," Groucho Marx's "You Bet Your Life").
Buddy Hackett
Shirley Jones
Jennings Lang: Senior executive vice-president in charge of feature films, MCA Incorporated, a large entertainment concern.
Walter Matthau
Liza Minnelli
Thurman Munson: Catcher, the New York Yankees.
Ozzie Nelson
Mike Nichols
Tony Roberts
Buffy Sainte-Marie
Barbra Streisand
Calvin Tomkins: Writer, *The New Yorker.*
Brenda Vaccaro
Barbara Walters
Frank G. Wells: President, Warner Bros.
Andy Williams
Jonathan Winters

POLITICS

Ernest F. Hollings, senator from South Carolina
Jacob K. Javits, senator from New York
Claude R. Kirk, Jr., former governor of Florida

BUSINESS

In most instances, titles and corporate affiliations are listed as they were when these people made their investments. Some later changed jobs or retired.

Hoyt Ammidon: Chairman, United States Trust Company of New York.

Eaton W. Ballard: Executive vice-president, Carter Hawley Hale Stores Incorporated (Neiman-Marcus, Bergdorf Goodman).

George L. Bartlett: Partner, Thomson McKinnon Securities Incorporated, a securities firm.

Bernard D. Broeker: Executive vice-president, Bethlehem Steel Corporation.

Howard D. Brundage: Executive vice-president, finance, J. Walter Thompson Company.

E. T. Collinsworth, Jr.: Executive vice-president. Armour & Company.

John C. Dawkins: Partner, Faulkner, Dawkins & Sullivan, a securities firm.

Disque D. Deane: Partner, Lazard Freres & Company, an investment banking firm.

John Ellis: Partner, Eastman Dillon, Union Securities & Company, a securities firm (now part of Blyth Eastman Dillon & Company).

John M. Evans: Vice-president, general counsel, and secretary, Western Union Corporation.

Dean P. Fite: Vice-president and group executive, Procter & Gamble Company.

Lewis W. Foy: President, Bethlehem Steel Corporation.

Thomas S. Gates: Former secretary of defense and United States envoy to the Peoples' Republic of China; former director and chairman, Morgan Guaranty Trust Company of New York.

Morgan H. Grace: Partner, Sterling, Grace & Company, a securities firm.

John W. Hanes, Jr.: Partner, Wertheim & Company, a securities firm.

Jack Hanson: Senior vice-president and treasurer, R. H. Macy & Company.

Reese H. Harris, Jr.: Executive vice-president, Manufacturers Hanover Trust Company.

Ralph A. Hart: Director and former chairman, Heublein Incorporated.

Harold M. Hecht: Retired chairman, J. W. Robinson Company, a large Los Angeles department store chain; director of its parent company, Associated Dry Goods Corporation.

Victor Holt, Jr.: Former president, Goodyear Tire & Rubber Company.

Gerald A. Hoyt: Former executive vice-president, Western Union Corporation.

Charles O. Johnston: Executive vice-president, Western Union Corporation.

George S. Jones: Partner, Wertheim & Company.

Matthew W. Kanin: Independent investment analyst and manager.

Donald M. Kendall: Chairman, PepsiCo Incorporated (formerly Pepsi Cola Company).

William D. Kerr: Partner, Wertheim & Company.

Joseph Klingenstein: Partner, Wertheim & Company.

William S. Lasdon: Director and former chairman of the executive committee, Warner-Lambert Company.

Robert L. Loeb: Partner, L. F. Rothschild & Company, a securities firm.

Peter Paul Luce: Son of Henry R. Luce, founder of Time Incorporated.

David J. Mahoney: Chairman, Norton Simon Incorporated.

Richard L. Maloney: Vice-president, Salomon Brothers, a securities firm.

John G. Martin: Director and chairman of the executive committee, Heublein Incorporated.

Neil H. McElroy: Former secretary of defense and former chairman, Procter & Gamble Company.

Russell W. McFall: Chairman and president, Western Union Corporation.

Paul Miller: Chairman, Gannett Company, a newspaper chain.

Paul L. Miller: President, First Boston Corporation, a securities firm.

Ernest L. Molloy: Director and former president, R. H. Macy & Company.

George S. Moore: Former chairman, Citicorp and Citibank (formerly First National City Corporation and First National City Bank of New York), the nation's second largest bank.

William H. Morton: Chairman of the executive committee, Singer Company; former president, American Express Company.

Chester W. Nimitz, Jr.: Chairman, Perkin-Elmer Corporation, a Connecticut scientific instruments concern; former Navy rear admiral and son of the World War II naval hero.

Norwood Norfleet: Partner, Reynolds Securities Incorporated, a securities firm.

Robert S. Oelman: Chairman, NCR Corporation (formerly National Cash Register Corporation).

Redvers Opie: Independent businessman, Washington, D.C., and Mexico City.

Andrew N. Overby: Vice-chairman, First Boston Corporation.

Emil J. Pattberg, Jr.: Chairman, First Boston Corporation.

Milton Pauley: Partner, Troster, Singer & Company, a securities firm.

Henry R. Roberts: President, Connecticut General Insurance Corporation.

Thomas B. Ross: Vice-president, Merrill Lynch, Pierce Fenner & Smith Incorporated.

James R. Shepley: President, Time Incorporated.

Muriel Siebert: Wall Street securities broker and the first female member of the New York Stock Exchange; named New York State Superintendent of Banks in 1977.

Louis P. Singer: Partner, Troster, Singer & Company, a securities firm.

Donald B. Smiley: Chairman, R. H. Macy & Company.

J. Stanford Smith: Chairman, International Paper Company; former vice-president, General Electric Company.

William I. Spencer: President, Citicorp and Citibank.

Thomas F. Staley: Former chairman, Reynolds Securities Incorporated.

Jack I. Straus: Chairman of the executive committee, R. H. Macy & Company.

Judson L. Streicher: Partner, J. Streicher & Company, a securities firm.

Oliver J. Troster: Partner, Troster, Singer & Company, a securities firm.

George E. Vandenhoff: Partner, Dean Witter & Company (Beverly Hills branch), a securities firm.

Harry J. Volk: Chairman, Union Bank (California).

Charles R. Walgreen, Jr.: Director and former chairman, Walgreen Company.

Hicks B. Waldron: President, Heublein Incorporated; former vice-president, General Electric Company.

Ted B. Westfall: Executive vice-president, International Telephone & Telegraph Corporation.

Dean Witter, Jr.: Partner, Dean Witter & Company.

J. Howard Wood: Director and former chairman of the executive committee, Tribune Company, owner of the Chicago *Tribune* and the New York *Daily News*.

Walter B. Wriston: Chairman, Citicorp and Citibank.

GENERAL ELECTRIC COMPANY

All the people below are or were vice-presidents or managers of GE, except where otherwise noted.

A. Melcher Anderson
Christy W. Bell

Arthur M. Bueche
Fred J. Borch: Former chairman.
S. Wellford Corbin
Hershner Cross
Walter D. Dance: Vice-chairman.
William H. Dennler: Vice-chairman.
Virgil B. Day
Robert M. Estes
Stanley C. Gault
J. H. Gauss
James H. Goss
Hubert W. Gouldthorpe
Reuben Gutoff
Reginald H. Jones: Chairman.
Milton F. Kent
John D. Lockton: Former treasurer.
Francis K. McCune
J. B. McKitterick
Charles Meloun
Halbert B. Miller
Carl W. Moeller
Thomas O. Paine
Jack S. Parker: Vice-chairman.
Gene R. Peterson
Charles E. Reed
Donald D. Scarff
A. E. Schubert
Cecil S. Semple
J. Stanford Smith
Gordon K. Stebbins
Hicks B. Waldron
Herman L. Weiss: Vice-chairman.
Russell E. Whitmyer

LAW

All the people below are or were partners in New York law firms, except where otherwise noted.

R. Burdell Bixby: Dewey, Ballantine, Bushby, Palmer & Wood.
L. R. Breslin, Jr.: Cravath, Swaine & Moore.

John W. Castles III: Lord, Day & Lord.

Norris Darrell, Jr.: Sullivan & Cromwell.

Thomas E. Dewey: Dewey, Ballantine, Bushby, Palmer & Wood.

Robert B. Fiske, Jr.: Davis Polk & Wardwell (later appointed U.S. attorney in Manhattan).

Henry J. Fox: Arent, Fox, Kintner, Plotkin & Kahn (Washington, D.C.).

Justin L. Goldner: Trachman and Goldner (Beverly Hills).

Nathaniel L. Goldstein: Former attorney general of New York.

Murray I. Gurfein: Judge, U.S. Court of Appeals for the Second Judicial Circuit (author of the original Pentagon Papers decision).

Peter L. Keane: Lord, Day & Lord.

Henry L. King: Davis Polk & Wardwell.

Earl W. Kintner: Arent, Fox, Kintner, Plotkin & Kahn (Washington, D.C.).

George N. Lindsay: Debevoise, Plimpton, Lyons & Gates (brother of John V. Lindsay, former mayor of New York City).

Dennis G. Lyons: Arnold & Porter (Washington, D.C.).

Robert J. McDonald: Sullivan & Cromwell.

William Edwards Murray

Harry M. Plotkin: Arent, Fox, Kintner, Plotkin & Kahn (Washington, D.C.)

Philip C. Potter, Jr.: Davis Polk & Wardwell.

James H. Rowe: Corcoran, Youngman & Rowe (Washington, D.C.); high White House aide under Franklin D. Roosevelt.

George C. Sharp: Sullivan & Cromwell.

William A. Shea (for whom Shea Stadium is named).

Michael I. Sovern: Dean, Columbia University law school.

Richard S. Storrs: Sullivan & Cromwell.

Sherman Welpton, Jr.: Gibson, Dunn & Crutcher (Los Angeles).

John E. F. Wood: Dewey, Ballantine, Bushby, Palmer & Wood.

ROSENFELD, MEYER & SUSMAN (Beverly Hills)

Peter R. Cohen
Norman H. Garey
Lawrence S. Kartiganer
Marvin B. Meyer
Jeffrey L. Nagin
Edward J. Riordan
Donald T. Rosenfeld

Gary A. Schlessinger
Allen E. Susman
David D. Wexler
George C. Zachary

Source Notes

The primary source of the factual material in this book is the massive public record of the Home-Stake affair that is filed in the federal and state courts in Tulsa, Oklahoma. The record comprises the SEC's two cases against Home-Stake; the many lawsuits brought by private investors; the bankruptcy trustee's lawsuits; the bankruptcy reorganization effort; IRS actions; and the Justice Department's criminal case.

These proceedings have spawned thousands of documents: formal complaints and indictments and responses to them; court testimony, depositions, legal briefs, and affidavits; letters and memoranda; financial data, oil production reports, and analyses by certified public accountants; year-by-year rosters of individual investors' outlays; and much more. The record includes Home-Stake's annual shareholder reports from 1955 through 1972; minutes of its directors and shareholders meetings; and the company's prospectuses and sales literature.

The author has examined nearly all this material. In addition, he has conducted hundreds of interviews with people in Tulsa, New York, Los Angeles, and elsewhere who are familiar with one or more aspects of the Home-Stake case. He also has obtained a significant amount of nonpublic documentary material that has aided reconstruction of the story.

The following notes identify most of the important sources that are not explicit or evident in the narrative. Confidential sources, of course, are not named. Dialogue is taken from witnesses' sworn recollections of what they or others said.

The book's analyses and conclusions, as distinct from factual exposition, are the author's, and in most instances stem from his general knowledge of the case rather than from a particular source.

CHAPTER 1

The account of the events of Monday, May 24, 1971: Recollections of many people who were in Tulsa that day and over the preceding weekend for Home-Stake's annual shareholders meeting; Reg Dawson, whose good memory was further sharpened by the detailed recollections of others.

Description of the Fitzgerald home: Tulsa *Tribune* article detailing the interior decoration of the house, the accuracy of which was verified by Mary Anne Fitzgerald; photographs of the swimming pool and patio; the author's personal visit.

Description of the Crystal Ballroom of the Mayo Hotel: The author's personal visit.

CHAPTER 2

Robert Trippet's life through high school; capsule profile of parents: Interviews with several of Trippet's close friends who grew up with him in Bartlesville, Oklahoma, during the 1920s and 1930s and who knew his parents well; detailed obituary of H. W. Trippet in a Bartlesville newspaper.

Trippet's college, law school, and professional life to 1948: Interviews with several college and law school classmates; University of Oklahoma yearbooks for the period; deposition given by Trippet in early 1977 recounting the events of his early adulthood (in the case of *Savage* et al. v. *Trippet* et al., C-73-1764, Tulsa County district court, Oklahoma, September 11, 1973. [hereafter *Savage* v. *Trippet*]).

Trippet's law practice, personal life, and attitudes (1948–1955); decision to start Home-Stake: Interviews with several people who knew Trippet well during the period; Oklahoma Tax Commission, Cigarette Tax Warrant, January 29, 1953; release of Cigarette Tax Warrant and Lien, July 1, 1957.

Russell Cobb, Jr.: Interviews with acquaintances; Tulsa newspaper obituaries of Russell Cobb, Jr., and Russell Cobb, Sr.; court papers in the case of *Irwin Shaw* v. *Russell Cobb, Jr.*, No. 106700, Tulsa County district court and *Ralph Donahue* v. *Russell Cobb, Jr.*, et al., No. 110768, Tulsa County district court; court papers detailing the Russell Cobb, Jr., bankruptcy, U.S. District Court, Northern District of Tulsa, Oklahoma.

Paul C. Edwards: Indictment, *U.S.* v. *Paul C. Edwards*, Criminal No. 14230, Tulsa federal court; letter from court clerk indicating conviction was upheld on appeal and Edwards was delivered to a federal prison in Texas.

CHAPTER 3

Home-Stake, 1955–1957: Interviews with people familiar with the early years of Home-Stake; incorporation papers and corporate minutes.

Charles Plummer: Resolution of state legislator Robert Cunningham, *Journal of the House of Representatives,* Oklahoma legislature, February 28, 1951; numerous Tulsa newspaper articles.

Accountants' report on Home-Stake irregularities: Minutes of special board of directors meeting, February 25, 1957, signed by O. Strother Simpson and James G. Blount.

The firing of Keith Schuerman: Trippet's letter to Schuerman, September 18, 1957; Schuerman letter to O. Strother Simpson, November 5, 1957.

Home-Stake, 1958–1959: Interviews.

The Rosenblatt group: Affidavit of William Rosenblatt in the case of *Albert S. Lyons* et al. v. *Home-Stake* et al., Civil Action No. 6543, Tulsa federal court, September 26, 1966 (hereafter *Lyons* v. *Home-Stake*).

William Edwards Murray: Murray's testimony to a federal grand jury, Los Angeles, California, November 26, 1974. (All grand jury testimony to which these notes refer was taken at the Los Angeles federal courthouse in late 1974, unless otherwise stated.)

Harry Fitzgerald: Interviews with Fitzgerald; Tulsa newspaper articles about the controversy over the estate of his father; Fitzgerald's alcohol problem is mentioned in a number of court documents as well as in Fitzgerald's conversations with the author.

CHAPTER 4

The Home-Stake sale to the Rosenblatt group: William Rosenblatt's affidavit in *Lyons* v. *Home-Stake;* interviews with Rosenblatt and other knowledgeable people.

Home-Stake's dummy corporations and subsequent references to them: Complaint and exhibits in *Savage* v. *Trippet.*

Communication between Trippet and the Rosenblatt group: Quotations in this chapter and subsequent ones are taken from correspondence filed in *Lyons* v. *Home-Stake.*

Fred J. Borch's Home-Stake investment: William Murray's grand jury testimony; Kent M. Klineman's grand jury testimony; Borch's deposition and answers to interrogatories, *In re Home-Stake Securities Litigation,* Multi-District Litigation No. 153, Tulsa federal court (hereafter *In re Home-Stake,* MDL 153).

Elmer Kunkel's discoveries: Notes of interrogation of Kunkel by Wayne Whitaker, lawyer-investigator for the SEC, September 8, 1974 (hereafter the Whitaker-Kunkel notes), filed in *U.S.* v. *Trippet* et al., 76-CR-23, Tulsa federal court, February 20, 1976 (hereafter *U.S.* v. *Trippet*). The companies later alleged to be dummy corporations also were mentioned in grand jury testimony by Kunkel and by John Lenoir.

Stock market decline in 1962: *Wall Street Journal* accounts.

P. C. Simons estate: General Inventory and Appraisment, and Final Decree, *In the Matter of the Estate of P. C. Simons, Deceased,* County Court of Garfield County, Oklahoma.

CHAPTER 5

William Murray's role: Murray's grand jury testimony.

Fitzgerald's 1962 California effort: Interviews with Fitzgerald and other knowledgeable individuals.

Charles Ponzi background: "Where Are They Now?", *The New Yorker,* May 8, 1937; Donald H. Dunn, *Ponzi! The Boston Swindler* (New York: McGraw-Hill, 1975).

Home-Stake oil income projections: Company sales literature.

Reference to Secondary Recovery Operating Corporation: Complaint and exhibits, *Savage* v. *Trippet.*

Charitable gifts: Complaint and accompanying court papers in *Securities and Exchange Commission* v. *Trippet* et al., 73-C-306, Tulsa federal court, September 11, 1973 (hereafter *SEC* v. *Trippet*); alleged in three indictments, *U.S.* v. *Trippet;* testimony at trial of Norman C. Cross, Jr. (hereafter the Cross trial); alleged and documented in numerous lawsuits consolidated with *In re Home-Stake,* MDL 153; depositions, *In re Home-Stake,* MDL 153.

CHAPTER 6

The SEC contacts Home-Stake: Interviews; deposition of William Blum, Jr., *In re Home-Stake,* MDL 153, September 12, 1974 (hereafter the Blum deposition); Trippet's letter to the SEC; Sims's memorandum to Fitzgerald; the SEC's letter to the IRS.

Disproportionate payments and other fraud prior to 1964: Alleged in *Lyons* v. *Home-Stake;* complaint of John J. Shea et al., intervenors in *Lyons* v. *Home-Stake; Morrell H. Blesh* et al. v. *Home-Stake* et al., 74-C-224, Tulsa federal court, May 22, 1974; *Savage* v. *Trippet.*

Kunkel confronts Trippet again: The Whitaker-Kunkel notes.

Drafting the first Home-Stake prospectus: Memorandum of interrogation of Harry Fitzgerald by Cecil S. Mathis, chief enforcement attorney for the SEC's Fort Worth, Texas, office, October 2, 1974 (hereafter the Mathis-Fitzgerald memorandum), filed in *U.S.* v. *Trippet;* the Blum deposition, *In re Home-Stake,* MDL 153.

Trippet's attitude toward stockholders: John Lenoir's grand jury testimony.

The first California sales: Interviews.

Expansion of New York sales in 1964, particularly to the General Electric group: Interviews; William Murray's grand jury testimony; depositions, *In re Home-Stake,* MDL 153.

Martin Bregman, Kent Klineman, and the first sale to Barbra Streisand: Interviews; Klineman's grand jury testimony.

Trippet's life-style and family: Interviews.

CHAPTER 7

The sales network and payments to lawyers, accountants, and others: Home-Stake's general policy of offering compensation to all who aided sales is explained by Harry Fitzgerald in the Mathis-Fitzgerald memorandum; in formal testimony to the SEC; and in interviews with the author. The roles of William Blum, Redvers Opie, and Lyle O'Rourke are documented in extensive correspondence filed with *In re Home-Stake,* MDL 153. For the Blum and O'Rourke correspondence, see exhibits to the Blum deposition. For correspondence involving Opie and his clients, see exhibits to "Attorney Defendants' Brief in Opposition to Motion for Class Action Certification," filed August 11, 1975, *In re Home-Stake,* MDL 153. Unless otherwise noted, these exhibits include all correspondence involving Opie, Blum, and O'Rourke and their clients used in the book.

Opie's 1965 sales, clients, and commissions: Trippet's letter to Opie.

Other 1965 investments: Interviews.

Southeastern Massachusetts University foundation: Interviews; university records; newspaper accounts.

Home-Stake loans to William Murray: Murray's grand jury testimony; Home-Stake loan records.

Kunkel warns Trippet: The Whitaker-Kunkel notes.

Heller warns Fitzgerald: The Mathis-Fitzgerald memorandum.

Blum's role in the Zipco case: "Opinion, Findings of Fact and Conclusions of Law," *Moerman* v. *Zipco* et al., No. 63-Civ-922, 302 F. Supp. 439, U.S. District Court, Eastern District of New York, July 31, 1969. Affirmed by the U.S. Court of Appeals for the Second Circuit, April 2, 1970.

Bregman-Streisand contract: Dated and signed by Streisand on December 14, 1966; signed by Bregman on December 19, 1966.

California and New York 1966 investments: Interviews.

O'Rourke letter to Paul Dean: Exhibit with the Blum deposition.

Fred Borch's tax audit: Borch's deposition, *In re Home-Stake*, MDL 153, quoted in "Memorandum of Attorney Defendants with Respect to Adequacy of Class Action Representation," filed April 11, 1977, Tulsa federal court; Borch's answer to interrogatory.

Meeting in October 1966: GE officers' depositions, *In re Home-Stake*, MDL 153, quoted in attorney defendants' memorandum.

Trippet hires Arthur Andersen: GE officers' depositions; John Lockton's answer to interrogatory, filed May, 1976, *In re Home-Stake*, MDL 153.

Arthur Andersen's findings: Complaint and accompanying documents, including internal Arthur Andersen memoranda, filed in *Luce* et al. vs. *Arthur Andersen & Company*, 75-C-431, Tulsa federal court, September 19, 1975, consolidated with *In Re Home-Stake*, MDL 153. A portion of the April 15, 1967, memorandum was read into the record by William A. Wineberg, Jr., attorney for plaintiffs Ivan Anixter et al., during a court hearing.

Reaction to parting of Home-Stake and Arthur Andersen: Depositions of the First National City Bank and GE officers, *In re Home-Stake*, MDL 153.

Trippet-Greer discussion of responses to Sherrod, McKitterick, and Martin inquiries: Memoranda and letters filed as exhibits in *U.S.* v. *F. Conrad Greer*, Criminal 75-234 (A), U.S. District Court, Central District of California, Los Angeles (hereafter *U.S.* v. *Greer*). (All quoted communication between Greer and Trippet is taken from memoranda or letters, unless otherwise noted.)

Plummer's suicide: Tulsa newspaper account.

Home-Stake investments in 1967: Interviews.

The parting of Bregman and Streisand: Interviews; court files of lawsuits, *Martin Bregman Inc. against Barbra Streisand, Martin Bregman against Jemb Music Corp.* et al., and *Jemb Music Corp.* et al. *against Martin Bregman Inc.*, Supreme Court of the State of New York, County of New York, 1968 and 1969.

Gifts to Southeastern Massachusetts University foundation: University and foundation records.

CHAPTER 8

Payments to William Murray's company: Exhibit G, "Response to Application by the Trustee for Instructions Concerning the 1972

Program," *In the Matter of Home-Stake* (Bankruptcy Reorganization), 73-B-922, Tulsa federal court, September 20, 1973; Murray's grand jury testimony; schedule prepared by Arthur Andersen & Company, March 6, 1967.

Trippet-Landrith stock deal: Landrith's and Kunkel's grand jury testimonies; Kunkel's testimony at the Cross trial.

Trippet's reaction to the McKee-Atkins audit: The Whitaker-Kunkel notes; Kunkel's testimony to the grand jury and at the Cross trial.

Falsification of lease ownership: Indictments, *U.S.* v. *Trippet.*

Grant Anderson's experience: Interviews; Anderson's letter to Fitzgerald.

McKee-Kimball episode: Kimball's memoranda to McKee; affidavit of Robert T. Nixon, U.S. postal inspector, filed in *U.S.* v. *Trippet.*

Investments in 1968: Interviews.

Walter Matthau's investment and loan, and his lawsuit against bank alleging loan "fronting": Complaint and accompanying documents, *Helmer and Matthau* v. *First National Bank and Trust Company of Tulsa,* 75-C-430, Tulsa federal court, September 19, 1975.

Doris Day's judgment against Jerome B. Rosenthal: *Samet* v. *Day* and consolidated cases, No. 938,682, Superior Court of the State of California for the County of Los Angeles, Department No. 31, September 18, 1974.

Opie 1968 sales and commissions: Trippet's letter to Opie, December 17, 1968.

Alan Pope's resignation and report to the SEC: Letter from M. David Hyman, SEC chief enforcement attorney, to Pope's lawyer, January 24, 1969; Hyman's memorandum referring the matter to the SEC's Fort Worth regional office, same date.

Trippet-Klineman relationship: Klineman's SEC and grand jury testimonies; Trippet-Klineman correspondence.

Trippet-Goldblum meeting: Trippet-Klineman correspondence.

Talk of possible acquisition of Home-Stake and Ankony Angus by Equity Funding or a holding company: Trippet's deposition, *Savage* v. *Trippet;* Trippet-Klineman correspondence.

Puerto Vallarta land purchase: Home-Stake records.

Loans by Home-Stake and Trippet to Klineman and Dryfoos & Company: Klineman's grand jury and SEC testimonies; Home-Stake loan records.

John Lenoir brings Norman Cross to Home-Stake: Lenoir's grand jury and trial testimonies.

Cross and Trippet confer: Cross's grand jury and trial testimonies.

Backing into earnings: The Whitaker-Kunkel notes; Kunkel's grand jury and trial testimonies; Don Richards's trial testimony; Fitzgerald's SEC testimony.

The Santa Maria showcase: Interviews; testimony of L. B. Malkin at Greer's trial; testimony of Harvey L. Garland at the Cross trial; testimony of Arnold H. Nadlman at the Greer trial; work orders and invoices covering painting of irrigation pipes; indictments, *U.S.* v. *Trippet;* statistics compiled by the Conservation Committee of California Oil Producers; affidavit of Harry E. Bonetto; complaint, *Streicher* et al. v. *Home-Stake* et al., 73-C-175, Tulsa federal court, April 23, 1974 (hereafter *Streicher* v. *Home-Stake*), consolidated with *In re Home-Stake*, MDL 153.

Greer resists giving less information to Lewis & Ganong: Greer's memorandum to Trippet.

CHAPTER 9

The Trippet-Klineman reversionary interest transaction: Interviews; extensive documentation throughout the public record.

Use of the phrase "Great Train Robbery": The Mathis-Fitzgerald memorandum; interviews; Trippet's deposition, *Savage* v. *Trippet;* statement of prosecutor William R. Hawes during the Cross trial.

Value of 1968–1969 properties: Lenoir testimony at the Cross trial.

Trippet's management contract: Complaint and exhibit, *Savage* v. *Trippet.*

Evaluation of T & F Oil and Realty: Exhibit attached to Trippet's letter to Klineman, December 15, 1969.

Circumstances of Klineman's Bahamas loan and purchase of T & F Oil and Realty: Klineman's SEC and grand jury testimonies; Trippet's deposition, *Savage* v. *Trippet.*

Trippet pays Fitzgerald $15,000: The Mathis-Fitzgerald memorandum; interviews.

Arrangement for Klineman to obtain reports on his clients' oil income: Trippet's memorandum to Home-Stake's accounting department, April 29, 1966.

The quid pro quo: Klineman's SEC and grand jury testimonies.

Trippet's disposition of $2,635,000: Statement of account, R. S. or Helen Grey Trippet, Account No. 0040-86-5, First National Bank and Trust Company of Tulsa, January 22, 1970.

Payments to Siegel & Goldburt: Louis Goldburt's and Nicholas Marsh's testimonies in Home-Stake's bankruptcy case, July 15, 1975.

Meeting with Andy Williams: Interviews; Greer's testimony at his own trial.

Arrangements with Rosenfeld, Meyer & Susman: Interviews; documents filed in *U.S.* v. *Greer.*

Barry Tarlow's experience: Interview.

Purported arrangement with Bregman: Klineman's letter to Trippet, August 6, 1969.

False oil-production reports: Indictments, *U.S.* v. *Trippet*; comparisons of reports to investors and reports filed with the California state government.

Mary Lou Patrick's complaint: The Whitaker-Kunkel notes; Kunkel's grand jury and trial testimonies.

Greer-Davies calculation: The Mathis-Fitzgerald memorandum; Fitzgerald's SEC testimony.

Meeting with Richard Taft: The Whitaker-Kunkel notes; Kunkel's grand jury and trial testimonies.

Carl Clay's discoveries and the payment to him: Clay's testimony at the Cross trial.

Trippet inherits $434,000 from his father: Washington County, Oklahoma, court records.

Home-Stake buys a California apartment complex: Minutes of Home-Stake directors meeting, March 18, 1970.

Don Steinmeyer resigns: Steinmeyer's grand jury testimony; the Justice Department's Statement of Facts and Memorandum in Aid of Sentencing, *U.S.* v. *Trippet*; indictment, *U.S.* v. *Trippet*; interviews.

Early IRS audits: Greer's memorandum to Trippet.

Reducing Home-Stake's California operations: Greer's memorandum to Trippet.

The SEC summons Home-Stake to Washington: Affidavit of Richard B. Nesson, filed with *SEC against Home-Stake 1970* et al., 71-Civ.-348, U.S. District Court, District of Columbia, February 11, 1971 (hereafter *SEC against Home-Stake 1970*).

Trippet's comment to Fitzgerald: The Mathis-Fitzgerald memorandum.

Home-Stake buys Equity Funding stock: Klineman's SEC testimony.

Trippet's activities in 1970 sales effort: Trippet's expense account records.

Bernhardt Denmark retains counsel to threaten Home-Stake: Court records of Denmark's threat and Home-Stake's buying back his units; interviews.

Loans to Klineman and Bregman, and commissions to Dryfoos &

Company: Trippet-Klineman correspondence; Home-State loan records.

Lobbying in Venezuela: Interviews; Herbert R. Smith's grand jury testimony.

Trips to Venezuela: Louis Goldburt's testimony in Home-Stake's bankruptcy case.

The SEC's investigation and lawsuit: Complaint and accompanying documents in *SEC against Home-Stake 1970.*

Trippet warns his salesmen to use the *Tale of Two Cities* memorandum with discretion: Memorandum to a salesman, February 13, 1971.

Lawsuit against Home-Stake in 1960: *Viersen & Cochran* v. *Home-Stake,* No. 100697, Tulsa County district court, December 30, 1960.

Goldburt and Marsh comments on rescission offer: Testimony in Home-Stake's bankruptcy case.

Tarlow comment: Interview.

Trippet's personal loan to Home-Stake: Form 10, General Form for Registration of Securities, filed by Home-Stake with the SEC, August 23, 1971.

Negotiations with Sherman Welpton: Welpton testimony at the Cross trial; Court records of Home-Stake's buying back Welpton's units.

Carl Clay resigns from the Cross firm and joins Home-Stake: Clay's trial testimony.

Landrith's legal opinions: Landrith's affidavit, filed in *U.S.* v. *Trippet.*

Hollis calls extra pay hush money: Hollis's testimony at the Cross trial.

Walker analyses of tax audits: Walker memorandum to Procter & Gamble executives, June 23, 1971.

Payment to Blum: Exhibit with the Blum deposition.

Trippet's complaint about Simpson, Thacher & Bartlett's bill: Exhibit with the Blum deposition.

Cases involving John Pogue: Complaint, C. A. No. 68-H-738, U.S. District Court, Southern District of Texas, Houston Division, dismissed as to Pogue; indictment, 69-CR-127, 70-CR-43, U.S. District Court, Chicago, dismissed as to Pogue; interviews; Home-Stake employment records.

CHAPTER 10

Fitzgerald's resignation and related events: Resignation letter; Fitzgerald's SEC testimony; interviews.

Greer-Heller-Blum conversation, August 12, 1971: Greer's diary.

Clay-Heller discoveries: Clay's testimony at the Cross trial.

Klineman-Trippet relations deteriorate: Klineman's grand jury and SEC testimonies; Klineman-Trippet correspondence.

Trippet discusses the reversionary interest with Landrith, Metcalfe, and Gutelius: Landrith's grand jury and trial testimonies; Metcalfe's and Gutelius's trial testimonies.

Home-Stake buys Oil & Realty Remainders from Klineman: Klineman's SEC testimony; Home-Stake records of the transaction.

Caponegro meets with Trippet and then recommends that Faye Dunaway's gift deduction be reduced: Caponegro's memorandum to his IRS superiors, October 28, 1971.

Home-Stake sells its Equity Funding stock: Klineman's SEC testimony.

The November crisis: Clay's trial testimony; Landrith's trial and grand jury testimonies; Landrith's memorandum of record and letter to Trippet; Home-Stake's financial records; the Blum deposition and exhibits; the Heller and the Kothe and Eagleton resignation letters.

Greer-Trippet communication in late 1971: Letters, memoranda, and transcript of taped telephone conversation.

Decision to audit books of Southeastern Massachusetts University foundation: School and foundation records; interviews.

Home-Stake investments in 1971: Interviews.

Cross's assistants react to Home-Stake irregularities: Assistants' and Cross's trial testimonies.

Climax at Southeastern Massachusetts University: School and foundation records; interviews.

Siegel & Goldburt retain the Lybrand accounting firm: Goldburt's testimony in Home-Stake's bankruptcy case.

Tarlow-Trippet negotiations: Interviews; court records of Home-Stake's buying back Tarlow's units.

Walter Matthau's investment: Stiglitz-Goodkin correspondence.

Marsh and Goldburt transfer their investments to the 1972 program: Marsh's and Goldburt's testimonies and attached exhibits in Home-Stake's bankruptcy case.

Charitable gifts in 1972: Bregman's letter to the Library of Congress; interviews.

CHAPTER 11

The payout system: Home-Stake record of payment categories in early 1973; Ouida Mae Back's SEC and trial testimonies and deposition in *Streicher* v. *Home-Stake;* Lenoir's trial testimony.

Trippet's bank deposits and withdrawals: IRS summons served on the First National Bank of Tulsa, December 2, 1975, listing 1973–1974 deposits and withdrawals, filed in *Helmer and Matthau* v. *First National Bank.*

Klineman assembles investor group: Interviews; Kronish Lieb letter to Trippet, filed in June, 1977, *In re Home-Stake,* MDL 153.

Trippet meets Riebold; background and events of March, 1973: Indictment, trial transcript, grand jury testimony, and accompanying documents, *U.S.* v. *E. M. "Mike" Riebold* et al., Criminal No. 74-353, U.S. District Court, District of New Mexico (hereafter *U.S.* v. *Riebold*).

The Anixter-Dickinson-Yoshida lawsuit: Complaint, interrogatories and answers, and other documents in *Anixter* et al. v. *Home-Stake* et al., 73-C-382, Tulsa federal court (hereafter *Anixter* v. *Home-Stake*), consolidated with *In re Home-Stake,* MDL 153; interviews.

Trippet and Riebold make a deal: Testimony in *U.S.* v. *Riebold.*

Sims warns Trippet about Riebold: Sims's memoranda to Trippet, attached as exhibits to Donald C. Larrabee's SEC testimony.

Robinson and Melendy become Home-Stake directors: Home-Stake letter to stockholders; testimony in *U.S.* v. *Riebold.*

The abortive $2.75 million loan: Testimony in *U.S.* v. *Riebold;* Larrabee's SEC testimony; Larrabee's narrative, written for his lawyer, of his Home-Stake involvement; interviews.

Larrabee visits Riebold: Larrabee's SEC testimony and narrative for his lawyer; interviews.

Riebold secures control and transfers $3.75 million to Albuquerque: Trial testimony and accompanying exhibits, *U.S.* v. *Riebold;* minutes of Home-Stake directors meetings; depositions and other documents, *Streicher* v. *Home-Stake.*

CHAPTER 12

The SEC begins a full investigation: Interviews; newspaper clippings on the Four Seasons and Sharpstown cases.

The $3.75 million is returned to Tulsa: Trial testimony, *U.S.* v. *Riebold;* depositions and other documents, *Streicher* v. *Home-Stake.*

Wineberg examines Home-Stake's and Cross's files: Documents filed in *Anixter* v. *Home-Stake.*

Trippet consults Gary Glanz: Glanz's sworn affidavit, June 28, 1976; interviews.

Insurance claim is filed with Aetna Casualty and Surety Company: Attached to complaint, *Savage* v. *Trippet.*

CHAPTER 13

Mathis questions Roy Foulke: Subpoena requiring Foulke to appear; Foulke's expense account records.

A federal investigation begins in Albuquerque: Trial testimony, *U.S. v. Riebold.*

Trippet confers with Larrabee: Larrabee's SEC testimony and accompanying exhibits; interviews.

Trippet confers with Nathan Graham: Interviews; newspaper account.

The General Electric group assembles: Minutes of a meeting held on January 4, 1974.

CHAPTER 14

SEC transfers the Home-Stake case to the Justice Department for prosecution: SEC Criminal Reference Report, July 2, 1974; letter from the Los Angeles U.S. attorney to the SEC's Fort Worth office, June 26, 1974.

Defendants' complaints about government tactics: Affidavits filed by Kunkel, Fitzgerald, and the lawyer for Klineman in *U.S. v. Trippet;* government rebuttals.

William Murray interrogation: Transcript of Murray's testimony.

Events leading up to the indictment: Interviews.

Appeals court criticizes Judge Hauk: *U.S. v. Marshall, Eischen, and Morgan,* Nos. 72-3195, 72-3185, and 72-3186, U.S. Court of Appeals for the Ninth Circuit, September 7, 1973. (488 F. 2d 1169).

Hawes-Glanzer communication: Affidavits filed in *U.S. v. Trippet.*

Events leading to the third indictment: Interviews; Oklahoma newspaper accounts (for example, Jack Taylor, "Home-Stake Case: Spectacular, Tangled," the *Sunday Oklahoman,* 23 May 1976).

Riebold is questioned on July 15, 1976, about his dealings with Trippet: Memorandum of interview.

Events leading to the change of plea by Trippet, Sims, and Fitzgerald: Interviews; Oklahoma newspaper accounts.

CHAPTER 15

The Cross trial: Transcript.
The day and night in jail: Interviews.
The sentencing proceedings: Transcript.

CHAPTER 16

Trippets' notes and Christmas card to Judge Barrow: Filed by the judge in *U.S.* v. *Trippet*.

Analysis of losses and disposition of funds: Author's estimates based on extensive examination of documents and consultation with experts.

Epilogue

By the autumn of 1982, five years after the initial publication of this book, the Home-Stake litigation had grown into one of the most complex, protracted securities and tax-fraud cases in history. Depositions had been taken from more than one hundred witnesses and generated more than one hundred thousand pages of transcript. Tens of thousands of documents had been analyzed. But only mixed results had flowed from the investors' attempts to recover funds from convicted conspirator Robert Trippet, the Home-Stake Corporation, and the other alleged swindlers. The IRS's efforts to collect back taxes both from Home-Stake and the investors had fared no better.

After initially pressing a tax claim of $31.3 million against the Home-Stake Production Company, the IRS settled for only $3.2 million, or about ten cents on the dollar—a settlement typical of IRS capitulation to corporate taxpayers.

Robert Trippet, attorney William Edwards Murray, the CPA firm of Arthur Andersen & Company, and thirteen other defendants who were accused of fraud by the investors continued to contest the charges. However, a second group of defendants—fourteen individuals, law firms, and assorted entities associated with Home-Stake—agreed to pay $12 million to settle the investors' claims. The latter group included Harry Heller, the senior Washington partner of the renowned Wall Street law firm of Simpson Thacher & Bartlett; Heller's longtime colleague, Washington attorney William Blum, who wasn't connected with Simpson Thacher but worked with

Heller on Home-Stake's prospectuses; and the Oklahoma City law firm of McAfee, Taft, Mark, Bond, Rucks & Woodruff, which had done legal work for Home-Stake. Heller, Blum, and the McAfee Taft firm contributed most of the $12 million, making their share one of the largest amounts ever paid by lawyers or law firms— perhaps *the* largest—to settle damage claims against them in a single suit. (The exact amounts of Heller's and the other defendants' payments were kept confidential.) As part of the settlement, charges against the fourteen defendants were dismissed, they maintained their innocence, and no judgment against them was rendered. (Even though Simpson Thacher & Bartlett's professional liability insurance paid much or all of its partner Heller's contribution, the law firm insisted on being designated as the "dismissed defendant" in the settlement agreement, while Heller and the others were called "settling defendants.")

In addition to the $12 million from the Simpson Thacher group, the Home-State bankruptcy trustee agreed to contribute $11.6 million to the settlement fund for a total of $23.6 million as of the end of 1981. Up to a third of that amount—about $8 million—was expected to go to the investors' lawyers as fees and expenses, leaving between $15 million and $16 million, plus accruing interest, to be paid to the investors, probably beginning early in 1983. (Charities that had received Home-Stake shares as donations were to receive settlements of 40 percent of amounts they would have gotten had they purchased their shares.)

A $16 million settlement payment represented about 18 percent of the investors' previously calculated $90 million out-of-pocket loss on their total outlay of $140 million (see page 301), reducing the loss to about $74 million. That figure understates the enormous dimensions of the loss, however. Each dollar of the $16 million recovered in 1983 was worth far less than each dollar of the $140 million that Home-Stake had collected from 1955 through 1972. Moreover, had the $140 million been invested over the years in secure, high-interest bank instruments, instead of being turned over to Home-Stake to steal and squander, it would have been worth vastly more than $140 million by 1983.

The tax status of the investments and losses remained unresolved. The investors, through their lawyers, continued efforts to collect damages from Robert Trippet and the others who did not participate in the settlement.

The Home-Stake bankruptcy trustee laid plans to reconstitute the company's remaining assets under the name of the Resource Recovery Corporation, continue to engage in the oil business, and distribute stock in the new company to the old Home-Stake investors. The stock's value remained to be determined.

The IRS announced that the amount lost to the U.S. Treasury from "abusive" tax shelters had risen to $3 billion annually by late 1982.

Index